SHOCKED

Life and Death at 35,000 Feet

David K. McKenas MD, MPH
Former Corporate Medical Director, American Airlines

With
Dan Reed

Foreword by Robert L. Crandall
Former CEO American Airlines

Printed in the United States of America

ISBN 978-1-953910-46-2 (paperback)
ISBN 978-1-953910-42-4 (ebook)
ISBN 978-1-953910-47-9 (hardcover)

**Canoe Tree
Press**

4697 Main Street
Manchester Center, VT 05255

Canoe Tree Press is a division of DartFrog Books.

ABOUT THE AUTHORS

Dr. David McKenas

Dr. McKenas is a board-certified specialist in both Aerospace Medicine and Occupational Medicine. He served as Corporate Medical Director for American Airlines from 1992 to 2002, a period that included the final years at the helm of legendary American CEO Robert Crandall. In his early years, Dr. McKenas was a near musical prodigy who studied music composition, piano and voice, and who performed in a professional choir and as a piano soloist and accompanist as a child. He minored in college in music but earned his undergraduate degree in biochemistry before studying medicine at SUNY Upstate Medical Center and the Harvard University School of Public Health in Boston, MA.

As the son of a widowed mother, McKenas paid for his medical education by earning a scholarship and a commission from the United States Air Force. As an Air Force Officer, Dr. McKenas became a board-certified specialist in the unique field of Aerospace Medicine. He served as the lead aerospace medicine doctor in the Department of Defense's Manager Space Transportation System Contingency Support [DDMS] program at Cape Canaveral, Florida, where he coordinated world-wide emergency care for NASA's Astronauts in the event of a space shuttle catastrophe. As an aerospace medicine flight surgeon, Dr. McKenas also received full flight training, up to the point of soloing on a T-37 jet airplane.

Upon leaving the Air Force in 2002, Dr. McKenas joined American Airlines, first as a staff physician then, shortly thereafter Corporate Medical Director. He is one of the world's leading experts in Aviation and Aerospace Medicine. Today he practices medicine part time with the Carrollton, TX, Fire Department, where he makes sure firefighters are medically safe to perform their strenuous work, and screens for illnesses such as cancer that can harm firefighters. He composes music and is involved in various church-related mission efforts around the globe.

Dan Reed

Reed is an award-winning business and financial journalist who has spent three decades focused primarily on the U.S. airline industry and related aviation and travel service companies – plus all the workers, unions and legal and legislative issues related to those industries. He worked for the Arkansas Democrat (today the Democrat-Gazette) from 1978 to 1981, the Fort Worth Star-Telegram from 1981 to 2002, and USA TODAY from 2002-2010.

Today he is a senior contributor for FORBES.com, where he continues to focus on the airline and related industries and is a frequent contributor to other aviation and general interest publications. Reed also operates his own communications consulting firm, advising clients on communications, media, and strategy matters. He is the author of *American Eagle: The Ascent of Bob Crandall and American Airlines* (1993, St. Martin's Press/Thomas Dunn Books) and co-author of *American Airlines, US Airways, and the Creation of the World's Largest Airline* (2014, McFarland). Reed earned his bachelor's degree in Journalism at the University of Arkansas and his master's degree in Divinity at the Southwestern Baptist Theological Seminary.

ACKNOWLEDGEMENTS

There are so many people to thank, as putting defibrillators onto all US air carriers, and convincing Congress to make it a law was no small feat, and took an awful lot of people. These are but a few.

Dan Reed would especially like to thank his wife for putting up with him over all of these years of being at the keyboard writing all day and night as a journalist, and for Dr. McKenas for asking him to help with the book.

Dr. McKenas would like to thank his daughters, Erin McKenas Joyner, and Catherine Grace McKenas PhD, and his sister, Barbara A. McKenas, for being shining lights and staying with him through all of the turbulence. And Dan Reed for agreeing to help write the book!

Much thanks to the American Airlines Medical Department, and Flight Attendants everywhere, who are the true safety officials on airplanes by saving lives and keeping travelers safe.

And special thanks to Firefighter/Paramedics, and paramedics everywhere who save lives wherever they may be, so often placing the care of others ahead of their own safety.

Finally, this book is dedicated to Linda A Campbell, the Aeromedical Nurse at American Airlines, who was Dr. McKenas' right-hand person and program trainer. Linda died on May 6th,

2020. As Dr. McKenas would often joke to Linda during the training of 25,000 flight attendants, while handing her a CPR dummy's arm:

"Let's give Linda a hand!"

CONTENTS

FOREWORD

Robert L. Crandall
Former CEO American Airlines

One of the realities of life is that those who lead large and successful organizations – whether military, political or commercial – get a disproportionate amount of credit for the organization's successes. During my nearly 20 years as President and Chairman/CEO of American Airlines, the Company introduced an impressive number of business innovations, concepts, practices, tools, product offerings and technologies. I got lots of credit for those successes.

The credit was certainly welcome and to some extent, deserved. I was a very hands-on manager, was involved in every big decision and did my best to create an environment in which new ideas were valued and innovation was encouraged. Nonetheless, it is impossible for the CEO of a major company to be the key catalyst in everything new and successful that the organization does. Achieving success in today's complex society requires a team of dedicated, talented, and creative people working effectively together.

Fortunately, I had lots of really good people – not just a handful of top corporate officers but a small army of executives, technical subject matter experts, sales and marketing people, pilots, flight attendants, mechanics, fleet service workers and many others – who were collectively as proud of being part of American as I was to lead it. Without their deep commitment, American would not have been nearly as successful as it was.

Building an elite team required that we make it clear to everyone at the company that we were eager to hear all ideas about managing our business more effectively. Lots of our technical and managerial innovations, our advances in scheduling and route planning and lots of our tactical moves to contain costs and increase revenues bubbled up from rank-and-file employees. They quickly caught on to the fact that American was open to new ideas about tackling long-standing airline operational challenges.

That openness to new ideas extended into every department, including our medical department. Few people know it, but big airlines like American typically have – or at least had in my day - sizeable medical staffs. Back in the 1980s and early 1990s, when American was growing very rapidly, our medical staff was performing thousands of physical exams each year for both existing employees and job seekers. Pilots must pass a federally mandated exam prior to being hired and annually thereafter. Moreover, with thousands of employees in continuous contact with fellow employees and travelers, common sense dictated that we should do all we could to keep our people healthy. To deal with these realities, we had a team of nurses and doctors at each of our major hub cities.

American's Chief Medical Officer at the time of my retirement was Dr. David McKenas, a uniquely qualified doctor who had come to American from the U.S. Air Force in 1992. As an Air Force and NASA Flight Surgeon, David had learned to fly himself, which made him very aware of the effects of flight on the human body. Dave had various unique capabilities that fit very well with the airline industry including managing a NASA/DOD program intended to equip the agency to deal with an abort of a space shuttle mission. Doing so made Dave something of an expert in planning for emergency medical care in tense and fluid circumstances. Additionally, the Air Force had put Dave through Harvard University's T.H. Chan School of Public Health, where he earned a master's degree on top of his medical degree. So, in addition to being a highly qualified aviation medicine specialist David was, in effect, a Public Health doctor skilled in the research and tracking methodologies necessary to diagnose and respond to any rapidly spreading disease or health challenge within our huge corporate family or our enormous population of passengers. For obvious reasons airlines, especially those like American that fly to many foreign destinations, are keenly aware of the potential for spreading dangerous diseases.

As the years passed, I saw Dave frequently in our headquarters and enjoyed the annual events when he used his musical talents to play the piano and sing Christmas carols in the headquarters lobby. However, since there were relatively few medical crises to deal with, I saw him infrequently on professional matters and interacted primarily when he gave me my annual physical. When I got my check up in 1996, Dave asked me whether I was aware that around 50 or so people died every year aboard American flights; not from anything we did to them or caused, but just because they died. Sudden cardiac arrests were then, and I think still are the most common reason that passengers die aboard a commercial plane. And it does not happen only on American. The same thing happens on all airlines, though the numbers who die each year vary based on the relative size of the carriers involved.

To be sure, I was aware that people died on our airplanes from time to time. Each time it happened it was included in the daily reports delivered to me and all officers. It was always sad, and I would generally write a note of condolence to the family of the deceased passenger. But I, and pretty much everyone in the industry, chalked it up as just one of those things. We are all going to die. Some die at home. Some die at work. Some die in hospitals or nursing homes. And some – just a tiny fraction of all passengers, really – die aboard commercial jetliners.

Fresh out of the Harvard School of Public Health, Dave apparently started thinking seriously about the problem after he delved into passenger medical event statistics, and teased out how many people had died aboard our planes the previous year. Instead of simply taking note of it and moving on, Dave began wondering whether there was something that we could do to prevent so many passengers from dying on our planes.

Turned out there was – but if I told the rest of the story, I would be stealing Dave's lines. Dave wrote this book specifically to tell the story of what he suggested and what we did.

I commend this book to you, especially if you are now or once were an American employee. You'll be proud of the way Dr. McKenas and his team not only figured out how to save hundreds of lives on American flights over the last 20-plus years, but how they literally changed the world by pushing to get the solution American adopted out to the rest of world - and way, way beyond just the airline industry. If you work or worked for other airlines, I also think you will enjoy learning how impactful our industry can be when it seeks to do well by doing good. If you are a medical professional, you will be happy to learn the inside story of how a particular new technology has helped extend the lives of tens of thousands of people all around the world. And if you are a frequent, or even infrequent flyer, you might well be intrigued and maybe even a little inspired by the efforts of Dr. McKenas and his team to go beyond "the way we've always done it before" in order to have a positive impact on the world.

Dave chose as his professional writing partner for this book a business journalist I have known and respected for 35 years. Dan Reed began covering American and the larger airline industry in the early 1980s for the Fort Worth Star-Telegram, American's hometown newspaper. He later joined USA TODAY, where he continued to cover the airline industry, on which he still focuses today as a senior contributor at FORBES.com. As a reporter he sometimes proved to be a terrific pain in the neck to those of us managing American because he too often was able to report what we were going to do before we were ready to disclose what we were up to. Of course, he was just doing his job. And fortunately, for him, he mostly got it right. So, while I did not like our still-secret corporate plans being pasted across the top of the front page of the newspaper delivered to my office every morning, at least most of those stories were about our growth and successes. Dan worked to become something of a journalistic expert on it and on the many subjects like finance, markets, legal and government matters and more in which airlines must be involved. That is not quite the same as being a true expert on the airline business, but he worked hard to make sure he asked the right questions so that he could provide some additional insight to his readers. That understanding and knowledge, combined with his skill as a writer allowed him to explain very clearly the complexities and drama often found in our business. Eventually he even wrote a book about American's turnaround during my time there. Again, while he neither spared me from criticism nor left out some stories I would have preferred he not mention, Dan's book was largely fair and accurate.

I retired from American more than 20 years ago, but I have been happy to visit occasionally with both Dave and Dan about old times and, more interestingly, about current events in the industry to which all three of us devoted big slices of our lives. So now I am pleased to commend this book to anyone interested in the commercial airline industry, as well as to those interested in saving lives, and the advancement of medicine, especially heart-related medicine. I am also pleased to recommend this book to those who just enjoy good stories about those who go above and beyond to make life better – and in this case, longer – for others.

Robert L. Crandall
Retired Chairman, President and CEO of American Airlines and AMR Corp.
July 4, 2019

CHAPTER I

Sudden Cardiac Arrest
The Lethal Assassin

On the average day about nine million people fly aboard commercial airlines, thanks to the rapid growth of air travel around the world. Back in 1995 when our story begins, that number was closer to seven million a day—still an impressively large number, even on a global scale.

On April 24, 1995, Ben Talit was one of those seven million people to travel by plane. But he was one of only a few—maybe even the only one that day—who died while aboard his flight. Mrs. Lynn Talit, his widow, in congressional testimony[1] noted he was a senior analyst and frequent business traveler. His sudden cardiac arrest occurred on Northwest Airlines Flight 339 from Detroit to Los Angeles. Because he was seated in first class Ben had received the highest level of customer service, food, drink, and attention that Northwest could provide. Yet, he still died. Mrs. Talit informed

---

[1] Wednesday, May 21, 1997, U.S. House of Representatives, Subcommittee on Aviation, Committee on Transportation and Infrastructure, Washington, D.C. Medical Kits on Commercial Airlines

House *Members on Committee* on Transportation and Infrastructure in May 1997 that Ben's flight lacked such simple essentials as oxygen canisters, a length of endotracheal tubing, and lidocaine. Furthermore, there was no life-saving defibrillator onboard. And, she explained, the reason none of that critical life-saving gear was aboard her husband's flight that day – or aboard any U.S. commercial airliner - on that or any other day, for that matter, was that none of it was required. Not by the Federal Aviation Administration. Not by the Food and Drug Administration. Not by individual airlines or industry groups. Not by ICAO, the International Civil Aviation Organization, a United Nation's agency charged with coordinating and establishing internationally agreed-upon aviation operating standards. And certainly not by a Congress that had never given much, if any thought to the subject previously.

Ironically, Ben Talit was a fire/rescue volunteer his whole life. He was a deputy fire chief and an emergency medical technician (EMT). He was only 43 and had no known health problems on that fateful morning. Mrs. Talit, with tears in her eyes, said he was a thoughtful and loving husband of 20 years, an exemplary father, a valued professional, a truly good citizen who died for the lack of exactly the kind of preparedness he supported and practiced every day of his life.

But a sudden heart stoppage, or cardiac arrest, on an airplane is a certain death sentence. So, Ben Talit died. It did not matter that he was a First Class passenger and a high mileage frequent flyer. Indeed, it never matters where a passenger sits, in First Class or Coach, when a sudden cardiac arrest occurs in-flight. If it is not addressed immediately and with the proper tools it is a death sentence.

In March of 1995, Bill Rose, age 57 from Simsbury, Connecticut, was traveling on a Northwest flight from Detroit to Phoenix. He, too, was a firefighter and the chief of his local department. Bill Rose also died aboard that plane from a sudden cardiac arrest, though his death certificate never noted that. Instead, it listed his place of death as Phoenix, which is where his lifeless body was removed from the plane[2].

Thus, while Bill Rose, like hundreds and hundreds of others over the years did die in flight there is no official record of it having happened in the air. Death in flight was not, in those days, a statistic kept, at least not officially, by the airlines, the FAA, the Department of Transportation, the Surgeon General, local, or state medical examiners, medical researchers or anyone else. But he – they all - did die in flight; and in Rose's case, as in Talit's and the cases of many, many others, it was the result of sudden cardiac arrest. His heart – their hearts - suddenly stopped. And there was no defibrillator on board that could have gotten it/ them going again.

In the same hearing in May 1997 Jamie Soms, the widow of Steven Soms of Wellesley, Massachusetts, related how the father of two in his late 30s was seated in First Class aboard a United Airlines flight from San Francisco to Boston in October of 1995

---

[2] Under most airline protocols, it is exceedingly rare in the airline industry for anyone to be declared dead on an airplane. Even when a passenger does die on a flight – meaning there's obvious and incontrovertible evidence that the passenger is really dead - flight attendants are trained in most cases to continue their resuscitation efforts until the plane lands and the "passenger" is handed over to paramedics. Only when that passenger is transferred into the care of local paramedics or other medical personnel on the ground is he or she officially declared dead. Regardless of where the plane was – 35,000 feet over Missouri or someplace - when his or her death actually occurs, their death certificate will not say that they died in flight. Instead it will list the place of death as the city where their body is removed from the plane.

when he, too, had a sudden cardiac arrest. And, yes, Steven Soms, like Ben Talit and Bill Rose, died.

On April 19, 1997 on a Northwest Airlines Los Angeles to Detroit flight Mr. Sandy Peters, of Sterling Heights, Michigan, also suffered a cardiac arrest. This time the plane was on the ground in Detroit. But again, no defibrillator was available. Though two doctors tried to save Mr. Peters they could not give him the one lifesaving treatment that the situation demanded, a shock to the heart from a defibrillator.

The two doctors were of the highest caliber. One was a cardiothoracic surgeon, the other an intensivist (a doctor who specializes in Intensive Care Unit complex care). If you knew you were going to have a sudden cardiac arrest - anywhere – you could not pick a pair of doctors more qualified to treat you than the two who responded to Mr. Peters. But, again, their credentials, experience and skill did not count for much without the right tool being available to them. Both doctors later wrote to Sandy Peters' grieving widow that he likely could have been saved if only they had had a defibrillator to use on him aboard that plane. Instead Sandy Peters died at age 45, leaving behind not only his wife but also young children.

Another person who testified in Congress that day was Carolyn McDowell, of Montclair New Jersey. On May 18, 1996 her husband John suffered a heart attack and sudden cardiac arrest aboard a Continental airlines flight. He was formally declared dead after the plane landed in Nassau in The Bahamas, though in reality he died nearly an hour before landing. A doctor who had been on the McDowell's flight heroically had performed chest compressions unassisted for more than 45 minutes (try it sometime... few people could keep that exhausting activity up for even five minutes without a break). But no defibrillator was available on that plane either. Additionally, while the meager FAA medical kit onboard did contain a potentially usable medicine for the heart called epinephrine, there was no way to administer it because the kit did not include the syringe and needle necessary to deliver a potentially life-saving dose. As was nearly always the case back then, the onboard medical kit was woefully inadequate.

The doctor who worked so diligently but vainly to save John McDowell, a fellow passenger/medical doctor identified only as "Dr. Pinder" also had wanted to intubate Mr. McDowell. Intubation is where a doctor or other medical pro puts a tube into a patient's windpipe via their mouth so that oxygen can get directly to the lungs. It also protects the lungs from vomit, which is a common occurrence in cardiac arrest and other emergency health situations. But, once again, the Good Samaritan doctor did not have access to those rather commonly-required medical supplies. Carolyn McDowell tearfully told the members of Congress at the hearing that her husband would have been saved if only a defibrillator had been aboard. She added that the situation that took her husband's life likely would be repeated many more times because the FAA did not require airlines to report in-flight medical emergencies and, therefore there was really no one responsible for tracking any data about such events or looking into possible ways to reduce or eliminate them. Thus, having a heart attack or sudden cardiac arrest on board would continue to be a certain death sentence for future passengers, she said, and more people like her and her children would be left with a huge, unnecessary hole in their lives.

The message from that day of testimony in Congress had been a frustratingly somber one: "How long would this march of death continue? Especially for a potentially treatable condition?"

And who knows how much longer that message would have remained so somber and so frustrating had the events of February 18, 1998 on board an American Airlines jet departing from Dallas-Fort Worth International Airport not occurred? It was then and there that a historic change in air travel – and really in modern life on this planet – began unfolding.

Sudden Cardiac Arrest

What was happening to these people? What was happening was a frightening, lethal, but little-known medical condition, known as Sudden Cardiac Arrest. Just as the name implies, the heart suddenly, without any warning, stops. It stops beating, and stops pumping blood effectively, and the victim most assuredly will die without warning. You may have heard of this with that case of a healthy, young football player out on the high school football field, who collapses and dies. It happens too after electrocution of an electrician working on power transformers, or the sad case of someone struck by lightning.

In the case of otherwise healthy people like athletes, without a shock or lightning strike, why it occurs is often a mystery. It is no respecter of social status or age, and there is no warning. It certainly is some issue with the heart that causes it to go into a chaotic rhythm where it stops pumping blood. It is probably due to at least two things: either a defect in the heart's conduction bundles, or a problem with its blood supply.

Many people do not know that the heart, simply stated, is both a plumbing system with arteries and veins, and an electrical system containing lots and lots of electrical pathways called nerves or conduction bundles. Not only can the heart stop because the 'plumbing' clogs up, stopping blood flow to the heart, but sometimes the electrical system of the heart goes awry, and its rhythm becomes chaotic. That leaves it unable to pump an adequate amount of blood through the body, or, in a worst-case situation, to pump any blood at all.

Regardless of the cause, what happens is a heart rhythm called ventricular fibrillation. The word" fibrillation" comes from the Latin and means 'bag of worms'—which is exactly what a fibrillating heart looks like! If one could look at a person's heart while they are having a sudden cardiac arrest, it would look like a quivering mass of muscle, not a regular beating pump. Ordinarily, an electrocardiogram measures the heart's activity and it works in a very orderly fashion that when shown on a graph looks like this:

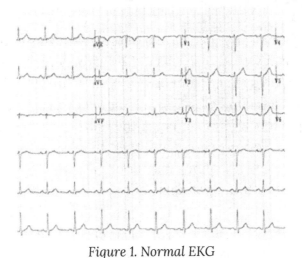

Figure 1. Normal EKG

Instead of the rhythmic pattern of spikes we are used to seeing on an electrocardiogram screen, we see nothing but a chaotic, wavy line, like this:

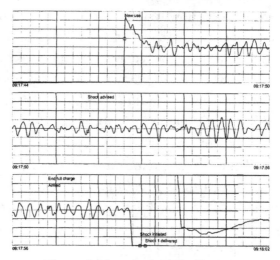

Figure 2. Ventricular Fibrillation

The only thing that can save a person with this condition is a shock from a device known as a defibrillator, which works sort of like the way the battery from one car can be used to "jump start" the engine of a second car via set of jumper cables. Only when you are dealing with the human heart the battery and jumper cables are a lot more sophisticated, and the "jump" or shock to the still heart must be given within a matter of minutes. This condition is otherwise lethal. If the person is not shocked within a very short time of the heart's stopping, the person dies. It is that frighteningly but realistically simple. The sad fact is that for every minute this lifesaving shock is delayed, the odds of survival drop by 10%.

Up until the mid-1990s defibrillators had been big and bulky (remember paramedics John and Roy from EMERGENCY! lugging around that huge box containing their portable defibrillator?). But advancements in the design, size, and quality of defibrillators in the few years just prior to them becoming widely available in public settings, manufacturers shrunk the devices to the size of a book. Furthermore, these new, smaller defibrillators were "automatic," hence their name, "Automatic External Defibrillators," or AEDs for short. They came with audible talking instructions on how to attach them to a patient's chest, and then on how to turn them on. From that point on the machine took over; monitoring the patient's heart beat and pulse and using its expert internal programing to determine if, when and how much of a shock should be delivered to the patient. That made it possible for almost anyone to use it to potentially save the life of a person suffering a sudden cardiac arrest.

Although there are many kinds, this is what one type of an Automatic External Defibrillator (AED) looks like:

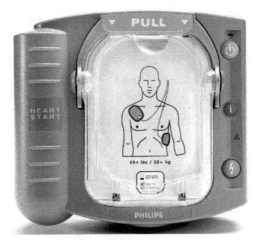

Figure 3. Automatic External Defibrillator (AED)

It is bad enough when a sudden cardiac arrest occurs on the ground. Afterall, every minute of delay from them receiving that life-saving shock decreases their chances of living by about 10%. Even if a paramedic responds with a defibrillator in 8 minutes, and then applies the defibrillator, the odds are that the patient has already died.

So, you can understand why it would be a particularly daunting challenge when a commercial airline passenger's heart stops. By the time a plane could get back down to the ground, let alone taxi back to the gate - at best a 30-minute process - the passenger would be long dead.

Yet it is odd that what is known as Public Access Defibrillation, the idea of placing the defibrillators everywhere, like fire extinguishers, so anyone could quickly respond and save a life, started in the United States on a large scale with a single airline: American Airlines.

Up until American placed them on all their planes, and trained 25,000 flight attendants to use them, there was no such large-scale usage of the devices. But the notion of putting these life saving devices everywhere took off quickly after American's tremendous success.

I think the rapid deployment of Automatic External Defibrillators eventually would have taken place without what I brought to American Airlines. Still, American's story was unusual as to how and why it happened. Looking back on my life in this memoir, I feel the events and circumstances in my upbringing and training contributed to the development of a country-wide and world-wide move toward the rapid placement of AEDs in public places all around the world in the late 1990s and early 2000s. Furthermore, the rapid deployment of AEDs in public places around the world would not have happened without the foresight and support of a visionary CEO, like Robert Crandall, and a dynamo nurse who worked at American, Linda Campbell. They however were only catalysts...this program came about through the efforts and contributions of teams of some of the finest Medical Personnel, flight attendants, flight attendant trainers, pilots, maintenance workers, and purchasing experts at American. It truly was a tremendous team effort that made this program fly.

This is the miraculous story of how AEDs and Enhanced Medical Kits got onto airplanes, and ultimately, everywhere in the United States. American's venture took away the excuse from all other industries for public access defibrillation. If a business with 700 aircraft that rove around the world could supply and maintain these life-saving devices, so could any business or public setting...and they eventually did!

Let me now tell you the story of the true, near miraculous first use of this remarkable device for the first time on board a United States plane.

CHAPTER II

THE FIRST SHOCK

Four people unexpectedly crossed paths on American Airlines Flight 2017 from Dallas Fort Worth Airport to Mexico City on February 18, 1998 flying themselves into history in the fight against the silent assassin Sudden Cardiac Arrest.

Carmen and Robert Giggey

Carmen and Robert were college sweethearts. They met at the Baltimore Bible College, a now-defunct college operated by the American Evangelistic Association. They were deeply Christian people, who trusted God for everything in their lives.

Their personalities are distinctively different. Carmen is a vivacious, lively, talkative lady from Santa Ana, California; Robert a reserved, calm, cool and collected gentleman from Maine. Robert also was a big man. Standing 6 feet, 4 inches, and weighing over 350 pounds, it is easy to understand how he earned the nickname "Big Gig."

They dated while in college, but they did not marry each other at first. Instead, Robert married another coed and graduate of Baltimore Bible College. They moved to Connecticut and adopted two children. But Robert's wife soon determined that marriage and the life of a mother were not for her. They separated and eventually divorced.

Carmen, meanwhile, met and married a man with whom she had children. They moved to Florida for her work. But, sadly, her first husband died, making her a young widow.

Ultimately, Carmen and Robert were reunited at a college reunion. Knowing of their past fondness for each other, members of the reunion committee played Cupid to get them back together. Thereafter Carmen and Robert began calling each other frequently and rather quickly rekindled their love.

They started dating once again in 1994, and wed on September 9, 1995, at Davidson Park in Burlington, North Carolina. It was a huge, joyous event with friends past and present joining in their celebration. They then moved to Roxboro, North Carolina. Carmen continued in her job as an expert in payroll systems for Human Resources departments. Robert worked in the Machining and Fabrication business.

Two-and-half years into their marriage the Giggeys decided to travel to Mexico. Carmen had earned a "use it or lose it" vacation award from her employer. Her company would not pay Carmen cash in lieu of taking the trip, so they had to go or lose the value of that trip. Besides, the Giggeys thought, it would be fun. Carmen was a critical contributor to various payroll and computer system support projects that her company was working on at the time; the kind of projects that would require her presence on certain days, particularly weekend days which companies often use to make major changes to their data systems. So, she and Robert picked a mid-week date of departure for their Mexico trip to work around those requirements. That is how their historic trip on American Flight 2017 came to be on Wednesday, February 18, 1998.

They flew out of Raleigh Durham Airport to the sprawling Dallas-Fort Worth International Airport in Texas, where they changed planes to get on Flight 2017 bound for Mexico City

It was a cool day at Raleigh Durham; about 54 degrees, and not a cloud in the sky. Because of Big Gig's stature Carmen had purchased seats in the front of the coach section, where there was more leg room. When they got on board, however, they noticed a woman with a foldup wheelchair seated in Robert's assigned seat, and her travel companion was sitting in Carmen's. The flight attendant asked if they could exchange seats with this disabled traveler and her companion. The Giggeys had hearts of gold to begin with, so of course they were glad to make the switch even though it meant they had to sit near the back of the coach section, where Big Gig wouldn't have the extra leg room Carmen had tried to arrange for him.

As they were walking to the back of the plane Carmen turned to her husband and said, "This could bring good luck, Dear!"

Robert, smiling, responded with a whimsical "Harrumph."

When they arrived at their new seats, Robert took the window seat, which meant he would be unable to let his legs slip out into the aisle for a little more comfort. He commented to Carmen as he squeezed into the seat, with his knees up to his chest, "At least I don't need to squeeze into a wheelchair each day like that poor woman does." Carmen smiled, again loving deeply the kind, good hearted man she finally had married.

Sitting on the other side of Carmen, who was squeezed into the tight middle seat, was a leader from the Girl Scouts. The lady was traveling with several other management employees from the Girl Scouts organization. They were on their way to Mexico City for a convention. She had with her a travel guide book about Mexico, which she let Carmen peruse. Carmen did more than just peruse it; she gave it nearly all her attention during that first leg of the trip to DFW because it was such a thorough and tip-filled guide to their destination.

When the Giggeys arrived at DFW Carmen asked Robert to join her in finding a bookstore because she wanted to get a copy of that travel guide. They succeeded in finding a book store. Alas, it did not stock the Mexico guide book she had enjoyed on the flight from Raleigh Durham. So, they proceeded to their gate to catch the Flight 2017 to Mexico City.

On their way to the gate they stepped onto a moving sidewalk. It did not move all that fast, but at least it kept a steady pace and saved their legs a bit. Oddly, Robert started complaining about his ears hurting.

Carmen dismissed his complaint and admonished him: 'You didn't chew gum and got some ear pressure from the previous flight. You need to start chewing gum! Start chewing—I don't want to hear about it when we have dinner tonight in Mexico City!"

Minutes later they boarded Flight 2017. To their surprise they were in the same seats as before, again next to the same group of Girl Scout leaders. Carmen again was able to look at the travel guide she had searched for at DFW but could not locate. She also began handing sticks of gum to Robert, for his ears, as the plane started its taxi out to the runway. She also carried on a fun conversation with the Girl Scout leader seated next to her, even as she kept on funneling gum to Robert.

After a time, she noticed he had stopped taking the gum. She turned to look at him, and said, "Keep taking the gum, or your ears will pop!"

He did not answer. His eyes looked funny. She had never seen eyes like that --"they were not alive" she later said. They were open and fixed in a gaze looking up, like he was going to turn on a ceiling fan or a light.

The seat belt sign was still on, but she stood up while the plane was moving and slid directly in front of her husband. He did not respond at all to her movements in that very tiny space between his long-but-compressed legs and the seatback in front of him. He appeared dead.

She let out a scream for help so loud that all passengers turned to them. She screamed for help again.

Despite the FAA mandate to stay in one's seat during the takeoff phase of flight, a flight attendant and an off-duty paramedic released their seatbelts, got up, and ran to Carmen as she stood over her stricken husband. A Mexican doctor seated ahead in the First Class section also responded.

Shawn Lynn, the Flight Attendant

Shawn was a beautiful, young flight attendant with the clearest, most peaceful face, brown hair, and brown eyes. She was a seasoned flight attendant for American, having graduated with the flight attendant class of 1990-1991. Yet, like so many people, Shawn silently struggled with the deep darkness of depression. She, in fact, was at her darkest low on that very day. Her husband had told her the day before that she should not come back home after her next trip. Also, one of her closest girlfriends had just died.

Shawn had reached the point where she did not feel life was worth living any longer. She no longer had a home to go to once she went off duty. She felt more alone than she ever had been. She simply could not take the pain any longer, she thought. Indeed, she already had been thinking about suicide for some time. And these most recent circumstances were just more than her heart could bear. She, in fact, had determined to take her own life that very day.

As she was starting to implement her plans, Shawn got a call from American's Systems Operations Control (SOC) center, where teams of experts manage the day-to-day, hour-to-hour operations of the huge airline with, in those days more than 700 big and small planes. The flight attendants' team at SOC, whose job it is to make sure enough attendants with enough remaining monthly duty hours are onboard each flight, called Shawn, asking if she could cover a trip for which some other attendant had called in sick.

The timing of that call was uncanny. Had it come a few minutes later Shawn might not have been alive to answer the phone. She thought to herself, "Well, I will go on this trip, and then make some decisions after that."

You see, Shawn had been assigned that month to "stand-by" duty, meaning she did not have a pre-determined duty and flight schedule for the month. Rather, on certain days and at certain times that month she had to be ready at a moment's notice to fill in on any flight that was short a flight attendant, for whatever reason. And, truth be told, Shawn had enough seniority that she could have rejected the SOC's first attempt to assign her to a flight at the last minute. She could have waited for a second, hopefully preferable duty assignment. And for a few minutes she half-way tried to bargain herself into a better trip assignment. But, oddly, this time she failed in using her rank to get an assignment that she liked better.

In any case, she viewed her new assignment that day to Flight 2017 to Mexico City, with a return trip - as "a real dog trip." If it is not already made clear by the term she used, a "dog trip" is a very undesirable assignment in flight attendant-lingo. But she had no place else to go. She certainly could not go home again. So, she thought, "why not?"

Shawn was assigned to the third flight attendant position for the DFW-Mexico City flight. That means she was responsible for serving passengers in the back end of the plane.

Shawn first had to catch a flight to DFW, "deadheading" as airline people call it when they take a vacant seat (for free) on a company plane in order to reach the airport where they are to begin their duty, or when they are returning home from a few days on duty. Her deadhead flight landed at DFW with just enough time left for her to dash off the plane, through the airport and onto Flight 2017 before the plane's door closed behind her.

She quickly stowed her luggage, but as she did, a new item on the plane caught Shawn's eye. She noticed for the first time a logo of a heart pierced by a bolt of lightning. (It was the logo that I had designed when we were first developing the defibrillator program. I had even gotten it copyrighted. It or variants of it are now a commonplace logo for automatic external defibrillators.) It drew her attention instantly and she knew immediately what it was. She thought to herself, "Oh, so that is where the new on-board defibrillator is." She also thought: "What a neat logo!"

She had read in her periodic training literature about American's new effort to place defibrillators on planes. She also read a detailed article about the program that I had written for the Association of Professional Flight Attendants' union magazine, AAirmail. She remembered from the AAirmail article, and from her training material, that American was the first airline in the United States to place them onboard planes, or to place them in mass numbers anywhere for that matter. It was a novel, controversial move. People generally did not view flight attendants as being capable of this level of emergency response. She recalled that American had decided to place them first on international flights, and to train a cadre of senior flight attendants, called pursers, on their use. That made sense to her because such flights typically lasted many hours and often were hours away from a suitable runway near a hospital.

Because Shawn was classified as a domestic flight attendant, she had not yet been trained to use the Automated External Defibrillator (AED). She knew it was about the size of a book, and, per her recollection from my article, "had the wisdom of 100 cardiologists in a box, analyzing the passenger's heart rhythm." She also knew that the machine talked to the user, telling them exactly what to do. Yet, while DFW-Mexico City is more like a domestic flight in length and in the way American managed its operation, it technically was an international flight. Thus, it had been equipped with one of the new defibrillators. And, providentially, Shawn had happened to notice its location on the plane. It was the first time she had ever seen one. The container in which it was placed was locked, but she knew that could be opened with a key that all crewmembers carry.

This particular defibrillator had been placed on this particular aircraft just two days earlier. It had never been used. In fact, none of the AEDs installed to that date on American's planes had ever been used to provide an actual shock.

Curiously, Shawn had, for years, been having a recurring dream about performing CPR - cardiopulmonary resuscitation – during a flight. Of course, CPR involves delivering compressions to the chest of a person who is having a heart attack or sudden cardiac arrest. And if the patient is not breathing, CPR calls for someone responding to them to blow air directly into the patient's mouth.

Shawn's was not a nightmarish kind of dream, but in one sense it was a haunting one in that Shawn was not comfortable with the thought of doing mouth-to-mouth resuscitation. To her it seemed pretty disgusting. She had never actually been called upon in training to do it. And she was not entirely sure she could do it if real circumstances ever called upon her to try.

That recurring dream often came back to her during times of stress in Shawn's life. And certainly, she was experiencing an extraordinary amount of stress in her life as she boarded Flight 2017. In fact, she had had the dream just the night prior, before she even knew she would be on a flight the next day. In her recurring dream she always worked her way through steps of the resuscitation process before getting to the point where mouth-to-mouth resuscitation is called for. Then the dream would end with Shawn still not knowing if she could overcome her discomfort and negative inclinations to save someone's life. She wondered, as she thought about her dream, could this be a metaphor for me trying to bring life back to myself? Or is it preparing me for something...?

Don Grohman, the Paramedic/Firefighter

The fourth actor in our story of Flight 2017 was paramedic /firefighter Don Grohman. He was traveling with a team of men from his church in Richardson, Texas, a northern Dallas suburb. They were headed to Mexico City to do some construction work as part of a mission project. They were flying into Mexico City with all their construction equipment. Once they arrived, they were taking a bus to a destination about two hours away in central Mexico.

Don was raised on a farm near Walberg, Texas, an unincorporated community about 35 miles northeast of Austin that was settled in the 1890s by German immigrants. At age 12 he moved with his family to nearby Georgetown TX, then at age 16, to Richardson. He graduated from the Fire Academy in December of 1984 and joined the Garland Fire Department, another suburb of Dallas just to the southeast of Richardson. He went to EMT and Paramedic school at the University of Texas' highly-regarded Southwestern Medical School in Dallas in 1985 as part of an elite program for local fire departments. At the time, he was the youngest firefighter in the Garland Fire Department.

Grohman also was strikingly handsome. In fact, after the first shock event he was involved in, one of the American Airlines nurses and I went out to the Garland, TX fire station after the event to meet him and to thank him personally. The nurse muttered to me, "Boy, I would not mind being resuscitated by him!"

Don was the complete package! He not only had brawn, and good looks, but also brains. He was very smart and action oriented. On

38

Flight 2017 he and his fellow missionaries were sitting in the rear of the plane as the plane left the gate. He heard Carmen Giggey's ominous scream for help. Immediately he jumped out of his seat and made his way forward.

Shawn Lynn also heard that loud scream and noticed the commotion up the aisle ahead of her and on the right side of the cabin. The plane's overhead call system – chimes initiated by passengers touching the call button on the panel above their heads, started to go off repeatedly. Then she heard her No.1 flight attendant, seated near the cockpit, page for a doctor or medical professional to help. There was also a group of people who had gotten out their seats and were standing in the aisle despite the plane being in motion as it taxied out.

Yet, it seemed to Shawn that no other flight attendant had moved in response to whatever was going on. Perhaps it was because American's flight attendant trainers had hammered into their minds the way they had hammered it into hers that it is a strict Federal Aviation Administration Rule that passengers - and especially flight attendants, the responsible safety officials in the cabin - must remain seated during taxi and takeoff. In fact, the No. 1 attendant was staying in her seat and using the PA system to order all passengers to re-take their seats.

But whatever was happening in front of her sure seemed to be unusual – and serious. So, Shawn unbuckled herself from the fold-down attendants' seat in which she had been strapped and responded to the growing chaos ahead in the aisle. "We can write up an FAA variance to procedure later," she thought as she moved into action. The other flight attendants seemed, momentarily at least, to be frozen in their place, unsure of how, or even whether to respond.

Scant seconds later, however, the No. 1 got on the PA again: "Again, is there a doctor or nurse on board, or anyone who can help? Please identify yourself," she pleaded, her voice cracking with anxiety.

By the time Shawn had made her way up to row 13, she had noted Mr. Giggey was in seat F, up against the window, unconscious. She also was impressed by how dead he looked. He was not moving, not breathing, and already was turning that ashen gray color so often associated with death.

A doctor from Mexico who responded said he could feel a pulse, but neither Shawn nor the young man who identified himself as a paramedic could find one. That paramedic was Don Grohman, trained and experienced in handling medical emergencies in all sorts of odd places. He took command of the scene naturally, the way a pro basketball player can take over a pick-up game with the neighborhood kids without saying a word.

He noted that Robert Giggey was so large that he could not be moved to the floor. So, Don and Shawn, perhaps with the help of other passengers, maneuvered him into position across the three seats in his row. By this time, nearby passengers had moved out into the aisle and into the empty row of seats ahead of Giggey. It was not much, but Don and Shawn at least had some room to work at that point.

Don quickly asked aloud whether anyone knew CPR. Shawn said, "I do!" just as she had so many times before in her recurring dream. He asked for a mask and oxygen. Shawn fetched at least the oxygen out of the main cabin overhead bin. The mask was nowhere to be found on that first run. When she got back, she again checked Giggey for a pulse. She could not find one. So, Don instructed her to begin CPR.

Meanwhile, Carmen Giggey, a devoutly Christian woman, was praying at Robert's feet. She said to herself, "I must touch him and pray. "Dear Jesus," she prayed, "please save the life of my husband." People kept trying to get her away from him, to provide more room.

She stubbornly refused, saying repeatedly, "I must touch him—I must pray: Dear God, please bring my husband back."

At the same time Shawn had to face her dream in real life and discover whether she really could perform mouth-to-mouth resuscitation on someone. And not only did she have to overcome that basic fear, she quickly discovered she would have to do it without a sanitary barrier because no such barrier or tissue was included in the onboard medical kit, and no mask was readily available.

Yet Shawn did not hesitate. The man was dying and needed her help. She delivered 2 full breaths directly into his lungs.

Even as she did so, Shawn remembered her dream clearly. He needed her help. Only this time the dream did not stop with the question of whether she could perform under pressure un-answered. In real life she was able to render that life-saving help without missing a beat. Robert Giggey's head was positioned per-fectly. She quickly achieved a perfect seal with her lips around his to give him powerful resuscitating blasts of air. She was not afraid at all. It certainly helped that her adrenaline was flowing.

Shawn continued the mouth to mouth resuscitation. But as she did, time oddly slowed down for her. Her awareness to things hap-pening around her increased yet she was able to sort the import-ant from the unimportant automatically. The shouting seemed to be quite distant from her.

Then during all the chaos, Shawn remembers hearing some-thing that caught her very much by surprise. At first, she thought maybe it was because of the stress stemming from the break-up of her marriage and her decision – aborted, temporarily that morning - to end her life. Or perhaps it was the result of having become lightheaded from performing mouth-to mouth-resusci-tation over and over.

But she clearly and unmistakably heard a voice, saying:

"Isn't life precious? Do not throw your life away. I am closer to you and care for you more than breath itself. If you have breath you have a chance to change. You have life. You have a chance to live."

Upon hearing it Shawn lifted her head to see who spoke those words to her. A lot of people certainly were talking and screaming. But no one was near her speaking those words. Still, she heard them. They were spoken clearly by a very real, audible voice. Shawn was stunned in disbelief, even as she continued with her mouth-to-mouth resuscitation efforts. Then, as she worked on Robert Giggey, an incredible 'peace that passed all understanding' came to her troubled mind.

While Shawn continued blowing breaths into Giggey's lungs, and seemingly having spiritual breath blown into her mind, Don Grohman performed a series of chest compressions. Giggey, however, was not responding to their efforts. His jaw already was locked, and Don feared that body fluids would start seeping from the mouth. He once again strongly advised Shawn to get protection to protect her from encountering the potentially dangerous body fluids that could come flooding out of Mr. Giggey's mouth and nose.

"Get me a mask!" Shawn screamed to her fellow flight attendants, to no avail. For the longest time, it seemed, they were still frozen in place in their seats, waiting for clearance from the flight's captain to get up. Then, when they could move, the other attendants could not find a mask anywhere onboard. A bit later, after Flight 2017 re-docked at the gate from which it had just departed someone brought a mask that they had retrieved from the American jet parked one spot over.

Shawn used it.

So, Don and Shawn worked, with no success, to revive Robert Giggey, Don's training told him to do what he always does when a patient remains unresponsive, unconscious, and not breathing he yelled "Get me a defibrillator."

He then quickly recalled, aloud, that airplanes do not carry defibrillators.

"This one does!" Shawn responded without missing a beat.

She ran and got it.

CHAPTER III

40 Years Earlier
Silverware and Space Shuttles

How did that defibrillator get on board?

Well, that is a long – and unique – story. I would like to take some time to tell you that story, if you will bear with me. So, this is both a cliff hanger AND a flashback! And I mean, WAY back about 40 years. After all, this book is in part my memoir! Then I promise we will jump back to what happened to Mr. Giggey, Carmen Giggey, Shawn, and Don.

They called me "Dr. Dave" around the headquarters of American Airlines in far east Fort Worth, just outside the gates of the Dallas-Fort Worth Airport. I was part of the airline's medical staff for about a decade, and Corporate Medical Director between 1994 and 2002. I am also one of those guys whose name, in print, often is followed by an alphabet soup of letters like "M.D." and "M.P.H." My now-grown daughters, Erin and Catherine, used to laugh at the "M.D." part, saying as children that it stood for "My Daddy," or, as they grew into sometimes sassy teenagers, "Mentally Deranged!" They, it seems, inherited at least some of their Dad's sense of humor. And, indeed, I pretty much always relied on humor in dealing with people. Mine was – and is - a dry sort of humor that others see as sly, or quirky but that would cause Erin and my wife, Laurie, to groan in disbelief. Catherine, on the other hand, is much like me and typically would laugh hysterically at my jokes and puns.

At the very moment that Shawn Lynn ran up the aisle or her airplane to fetch that new-fangled defibrillator, I was in my office at American's headquarters on Amon Carter Boulevard about three miles away, just across Texas State Highway 183, better known as Airport Freeway. Bettye Harris, my adept executive secretary and Linda Campbell, a human dynamo of a registered nurse who led some of my department's aeromedical programs, burst into my office at almost the exact same time.

"John Hotard from Corporate Communications called. They just got word through the System Operations Control that a defibrillator was just pulled to aid an unresponsive man on a flight to Mexico. They are trying to revive him," Bettye said, the words spilling excitedly out of her mouth like a rushing waterfall.

"The passenger is a 'Robert Giggey,' " Linda blurted out the next second.

"Has it shocked yet? Did he make it?" I asked, visibly shaking with excitement.

"We don't know," Linda answered. "I'll go out to the airport and get more details."

Moments later the phones in the Corporate Medical Office started ringing, and they kept ringing all day. Media inquiries started flowing in from the local news outlets – newspapers, news radio stations, local TV reporters, trade publications, even national news organizations. Bettye stepped out of my office to start fielding the phone calls. As a man of faith, I quietly prayed, and wept a bit as I did so. As I often did, I went alone into the small clinic we maintained at headquarters to find a quiet place amidst the sudden storm of activity happening in the office suite.

"Thank you, God, for letting this come to pass," I quietly muttered. "You know it has not been easy. I pray that Mr. Giggey comes back to life." My prayer was sincere. The fate of this "Mr. Giggey" really was foremost in my mind as I prayed. But I must confess, I also wanted him to survive for the greater meaning it would have on the biggest project of my career and of my life. If he lived, I thought, my work, and the work of the team I'd formed and worked so closely with for the past couple of years, would be vindicated against the professional – and sometimes unprofessional – criticism we'd received and the skepticism of some of our doubters and business competitors.

No sooner had I finished praying I began to experience something I had not quite expected. A sense of peace, and of quiet reverie came over me. The same 'peace that passeth all understanding' that was infusing Shawn Lynn the flight attendant at the time was infusing into my heart, mind, and soul. And I began to reflect on all the events that happened over the previous forty years that had led to this tragic-yet-momentous moment in medical history. Believe me, we will for sure get back to the main story, but let's digress for just a bit.

A Long Time Ago in Rural New York State

I was born in a small town in Upstate New York, called Oneida. You may be familiar with the Oneida Silverware brand.

Oneida, or more specifically, neighboring Sherrill was also the home of the mystical Oneida Community. That was the name of a 19th century utopian experiment with a lot of controversial practices which did not sit well with the traditional Christian community back then. The Oneida Community members practiced birth control, a rare thing in the mid-19th Century. They also practiced what most others saw as the scandalous practices of communalism and what is termed "complex marriage." In effect, because possessiveness and exclusiveness were frowned upon in their somewhat unique and highly unorthodox brand of Christianity, Oneidan society encouraged members to consider themselves to be married to all other adults in the community. That meant they could have, and did have sex with multiple partners within the community, typically under the oversight of the Community elders. What is more, matronly women often introduced young boys to sex in a kind of sexual mentoring process while older men did much the same with young girls. The practice, which certainly seems bizarre and even demented to modern readers, was intended to give young people experience without much risk of pregnancies resulting.

Their Community and faith dwindled in numbers in the 1860s and 1870s before eventually dissolving as a religious entity in 1881, three years after a tornado devastated most of their small town.

The Oneidans, however, still found a way to leave their mark on history and America. One of the ways they supported themselves and their Community was through the manufacturing of fine silverware. So successful was that enterprise that when the last few Oneidans legally dissolved their religion, they reorganized the entity as a business with the silverware factory as its primary asset. Across the late 19th and early 20th Centuries that business grew into one of the largest highly regarded makers of silver flatware and tableware. The company survived the Great Depression and both World Wars. It even converted its facilities to produce war time necessities like Army trucks, ammunition clips and shells, medical instruments, combat knives, survival kits and even aircraft engine parts during those wars.

I grew up knowing my entire family, including my Sicilian and Lithuanian immigrant grandparents, plus all their relatives - brothers, sisters, and children - had worked or were still working at the Oneida Silverware plant in Sherrill, an even smaller town a couple of miles outside Oneida. In fact, pretty much everyone in my family had spent at least some time in their lives working in that plant. Everyone, that is, except me. Descendents of the Community were well known. I even remember when the granddaughter of Community founder John Humphrey Noyes, Constance Noyes Robertson, would come to our house to get dresses worked on by my mother.

So, my brother Allen, my sister Barbara and I grew up in Oneida. It was a town with strong family values. Our house literally sat in the shadow of a huge Presbyterian church steeple. Our mother, Bessie, was the sixth of eight children born to Carmello and Maria Caputo Manaseri, who had immigrated to the United States from Sicily in 1910. Maria died in childbirth with her 8th child in 1916, and is buried in St. Patrick's Cemetery in Oneida with that eighth infant, who also died in the event, in her arms. That left Bessie motherless while still a child. She eventually married Allen McKenas Sr. a World War II veteran and son of Lithuanian immigrants.

Bessie worked out of our home as a seamstress. She made us kids go to Sunday School, complete with clip-on ties for the boys and pressed dresses for Barbara, every Sunday morning. She also helped with the church's kindergarten class during Sunday School. She was a kind-hearted lady with a passion for life - and a strong

Sicilian temper! She was the model of a Good Samaritan. One time, she found an elderly man in the snow out in the country. He was practically unable to move because of his prolonged exposure to frigid temperatures. Somehow, though, she managed to get him to our home, where she fed him and cared for him while finding out where his family was.

Our father, Allen Sr., on the other hand, was not a church goer at all. But he was very, very bright. Despite being, along with his parents, a relatively recent immigrant who spoke no English upon landing in American, Allen quickly mastered the language and became Valedictorian of his senior class at Oneida High School before heading out to war. He also was quite an accomplished violinist.

As is natural, both of my parents left big marks on my personality and character that continue to this day. My mother's imprint was the longest-lasting and most profound, for reasons that will become clear.

Notably, it was thanks to those Sunday mornings at the Presbyterian church that my mother insisted I attend that I, in a very circuitous and improbable way, eventually found myself in a position to have a lasting impact on global public health. That is because it was at that church just down the street in Oneida where I discovered my first passion – music. It is also where I became comfortable with, and learned a lot about God and the Christianity that remains at the center of my life today.

Indeed, some of my earliest and fondest memories revolve around hearing beautiful carols and hymns echoing through the snowy streets and neighborhoods of my home town as they rang out from the belfry in the church's steeple at 6 p.m. on Christmas Eve. Those wonderful old carols were played on actual bells back in those days in the 1960s instead of via some recording or electronic system. There's a subtle yet distinct qualitative difference between the sound of real bells tolling and the sound of some electronic facsimile of bells that a serious music lover and trained musician like me can appreciate - and that so many of others can enjoy more heartily even though they can't explain why.

I participated in every activity that church had to offer children growing up in Oneida, including Cub Scouts and Boy Scouts. One time I and a buddy, Dave Woodcock, found our way into the organ loft and to the small keyboard that controlled those steeple bells whose sounds I so fondly remember these days. It was the first –and probably the last - time ever that "Chopsticks" was heard all over Oneida as the bells resounded from that Presbyterian church steeple. The church janitor quickly came in and shooed us boys out even before he got close enough to see who the actual culprits of such mischief were.

It was because of my early, deep love of music that I began taking piano lessons at age six and progressed along the path of what some said was that of a prodigy. My first piano teacher was a woman by the name of Dorothy Brophy who lived on Main Street in Oneida. At first, I struggled to even learn where the notes were located on the keyboard. Mrs. Brophy, though was kind and patient. She kept saying: "Remember "F-A-C-E" and "Every Good Boy Does Fine!" That, in fact, is the first thing anyone taking piano lessons must learn. It is the road map to finding one's way around a keyboard and through a sheet of music. The letters E, G, B, D, F are the letters on a musical staff as printed on a sheet of music. And they correspond to the notes on the piano.

I wanted so much to be a "Good Boy," and to "Do fine!" But for a few weeks, I just did not get it! Then one day, out of the blue, I did "get it." I simply figured it out. And Mrs. Brophy was so impressed! Or at least she seemed impressed to this very self-impressed little boy.

51

From that point on I progressed through the piano books at lightning speed, surpassing my older sister's level, and she had begun taking piano lesson two years before I had. I quickly was playing the Chopin Minute Waltz in recital - to astounded audiences.

Mrs. Brophy then retired, only about a year after I had begun taking lessons from her. So, at age seven, I became the student of Mayola Warner. I not only learned a lot about playing the piano from her, she taught me about even more important things in life. One day, after a lesson, Mrs. Warner explained to me exactly who Jesus Christ was. After having attended the Presbyterian church every Sunday for years already, Mrs. Warner's explanation seemed to me to be a very natural and sensible explanation of the most important thing about life. So, at that time I fully accepted Jesus as my Savior. I felt then, as I do still today, that this decision that day to become a Christian was the most important decision in my life, and that it influenced all other decisions I made from that point forward.

In a bit of humorous symmetry this woman with the old-fashioned name, Mayola, also happened to be the organist at the Presbyterian Church – the one who played the keyboard that controlled those bells up in the church's steeple that I remember so fondly. She also had me, at the age of just seven, join her in a piano-organ rendition of the old hymn "Fairest Lord Jesus." Our duet became the talk of the town. Now well into her 90s, Mrs. Warner still lives in Oneida.

When I was 11, and in the sixth grade, a famous choir came to Oneida and grabbed hold of my thoughts – and my heart. The Columbus Boychoir (later re-named the American Boychoir) was known as America's answer to the Vienna Boys Choir. Not only did they perform all around the nation and internationally, too, the choir members attended their own boarding school in Princeton,

NJ. I was so taken with the Boychoir that I auditioned both as a vocalist and as a piano player. Not only did I do well on both auditions, I was accepted to the Boychoir and given a full scholarship to their school. That is how, at just 12 years old, I left my mother, father, brother, and sister and began preparing for a deeply impactful life as an adult.

I moved to Princeton, began studying music theory and became a member of a professional touring choir at the start of my 7th grade year, a time when most boys are stuck in the awkward stage when they are no longer a "little boy" but aren't yet quite a man. What's more, because I was so talented on the piano, I immediately was plugged into the touring Boychoir's performances as a featured soloist. Thus, while other choir members dashed off stage to make costume changes between sets of songs, I would keep the audiences engaged and entertained from the piano.

The choir would tour 10 weeks at a time, traveling around in a special bus equipped with a piano in the back, and a refrigerator. School was held right on the bus. The choir's academic teachers traveled with us, and we had to do their homework assignments on the bus. Motion sickness became a common companion for us all.

As a member of the Choir from age 12 to age 16, I found himself frequently in front of thousands of people, both singing as part of the group and playing piano pieces by Mozart and Sibelius as a soloist. Whatever stage fright I might have had as a kid quickly was extinguished. I often got standing ovations and excellent reviews from those performances. I accompanied the choir, too, on some songs, especially for the performance of an operetta by Benjamin Britten called The Golden Vanity. The piano score was complex and dissonant. And, because of the touring nature of the choir, the facilities and the equipment were of, shall we say, "varying" degrees of quality. During one performance in some long-forgotten city's civic auditorium I encountered my first, and only mobile piano. Whenever I would press one of the pedals with my foot, the piano itself would move two inches forward. By the end of the operetta, I - and the piano - had managed to move completely across the stage, from one side to the other – with no one else's assistance.

Life at the Boychoir school was, in many ways idyllic. Despite what you might expect from an organization that expects such a degree of discipline and maturity from youngsters who perform 200 or so shows a year, there was plenty of time for fun boy stuff. The estate at which the school was located in Princeton in those days used to belong to a pharmacist; Jordan Wheat Lambert, the inventor of Listerine and founder of the company that first made and sold the antiseptic mouthwash. It was a sprawling, beautiful southern-style mansion with Roman columns, gardens, fountains, and a wonderful hill for cardboard tobogganing. At the base of that hill there was a pristine fishing creek, untouched by civilization, where I and my buddies spent many a Huckleberry Finn weekend. We all also became convinced that there were secret tunnels that connected to other parts of the estate, where the school buildings were. Many a weekend was spent looking for those tunnels in the woods.

Still, as you also would expect of a young teenager living away at a boarding school, I missed my mother and father – and my siblings – fiercely. I cried every time I had to leave home to return to school, and I looked forward eagerly to going home whenever a vacation break was coming up. My mother rode the bus with me from Oneida NY, through New York City, and then on to Princeton the first time I left home to join the Boychoir. But after that I was on my own during my travels between Oneida and Princeton. Nowadays, few parents would even consider allowing a child my age back then to catch a bus to New York City, make a connection to another bus at the Port of Authority Bus Terminal, and then travel on to Oneida all on their own. But at 12, that was what I did, and what many other Boychoir members did. Times were far different then.

It was because of these experiences that I became fiercely independent and self-reliant, a trait that aggravated my wife. But as a result, I became very adept on the stage and developed a strong stage presence and the ability to talk freely to very large groups of people.

But life with the Boychoir was not without its challenges. I had been away at school at Princeton only a year or so when my father died. It happened on Saturday, April 5, 1969, the day before Easter. The odd thing was that I had dreamed repeatedly that my father had died, even pinpointing the day it would happen, months ahead of his actual passing. Allen Sr. was not ill, so there was no logical reason for me to believe – or dream - that he would die. Yet the dreams were so provocative, and so lucid that months before his actual death I had told my sister Barbara about my dreams and their apparent prediction that our father soon would die the day after Good Friday. I had three differently-themed dreams, each of which made it clear that Dad's death occurred on the day after Good Friday – which is also the day before Easter. Then I forgot about them.

Sure enough, my father had a stroke one week before Easter and died at the young age of 52 on the day after Good Friday, just as I had dreamed, and as I had told my sister many months in advance. I was away at school in Princeton and my mother had not even sent word of my father's stroke and hospitalization. And word did not reach me that Dad had died until the day after his passing, Easter Sunday. The Headmaster at the choir school called me down to his office that Sunday morning to give me the sad news.

It was frightening to be called into the Headmaster's quarters. Harvey MacArthur was a tall man who the Boychoir members genuinely feared, not only because of his imposing size but because we all knew he owned a large paddle and was well-practiced in its use. Mr. MacArthur sat down in an office chair. I sat on the couch across from him, dressed in my Choir dress blazer, we boys were all ready to be bussed into church in downtown Princeton.

"David, do you know what a stroke is?" the Headmaster asked.

"Yes, Sir, I do," I replied

"David, your father has had a stroke."

"Is he OK?" I asked fearfully.

Mr. Macarthur said: "David, your father has died".

At age 12 and living away from home for the first time I was ill-prepared to handle news that would have been staggering and gut wrenching even to the most mature senior boy at the school. I wept bitterly. Then I quickly made arrangements to get back to upstate New York to be with my family.

But then I realized that my dreams about my father's death must have been God's way of preparing me for this stunning loss. In that way my dreams somehow brought great comfort to me - and ultimately to my mother, brother, and sister - during a very tough time. And it renewed my faith that there is much more to this life than what can be seen or experienced via the physical senses. Despite eventually earning degrees in biochemistry, and statistical training at Harvard, I became unshakably convinced that science alone cannot explain "us," let alone "Him."

A year or so after Dad's passing, when I was back at the Boychoir School, where I participated in a piano concerto competition, the prize for which was the opportunity to perform a piano concerto as a featured soloist with the Garden State Philharmonic Orchestra in New Jersey. And, sure enough, I won that competition. It took nearly a year to happen, but while I was in the ninth grade and 16 years old, I finally got that chance to perform as a soloist with the Garden State Philharmonic in Tom's River, New Jersey, under Henri Elkan. They played the first movement of a Mozart Piano Concerto and I wound up being awarded the state of New Jersey Francis Hopkinson Memorial Medallion for that performance.

That achievement helped open up another music opportunity when I was offered the opportunity to audition for a slot at the Interlochen Center for the Arts in Interlochen, Michigan. Interlochen was sort of like the high school depicted in the short-lived 1980s TV show FAME, and in the movie by the same name. Except instead of being set in a gritty inner-city environment it was nestled in the beautiful forests of northern Michigan, near Traverse City. By now the reader will not be surprised to learn I excelled at my audition and was invited to attend that prestigious school, where I continued as a piano major. I had to practice four hours daily. It was grueling but, in my mind, very much worth it because I got to study under the famous Portuguese pianist, Fernando Laires. Laires is one of those wizards who had all the Beethoven Piano Sonatas memorized by the age of 18. I, by way of comparison, had only memorized just one.

We admired Laires greatly, but we were equally frightened of him. So to make him seem a little less intimidating we called him "Joe" – though never to his face. In our eyes that brought him down to the level of mere human being.

"How was your lesson with Joe?" we would ask each other while laughing.

"Is Joe in a good mood?"

The answer was usually 'No'. He was a tough, strict teacher.

Interlochen had beautiful Steinway grand pianos in cabins out in the glorious woods that covered the school's 1,200-acre campus. Although the practice as a piano major was long and hard, the experience to play beautiful music in such a marvelous and peaceful setting in the wild was uplifting, even breath-taking at times.

Of course, Interlochen was expensive, and my mother was now a widow with little money. So that wonderful town, the town of my birth and upbringing, through the Oneida Area Arts Council, sponsored a concert at which I performed to raise funds so I could continue at Interlochen. I gave the concert – playing entirely by memory for 90 minutes - at the High School Auditorium in Oneida. It seemed as though the whole town turned out. And I got a wild standing ovation. I did another concert at the Oneida Community Mansion House, again to a packed house, and at many local schools. Thanks to those concerts and the generosity of my hometown supporters I was able to stay at Interlochen all the way through high school.

Still, by the time I graduated from Interlochen, I had come to recognize that while I was extremely good at piano, I probably was not good enough to make it big as a concert pianist. It was a sobering, and in some ways sad realization, but one that many young people have to make eventually when they learn they can't hit well enough to make it in the big leagues, that they aren't physically strong enough to serve in the Marines, that they aren't talented enough a singer and dancer to make it on Broadway, or smart enough to be a physicist, an architect or a philosophy professor. Still, my clear-eyed, mature honesty with myself as my high school career wound down turned out to be a blessing. With that huge decision made, I could turn my attention toward the next, critically important phase of my life without regrets or a nagging sense of failure.

While music always had been my primary focus in school, I also had always been interested in science. I also excelled in school, where my grades always put me at or near the top of my class. So, I decided to pursue a biochemistry degree at the State University of New York at Binghamton, not too far from Oneida. It was an academic path that I expected to lead me toward medical school and a career as a physician. But, mainly for fun, I also pursued a second major in Music Composition. Turns out one of my music composition classmates at SUNY-Binghamton was Paul Reiser, who years later would gain fame as an actor on TV and in the movies.

During those years at college, while I focused mainly on my science courses, I also wrote many choral and instrumental works, including one called *The Creation of Narnia*. It was a 30-minute cantata based on how Aslan the Lion sang creation into existence. (Aslan, of course, is the central character of C.S. Lewis' beloved *Chronicles of Narnia* series and, especially of the first book in that series, *The Lion, The Witch, and the Wardrobe*. Throughout the Chronicles, Aslan serves as the Christ-figure who saves the kingdom of Narnia and all its inhabitants from the evil Witch whose goal is to defeat the noble Lion and rule an eternally grim and unloving world.) Still, despite my heavy academic load and my continuing love for and involvement with music during my college years I was able to graduate with Honors and a Bachelor of Science degree in biochemistry. I also was inducted into the prestigious Phi Beta Kappa honor society.

By the time I began college I knew I was med-school bound. But instead of applying to dozens of them, I sent an application to just one. And I did it as a junior, not as a senior. The reason: The Upstate Medical Center in Syracuse, New York, had an early admissions program and I was eager to move ahead.

And because my widowed mother still did not have the means to pay for my medical education, I made a grand bargain to get my schooling paid for. While many of my classmates took out thousands upon thousands of dollars in loans to pay for their medical education, I went a different route. In exchange for a full, four-year Health Professions scholarship, I agreed to become a doctor with the U.S. Air Force. In effect, I traded one year of my professional life after medical school for each year of medical school I attended on the Air Force's tab. I always considered it a great trade in my favor, and not only for professional reasons.

In my plan to get accepted into medical school early, and to get that schooling paid for by the Air Force, I began volunteering while in college at University Hospital in Syracuse. It was meant to be a resume-enhancing experience, but it ended up being much more than that. I was assigned to work in the hospital's clinical pathology department. One of the tasks I performed quite often was urinalysis. One day, while working in that lab my supervisors introduced me to a beautiful new lab technician named Laurie Hamlin. Part of my job included training her how to analyze urine. Laurie and I typically had to work our way through a row of 30 specimens at a time. It wasn't the most ideal way to develop a close relationship with a member of the opposite sex, but I joke these days that maybe the glow of all that urine reflecting up into our faces created an atmosphere that was conducive to building what, at least early on, became a close friendship.

I was always a bit kooky, and a prankster, so one day, as we prepared our usual lineup of urine specimens to work through, I secretly replaced one of the urine-filled vials with another containing iced tea. Then I said to the other lab techs:

"Did you know there is a new way to analyze urine?"

They looked at me quizzically.

Then, I picked up the one with the iced tea.

"Sometimes you can smell sugar in the urine," I said.

Then I proceeded to sniff it. They thought I was psychotic.

"Sometimes, by taste," I added as I dipped my finger in and tasted it. By this time, they were gagging.

Finally, I said, "Sometimes you have to drink it." And I gulped down the whole vial!

They screamed in disbelief! Then they laughed hard as I revealed the truth.

Of course, that earned me a stern "talking to" from the supervisor, Kathy Walker: "No horseplay in the lab!" she scolded me, wagging her finger. But even she laughed!

Laurie and I became friends as I went through medical school, often going to coffee together when I was on clinical rotations at the hospital. Our annual event together was the Upstate Medical Center Clinical Pathology Christmas Party. We would have a good time, but nothing romantic developed between us, at least not at that point. She would tell her friends I was too much of a nerd and was spending too much time becoming a doctor.

It was true. I had no life, except studying. My Saturdays were spent all day in the library, in the books. My Sundays permitted the morning for Church, but then more studying. I had no time for dating.

But that hard work payed off; I graduated from medical school in 1981 in the top 25% of my class, which of course reminds me of the standard joke: "What do the call the person who graduated at the very bottom of their medical school class? Doctor." So, class ranking did not matter too much. Still, I and my medical school colleagues were a competitive bunch, always jockeying for the best scores on tests. So, I found satisfaction in finishing in the upper quarter of my class.

But unlike other newly-minted physicians, I was not bothered with applying to residency programs or figuring out what specialty I wanted to pursue. I already knew I owed at least the next four years or more of his life to the U.S. Air Force. There were, however, several different tracks I could have followed through the Air Force's medical corps. And since I had always been fascinated by flying and outer space since he was a little boy, I applied to fulfill my obligation by serving as what is known in the Air Force as a flight surgeon.

No, that is not a doctor who does surgery in the sky. In fact, Air Force Flight Surgeons are not necessarily even "surgeons" in the common sense of the term. You can argue all doctors are surgeons in that any procedure that involves cutting into or stitching up the body, or somehow using instruments to penetrate the body could be classified as a bit of surgery. But most commonly a surgeon is thought of as a medical doctor who performs significant operations on the human body that require him or her to cut it open and re-wire, re-plumb, or rebuild it in some significant way, or to remove from it pieces of the body itself or other matter, infections or tumors that need to be removed. An Air Force Flight Surgeon, on the other hand, is a doctor who has special knowledge about what the physical act of flying does to the human body so that he or she may take care of the unique needs of pilots and crew members. Flight Surgeons also take care of the ordinary medical needs of pilots' families and those of other non-flying Air Force personnel assigned to flying units.

I spent my first two years as a flight surgeon with an elite F106 Fighter squadron, a KC-135 squadron and a B-52 squadron all based at the now-closed Griffiss Air Force Base in Rome, NY. Because I remained close to Syracuse, where Laurie worked and lived, she and I started dating more seriously. It did not hurt I also had more spare time on my hands than I had ever had before, and that I finally, for the first time, had more than a couple of pennies in my pocket. I shocked her one day at Green Lakes State Park in upstate New York, near Syracuse, with a diamond ring. After nearly falling into the lake from surprise, she said yes.

After working at Griffiss AFB, I applied to become a specialist in Aerospace Medicine It was, for me, a great opportunity to combine my childhood love for space exploration and aviation with my new passion for medicine. Aerospace Medicine is a medical specialty that is a sub-specialization under the oversight of the American Board of Preventive Medicine. It deals with the health care for aircrew members and astronauts and the people that support them in the extraordinarily hazardous environments in which they work. In traditional medicine, it is the patient who is usually sick, and care is directed to them, not the environment. In Aerospace Medicine, however, the "patient" – i.e., a pilot or an astronaut - is selected for his or her excellent health and near-perfect condition. What is "sick" is the dangerous or even toxic environment in which they work or, at times, live. There is radiation, vibration, low oxygen levels, low humidity, G-forces, motion sickness, space ship explosions, aircraft catastrophes, and other harmful environmental issues that can harm or kill an individual in a matter of seconds. The job of Aerospace Medicine Specialists is, in large part, to protect perfectly healthy people from their "unhealthy" environments.

In addition to paying for my medical school education, the Air Force also paid my way through more medical residency training after I graduated from medical school. And part of that came at one of the best institutions in the country: Harvard's School of Public Health. That is where I earned a master's degree in public health. And that is why on my curriculum vitae, my official correspondence, and my prescription pad my name is followed not only by the expected "M.D." designation but also by the letters "M.P.H."

During my year at Harvard I continued to court Laurie as we planned a wedding for June 1, 1985, right on the heels of my Harvard graduation. She was still in Syracuse, and I was in Boston. We would see each other when we could on weekends. Whenever it was her turn to drive to Boston to see me, she had to hold her nose when entering my apartment, which I shared with two other bachelors. The bathroom was "grody," in her words. She once opened the stove and found stacked dirty pots and pans. She tried to clean, but it was like trying to use a blow dryer in a hurricane. And there were the roaches; lots of 'em. Somehow, being a trained and licensed physician, and a budding expert on public health matters seemed to have no impact whatsoever on me and my roommates' hygienic practices at our apartment.

The master's in public health from Harvard is a great degree. But it's important to understand that in Public Health the doctor's human "patient" is replaced by an entire population, whether it be a work group, an entire state, an entire country, a squadron of pilots and their crew members, or, for that matter, all the passengers of an airline. The Public Health doctor or other public health professional then uses statistics to study that "population/patient" to discover what the entire group's health risks are, and to determine what programs might be implemented to affect positively the health of that population.

Immunization programs are probably the best example of public health intervention programs. You find out what diseases the population gets, then you determine what public health program is best to protect the largest number of people – all while introducing the smallest number of new risk factors possible.

My Master's program at Harvard included nearly a full year of learning how to use statistical analysis techniques, and studying what makes a successful, quality published paper. The sad truth is a lot of health-related "research" that is done and reported on publicly actually is the result of shoddy research or is research that is paid for by a group with a specific bias and desired outcomes. I learned how to spot such faulty work in published papers the way a hawk finds a field mouse.

Laurie would joke: "You know so much about public health! What are you going to do about your apartment? It is a public health nightmare!"

"Three bachelors are not large enough of a group to apply public health principles" I would reply wryly. "The 'N' is too small." (In statistical research "N" is the symbol used in mathematical formulas to represent the population being studied.)

We married, as planned, on June 1, 1985 in Sherrill, the town of the Oneida Community located right next door to Oneida. The night before the wedding, my brother Allen took me to get ice cream at a local upstate New York resort, Sylvan Beach on Oneida Lake at Eddie's Restaurant [still there today—delicious ice cream and food!]. While licking our ice cream we saw a man giving horse and carriage rides there. So, I walked over to him and asked what he was doing the next day.

"Nothing," the man replied.

"Can you bring your horse and carriage to our wedding church tomorrow, and take us to our reception in Vernon"?

"Sure!" he said.

And, as promised, the man showed up the next day, right on time, with top hat and all. He had a beautiful horse named Lucy and a white Cinderella carriage to carry the newly married couple to our reception down Route 5 at Dibble's Inn in Vernon.

Just like out of a movie, running alongside the carriage as Lucy trotted down the country roads was a herd of horses. Such herds running along fence lines is rather commonplace in upstate New York. Something about the sight of us riding in that glistening white carriage being pulled by that gorgeous horse with the driver dressed like an old Englishman with a top hat stimulated the herd. They ran along the fence line, following the carriage, as if to escort us newlyweds and wish us well. Laurie and I were filled with joy - and champagne. Someone had placed a bottle with two glasses in the carriage. I, especially, was not then, and still am not much of a drinker. But I had quite a bit in the carriage. To say the least, Laurie and I were stress free by the time they got to the reception!

After our honeymoon in Cape Cod, we moved to the United States Air Force School of Aerospace Medicine at Brooks Air Force Base, just outside of San Antonio, Texas, to complete more Aerospace Medicine training. We loaded our two cars with our clothes, books, some household items, and Laurie's cat, Bootsie. Then we drove for four days to San Antonio. At one point, one of our cars broke down. I took off my shirt to work on it, as it was so hot. I was unaware of the danger that awaited me, laid down right on a mound of fire ants while I tried to fix the car. As a New Yorker, I had never had any experience with fire ants. And laying down on a fire ant mound is most definitely not a good way to learn about them. I endured much pain for days!

While at Brooks. I published my first major statistical research paper, relying largely on the marvelous statistical tools I had learned at Harvard. My novel research involved studying all the pilots who had ever been in the Air Force, broken down by the category of aircraft they flew. I related the accident experience of those with medical waivers[3] to that of all other pilots in the Air Force's historical population. Surprisingly, I learned those who had been granted waivers were safer flyers and had fewer aircraft accidents that those pilots whose health and physical condition was so good that they did not need such waivers. That study showed the Air Force was not, in fact, violating the ancient medical aphorism, *Primum non nocere*, or "First, do no harm." By permitting pilots with certain known medical issues to fly anyway so long as they remained closely watched by medical teams, the Air Force was not making things worse, either for those individual pilots or for the branch's overall mission performance. In fact, my data and analysis showed that letting some pilots fly under such waiver conditions actually improved overall Air Force flight safety rather than making it worse. The result was fewer, not more incidents or crashes. I was awarded the prestigious Julian Ward Award in 1989 for Aerospace Medicine excellence by the Aerospace Medical Association for that work and other flight medicine activities.

At the School of Aerospace Medicine at Brooks in San Antonio, there was not only extensive classroom work and research, but lots of other interesting opportunities for these aerospace medicine doctors. I and the other doctors in my training cohort were called Residents in Aerospace Medicine, or "RAMS" for short. And our logo, naturally, was a horned ram in various configurations. We did lots of neat things, one of which was actual pilot raining up the point that we each soloed in a T-37 training jet. That included

---

[3] A waiver is a "permission slip" from the Air Force allowing a pilot to fly, albeit under closer monitoring by Flight Surgeons, despite certain known medical issues that otherwise would end their flying career.

doing lots of aerobatics. I never told my instructors, but I would get sicker than a dog when I flew. Although it was prohibited for an aviator to take any medicine before flying, unbeknownst to my Flight Surgeon I always loaded up with Dramamine prior to each flight lesson. It was all I could do not to vomit during each training session, even while I was on the Dramamine.

One time, however, I lost it while flying. But there was no barf bag available. So, I, an Air Force Captain, puked into my own flight suit, then had to live with it for the duration of that flight. The instructor pilot either did not know, or perhaps kindly ignored it to save me the embarrassment.

One time, I got the T-37 I was flying into what is known as a "prohibited maneuver" - an inverted spin. It was prohibited for a good reason. The T-37 has a gravity-fed fuel pump, and an inverted spin pushes the fuel away from the engines. So, the engines would sputter and die within a few seconds of the plane going upside down. That is when, as they say in the pilot vernacular, you stick your head between your legs and KYAGB (kiss your ass good-by). The spin experience is not pleasant, inverted or not, especially with vomit in your flight suit. It is sort of like being inside a running clothes dryer, looking out, but the dryer suddenly flips upside down, and the blood rushes to your head. This produces "red out," where the blood is forced into your head, and your vision turns red - just before you have a stroke or pass out. There are many ways to crash in this situation. Also, throw some rotten eggs into the dryer to simulate hot vomit, to make your experience complete.

I was starting to "red out" from eye hemorrhages and could barely get the words out to my Instructor: "You've got the airplane." That is the phrase pilots use to definitively transfer command and control of an aircraft to another pilot. In my head I started to think through the bailout procedures. Thankfully, the instructor got us out of that inverted spin just in time. I thought to myself "The things I do to pay for medical school!" Indeed, that became a common refrain for me.

Flight training was not the only "fun" thing that my group of Aerospace Medicine Specialists to-be did in San Antonio. We also did human centrifuge training. Again, it is sort of like being in a dryer, only this time, you are going 100 miles per hour, and you are smushed like a windshield bug up against the side of that dryer. Its purpose is to give one an idea of what high G forces feel like and what they do to the human brain and physiology. It is what astronauts and pilots are exposed to and must be able to function in during the launch and re-entry phases of their missions. And boy, did we experience some Gs! Some of my classmates could tolerate up to 15 Gs. I noticed that it usually was the short stocky guys and gals who had no neck to speak of, or who were body builders who could tolerate the most Gs. The shorter distance from the heart to the head gave these folks an advantage.

At high G-force levels pilots must do special breathing maneuvers. One well known one is the straining maneuver, or Valsalva - to help your heart force blood back up into your head so that you do not black out. The average person does this maneuver all the time without knowing it. Essentially, it is the process of straining with one's upper body and bowel muscles to initiate a bowel movement. Only for pilots experiencing high G-forces, the straining lasts longer and typically is much more intensely felt. And, oh yeah, it does not actually produce a bowel movement in flight, which is a really good thing.

When I and my colleagues rode in the human centrifuge, we had a video camera pointed right at our faces. Thus, we had no way of hiding anything that happened inside that little capsule at the end of a fast-spinning arm. Other pilots observing via the in-capsule camera would laugh as they watched their buddies go through the G-forces generated in that centrifuge.

"This is Joe 10 years from now...

"This is Joe 20 years from now...

"This is Joe 30 years from now..." they would say as the centrifuge accelerated with each lap. As the G forces increased, the flesh on the occupant's face would get pushed further and further back against the seat, and they would begin to look older and older. Most often, pilots in the capsule would black out, and they would not remember anything. Of course, those of us observing our friends go through that training stopped laughing when it came our turn to climb into the centrifuge.

Another "torture" we endured was known as "Helodunker" training. First, we had to swim 75 yards in full flight gear and boots. That was just to see if you even had the tolerance to do the training itself. Many of my classmates took one look and refused to do it. I HAD to do it though, since I already knew I was going to be assigned as a flight surgeon for a Pararescue Jumper, or "PJ" squadron at Cape Canaveral Air Force Station. That meant I had to be able to support PJs on the ground or in the water from a huge Sikorsky HH-53 Jolly Green Giant helicopter hovering above them. And that, in turn, required that I know how to exit one of those big boys if it were to ever tumble into the water. So, I performed the requisite swim and passed the first hurdle.

After the swim test, trainers would place four of us RAMS into a huge metal barrel that looked like a helicopter chassis with four positions, or seats. This was the dreaded "Helodunker." The trainees were strapped in. Then, the entire barrel was dropped into 20 feet of water... and turned upside down. In my case, as the water rose quickly over my face and above my head, I muttered again to myself, "The things I do to pay for medical school." But that was not even the hard part. Once in the water and upside down, trainees are told to patiently count to 10 before unlatching their seat belts and beginning to find our way to the exits. Only once you get out can you begin our 20-foot ascent to the surface. Try counting to ten when you are underwater, and feel like you are about to die! The first time, you go out the nearest exit, then the main exit on the second try. But it does not stop there. You then have to repeat these steps BLINDFOLDED! I remember getting kicked in the mouth on my way out the last time I went through the Helodunker training exercise. You must do it all by feel only. That is also why they have divers in the water to save your hide when you start to drown. Thankfully, I did not need the divers' aid. But, again, though I am not much of a drinking man, I drank heartily with my RAM buddies that night as we celebrated still being alive!

We RAMS also went through all the famous pilot survival schools: Arctic, land, and water survival. The thinking behind all that was if these specialist doctors were going to be experts in taking care of pilots and astronauts, they ought to go through what pilots and astronauts go through in their training and, potentially, in the performance of their jobs when things go really, really wrong. That way we docs would know better how to care for pilots and astronauts who have just had such an experience in the real world and so we'd better understand what those aviators must be conditioned to do.

During my RAM training days, I picked up two nicknames from my classmates. The first I liked: Top Gun.

"I sort of look like Tom Cruise anyway," I joked, at least back in those days.

71

Actually, the name came about because of my competitiveness. Though I was the youngest, and lowest ranking person in my RAMS class at the measly rank of Captain, I did very well in terms of my training grades. In fact, I earned the highest-grade point average among a group of mostly Colonels and Majors, and even other Captains who held seniority over me. And as a classic "achiever" – some would say "over-achiever" – my competitive nature was impossible to conceal. So, they called me "Top Gun."

Of course, since that was too high and mighty of a name for a lowly Captain, I quickly acquired a second, much less cool nickname: Ripcord. One day, while I and my colleagues were all getting our parachutes on for our jet pilot training at Randolph Air Force Base half-way across San Antonio from Brooks, I must have pulled the parachute deployment cord by mistake. Suddenly, everyone could hear a ticking sound, like a bomb about to go off. But the other guys all quickly recognized that it was a parachute about to deploy in a 12' x 12'room filled with RAMS and their flight gear. For a millisecond everyone froze. Then they all ran like those cockroaches exposed to the kitchen light in my old bachelor pad in Boston. I was left there alone with the device still ticking away. Thankfully, when that chute did explode out of its pack in the donning area there was nobody left in there for it to hit, except me. That is how I went from being known as "Top Gun" to "Ripcord."

Space Shuttle Challenger Explosion

The world changed quickly for me on Jan 28, 1986. On that day, as I neared the end of my residency at Brooks AFB in San Antonio, the space shuttle Challenger exploded. The team at Cape Canaveral Air Force Station, Kennedy Space Center and the adjacent Patrick Air Force Base, the complex of installations where I already was scheduled to be assigned, called and said they needed a specialist in Aerospace Medicine to come immediately to aid in body recovery and other post-Challenger issues. I, of course, was the natural choice for the assignment since I was headed there in a few weeks anyway. So, my first assignment as an aerospace medicine specialist came during a period of crisis. Once I arrived at the Cape, I became Chief of Aerospace Medicine.

"Frenchy" Beaulieu was the worldly-wise senior master sergeant that kept me out of trouble, especially early on, at this assignment. And that was a good thing because I had no time for a learning curve. I and my team initially were involved in recovering Challenger crewmembers' dismembered and scattered remains, and in helping NASA minister to those crewmembers' families.

While Laurie and I were living on the Florida Space Coast she had our first child, Erin. Erin was born on September 8, 1987 in Cocoa, Florida. She grew up watching the space shuttle and other rocket launches from the front yard of our home on Pineland Drive in Rockledge. I was most often on console for the shuttle launches at the military Cape Canaveral side of the launch complex, but sometimes in an Air Force Sikorsky HH-53 Jolly Green Giant rescue helicopter with four PJs to support potential shuttle emergencies. Laurie, meanwhile, would be at home with Erin. Each time their ritual was the same: they would feel the ground rumble, then see the space shuttle rocket take off on TV. Then they would run outside just in time to see the massive space vehicle rise above the trees.

"It's BEEEG," little Erin would say in wonder and awe.

I was only a Captain at the time, but Air Force rules said at the time the Aerospace Medicine Specialist, if present, oversees the Aeromedical Services regardless of his or her rank. So, I was in a position of being the boss of a Major, and at one point even of a full bird Colonel who were doctors, but not aerospace medicine specialists. It was an odd situation, one in which I was forced to develop both tact and diplomacy skills that would serve me well in later years.

In Florida, I also was the Aerospace Medicine expert assigned to the Department of Defense's Manager for Space Transportation System Contingency Support Office (DDMS). That is a mouthful. And it meant that DDMS, a joint NASA/DoD agency, was responsible for taking care of manned space emergencies of any sort, wherever they happen, around the world. For example, if the shuttle could not make it into orbit, and had to make the call to abort less than 20 minutes after launch, my job was to get the shuttle's crew to medical care at one of NASA's emergency landing sites in Africa – or wherever around the world the orbiter happened to come down.

It turns out that in our planning, we made the decision to make a big change in our medical treatment plans for astronauts forced to abort their launch. Instead of trying to quickly collect the astronauts and whisk them to some medical center maybe six to 12 hours away by jet airplane, it would be easier and better to bring the care on-site to the astronauts, at least if they landed at any of the Transoceanic Abort Landing sites in Africa or Spain. These sites were Banjul in Gambia, Ben Guerir in Morocco, or Moron AFB and Zaragoza, both in Spain.

The operations team coordinated Lockheed C-130 Hercules aircraft fully staffed with a trauma surgeon and pararescue specialists who could recover the astronauts, treat them both at the site and then, if necessary, in flight. The goal still would be to get the astronauts to a top DoD medical center in Landstuhl or Wiesbaden, Germany, or to any other military medical center. But the human and technological capabilities aboard those specially-outfitted C-130s would allow top flight Air Force and NASA medical personnel to deliver better and faster treatment than would have been the case under the previous plan. That's why, on most launches after Challenger, I was on console at Cape Canaveral Air Force Station and in communication with a wide range of world-wide medical resources ready to act on my command [really, first my Colonel's command, then mine] to respond to any shuttle emergency.

The building I worked out of was highly secure, complete with not only human guards, but also retinal identity scanning technology – pretty nifty stuff for the 1980s. I and my DDMS team were about three miles from the launch pad, meaning we were positioned closer to the Launch pad than anyone else. No one dared to set up a position any closer because if the space shuttle exploded on the pad fully fueled, the concussive damage and the toxic fumes would threaten the survival of anything within three miles.

Also, in that building were the people who could destroy the orbiter, if it were to veer off course and head toward populated areas. That why, in the days before scheduled launches the astronauts would come over to the DDMS facility and show pictures of their spouses and children, jokingly begging for the staff there to think twice before pressing that orbiter destruct button. On occasion, I and my team were permitted to watch a night launch from the roof of that building, called the Cape Canaveral Support Operations Center. From the rooftop the launch looked like a nuclear explosion, turning the night into the brightest day. And the noise sounded like 1,000 jets taking off at once.

At this point I also went through NASA's Flight Surgeon Training, which took the medical and procedures training I got at Brooks in San Antonio up a couple more notches. I worked closely with NASA's own, non-military flight surgeons. Their lead doctor was named Dr. Jeff Davis, who in the years ahead would play a critical role in my future.

Remember Howard Wolowicz on *The Big Bang Theory* wanted his NASA nickname to be *Rocketman*? Well, I wanted *Top Gun*. But the nickname bestowed on me by the NASA medical corps was "Spuds." The reasons were never clear to me. I might have been nicknamed after that dog in the Bud Light commercials at the time, Spuds McKenzie. In any case, I wrote all the training guidelines for responding physicians, who had to be prepared to work in very close proximity to the shuttle after it lands. Many of these doctors were military docs who happened to be stationed in locations where a shuttle in trouble might be forced to come down. Chances were they would be the first trained medical responders. But chances also were they would have little or no understanding of the very specific dangers and conditions related to working around the shuttle and with the astronauts aboard it. In fact, the shuttle vehicle is one huge, nightmarish medical hazard, especially just after it lands and is venting fuels and dangerous toxins.

My work with the space program paved the way for developing similar and massive plans some years later for American Airlines. As an Aerospace Medicine specialist, my first operational achievement that prepared me greatly for being American Airline's top doctor was designing those emergency responses for astronauts and providing rescue and medical care options in the event of a space shuttle catastrophe[4].

Designing programs to rescue astronauts, I quickly discovered, is both an extraordinarily difficult technical undertaking and a bureaucratic quagmire. The space shuttle, or any space vehicle, was and is an extremely hazardous vehicle, to say the least. It looks all pristine and white on top of the 747 flying back from an Edwards AFB landing, but during and immediately after a space flight such vehicles are filled with toxic and caustic substances. I had to design programs to train physicians and pararescue people how to treat people who get exposed to some of the nastiest compounds on earth.

Obviously, with all that toxic rocket fuel around if things ever were to go wrong on the ground before or after a shuttle flight the results would be catastrophic. While I was at the Cape I learned and always had to keep in mind there were many systems in the shuttle that, if they failed, could cause a catastrophe and that a catastrophic event, statistically speaking, could be expected in one out of every 25 launches. It was a risk people involved in the space program knew about, and a risk they all accepted. Still, they all

---

[4] These days, I occasionally deliver "career day" presentation about my work with NASA and the Air Force to students in my now-grown daughter Erin's class at an elementary school in a poor section of Dallas. I emphasize how I, with no money and a poor, widowed mother got an Air Force Health Professions scholarship, and became a doctor and eventually worked for the space program. Of course, each time I deliver this presentation I'm surprised all over again, and made to feel like an ancient fossil, by the fact that these students are so young, and so unaware of the broader world around them that many of them have never heard of the space shuttle or the shuttle program.

worked aggressively to avoid having ANY accidents or catastrophes. At DDMS, I and my Operational and NASA colleagues had all the vast resources of the Department of Defense at our disposal in the event of an accident. We could direct military vehicles and personnel to aid the flight crew literally anywhere in the world. But that also meant we first had to understand and define all those things that could go wrong, and then determine what were the best or quickest ways to respond to each type of potential emergency.

We developed several plans for responding to different types of emergency scenarios. We labelled these, giving each scenario an emergency response "Mode" number, and distributed the plans to those who potentially could be called upon to help. We also made sure they had the training and gear necessary to do what they could be asked to do. When anyone assigned to respond to a potential shuttle emergency heard over the radio me or one of my colleagues at the Cape calling out personnel and using any of these "modes" in our instruction they immediately knew whether they were being called to action and what, exactly, they had to do. Nothing was left to be determined until after an emergency with the shuttle happened – nothing, that is, but the precise location where the emergency response was needed.

First, there were several emergency modes focused on providing aid directly to the orbiter and flight crew. Modes I-IV referred to an event in which something went wrong with the space shuttle while it was still on the launch pad. Modes V-VII referred to emergencies that began once launch rockets had ignited and the shuttle was taking off, or while the space shuttle was in the landing phase at the end of a mission.

Here is a more detailed description of what could go wrong, and how we would respond:

Orbiter on Launch Pad

Mode I: An unaided egress. In this situation something catastrophic goes wrong, but the astronauts can get out and can get away from the orbiter to safety on their own. For example, when the shuttle is still connected to the service gantry, huge baskets attached to a zip line are adjacent to the shuttle's hatch. Pilots escaping the vehicle are trained to jump in and experience the thrill ride of their lives to get away from the vehicle as fast as possible.

Mode II: Aided egress. This is when the crew that shuts the door of the space shuttle after the crew is tucked in (the close-out crew) must help the crew out of the situation because the crew cannot help themselves. Then, hopefully, they all would take the basket ride to safety!

Mode III: Fire/Crash/Rescue personnel respond to the shuttle. Specially suited responders would have to get up the gantry quickly, in full gear, to perform a crew rescue. These responders would be screened for cardiovascular fitness because it is extremely exhausting to do anything in the kind of gear needed to protect you from shuttle toxins, especially in the high heat and humidity of Florida. They would have to be able to run up many flights of stairs in the gantry wearing all their gear and carrying heavy tools because it is possible, even likely that in an emergency situation the gantry's elevator would be inoperable. Then, upon reaching the hatch they would have to then be able to pry open a sealed hatch and rescue crew members who could be injured or incapacitated.

Mode IV: Shuttle and close out crews both need rescuing. This is a worst-case response scenario with the shuttle still on the pad. Anything worse on the pad would preclude even attempting a rescue.

Orbiter Landing

Mode V: An unaided egress after landing near a runway. The astronauts can escape such a situation via the side hatch, which can be opened by explosives built into it. So, we train our rescue crews to stand clear because that very heavy hatch can be thrown out at least 50 feet from the orbiter.

Mode VI: A shuttle mishap at or near the runway and a fire/crash/rescue crew must enter the orbiter to aid the flight crew. In this situation there is lots of potential for exposures to toxic hazards.

Mode VII: A mishap off the runway and within 25 miles of the Kennedy Space Center or other facility where shuttle landings are planned, such as Edwards AFB or White Sands Missile Range, New Mexico. This is a much more difficult rescue scenario because of the rugged conditions in the Californian and New Mexican deserts and the swamps or ocean that surround the Cape.

Mode VIII: Shuttle Crew egress in flight. This would be the most hazardous of all the scenarios, not only for the flight crew but also for potential rescuers. A Challenger-like explosion, if survivable at all, would be a Mode VIII.

Orbiter Aborts

Also, there potentially were emergencies that would not qualify as a "disaster" but would create enormous emergency challenges. For instance, if the orbiter fails to develop enough speed to reach orbit, or equipment failures make it necessary to abort the mission before reaching orbit, our medical team had to be ready to respond wherever the vehicle came down. We developed several response plans or scenarios for those type of events, as well.

Return to Launch Site (RTLS): if the shuttle ever lost power after takeoff its pilots were trained to release the external tank and rockets (if they had not already been jettisoned) and then do what is known in the pilot world as a "Split S" maneuver to reverse course and descend. In a "normal" jet aircraft, doing a Split S will cause the aircraft to gain speed during the descent portion of the maneuver. But executing any turn in a shuttle traveling at extreme post-launch speeds will cause it to begin shedding speed (additional maneuvers during its descent cause it to slow down even more as it glides rapidly back toward the Cape's extra-long runway at Patrick AFB). Once a shuttle in that situation neared the Cape, the orbiter was supposed to attempt to loop around the field to line up a landing on that long runway. In truth, however, no one knew for sure whether the orbiter structure could even survive such aerobatic and aerodynamically severe maneuvers at the kind of speeds achieved after launch, but that was what we planned. We also did not know quite what would happen to the astronauts inside when the orbiter tried to perform those radical maneuvers. Nor did we dare actually put astronauts through those conditions as part of our planning and training because the risk to them simply was too high. On top of that, an RTLS situation would mean the shuttle would be coming back heavy, with a full load of mission gear and its fuel tanks full (while it lacked propulsion engines, it did have small maneuvering jets that controlled it during docking procedures and other small maneuvers while in space). Still, if the shuttle ever found itself in an emergency RTLS situation we knew there was no other way of quickly getting it and its crew back on the ground at the Kennedy Space Center and the astronauts – and the team on the ground – would just have to risk it in such extreme circumstances.

Abort Once Around (AOA): We planned for the possibility of the orbiter losing some power or experiencing some malfunction after it had reached a high enough speed and altitude to make one lap around the earth before landing at the Cape, or at Edwards AFB in California. This of course, would mean that it would land "heavy." The presence of that maneuvering jet fuel, of course, still implied significant danger upon landing and crew egress. The maneuvers necessary to bring the shuttle back after a lap around the earth would be less severe than those required for a quick return to the launch site.

Abort to Orbit (ATO): The orbiter has enough speed to get into a low earth orbit, and go around the earth a few times, to buy time to figure out what to do next. At some point, though, this still implied a quick return to Earth either at the Cape or Edwards AFB, with all the attendant dangers related to landing heavy and with volatile fuel still aboard.

Now, to complicate matters further, the space shuttle, in aerodynamic terms, was a flying brick with stubby wings. Once separated from the rocket boosters and fuel tank on ascent, it had no power or thrust on its own, except for its small orbital maneuvering thrusters. That is why, when it landed, those present, and those watching on live TV could not hear the roar of jet engines that are the characteristic sound of jet planes coming in for a landing. The shuttle is completely silent. Without engines, it falls to earth both quietly and far more quickly than an airplane. In effect, it is a very, very fat, and un-aerodynamic glider. That means there is no possibility of a "go around" for a second try at landing. The hope is for a smooth landing on a long runway where it can roll to a dead stop. If that does not happen, the shuttle will still land, only it will stop much more quickly and violently than is good for either the spacecraft or the astronauts inside.

The Nasty Stuff

As previously explained, Aerospace Medicine, like Occupational Medicine deals not with a sick person, but rather a sick environment. There are thousands of things that could harm not only the astronauts but also any first responders to a shuttle emergency.

Most notable is among them are its rocket fuels. These fuels, due to the nature of space operations, must be able to burn in space where there is no oxygen. For that reason, they are called 'hypergolic' fuels. The good news is that they will burn predictably in outer space. The bad news is that because they can burn without oxygen simply dousing burning rocket fuel with water or some other common kind of fire retardant or extinguisher will have no effect on hypergolic fuel fires here on Earth. Effectively, once lit such fuel will continue to burn no matter what the fire-crash-rescue medical personnel do to try to put the fire out.

There are other, different chemicals onboard a shuttle that can make astronauts and others who must work near it immediately after it lands very sick or even kill them. Refrigerants are carried onboard to keep the atmosphere inside livable, experiment kits working, and certain equipment onboard the shuttle within the proper temperature ranges. And in some cases, radioactive isotopes could be present in or near a shuttle after landing. Satellites launched from a shuttle or captured by the shuttle for return to Earth where they can be examined and repaired, would be the most common sources of such dangerous radioactivity.

Nitrogen Tetroxide: That is the primary chemical in the rocket fuel the orbiter uses to maneuver in outer space. It is extremely hazardous to humans. It causes the lungs to disintegrate and produces severe chemical burns. In liquid state it is green and in vapor, it is brown and heavier than air.

Hydrazine: This is another hazardous chemical used in the rocket fuel used both by the orbiter's thrusters and the spacecraft's internal power unit. It is extremely corrosive. It also has a fishy odor, though by the time a person can smell it they have already been overexposed. It causes chemical burns of the skin, and lung edema, or swelling. In humans it can cause seizures and it destroys red blood cells. It also is a B vitamin antagonist that robs people of this vitamin (part of the treatment for hydrazine exposure is to replace these vitamins).

Ammonia: Many of us are familiar with this one. You may even have it some low-level concentration as a cleaner stored below your kitchen sink. In space operations it is used in full concentration in the orbiter refrigeration unit to keep things cool. It is flammable and has a pungent odor. And when people encounter it, they will suffer chemical burns and pulmonary edema that can prevent oxygen from getting into their lungs, and therefore into their blood.

Freon-21: This, too, is used in the shuttle's refrigeration units. And it also causes lung edema, plus frostbite on contact with human skin.

Radioisotopic Thermal Generators: These generators served as power sources for some shuttle payloads. The radiation they emit is potentially lethal, especially if the orbiter were to have to land with those payloads still aboard or, even worse, if those payloads wound up being exposed to the atmosphere because of a catastrophic crash or some physical damage that caused the shuttle's cargo bay to be ruptured.

Because of the potential or certain presence of these toxic substances, DoD shuttle first responder medical teams, working under my direction, had to be prepared to set up a good decontamination station wherever the shuttle came to a stop (or crashed). Anyone exposed to any of these chemicals would have to be hosed down, stripped down, and hosed down again. Then they would be passed to one of the full medical teams stationed around the world, where they would undergo similar and even more specific decontamination procedures and treatments.

Because the medical resources in those days at some of the remote locations where a shuttle might have to make an emergency landing were not of highest quality, and because the security of the astronauts could not be assured in all such locations, I and my response planners made sure a doctor with adequate training for the situations that he or she might encounter in a shuttle emergency landing was assigned to each site along with four specially-trained Air Force Pararescue Jumpers. The PJs were ideal candidates to fill that role because they already were trained paramedics and extraordinarily fit individuals. They could repel from helicopters to rescue people on the ground from circumstances that threatened immediate survival, and then get those people out of danger using the helicopter's hoist.

Such ability to evacuate astronauts or injured responders on the ground very quickly was absolutely essential because of the pulmonary edema that could result from breathing in even a whiff of some of the chemicals associated with the shuttle. Such patients absolutely had to begin receiving oxygen treatment very quickly. The pulmonary edema, or swelling caused by exposure to those chemicals would cause a victim's lungs to fill up rapidly with fluid. And that would block the ability of the lungs to oxygenate the person's blood. In addition to helicopters assigned to each location to perform close-in rescue work, I arranged it so each field doctor and PJ team also had immediate access to a C-130 equipped with a mini-emergency room that could be used to treat patients during their flight from the emergency landing location to the closest major military hospital. Such flights could be expected to take six to eight hours, or even more in certain circumstances.

Space Related Illnesses

This weird field of medicine that brought defibrillators to airplanes is based on the fact the environment to which people are exposed is 'ill' or adverse. If my medical treatment teams only got normal people who had been exposed to these toxic agents, that would be bad enough. But astronauts also can develop all sorts of space-related illnesses that could greatly complicate their medical response to injuries or chemical exposures suffered during an emergency landing and rescue scenario. That, naturally, would further complicate the treatment they would need on site at the landing location, in flight in one of those specially-equipped C-130s, or even at a major military hospital. The abnormal environment of outer space is intolerant and unforgiving. Here are just a few of these conditions that can result from space travel:

Decompression sickness: This is where the astronaut gets bubbles of nitrogen in their blood from too low of an atmospheric pressure. We all have nitrogen in our tissues, even right now as you are reading this book. But it is kept in the fluid in your tissues. However, should the atmospheric pressure suddenly drop, the nitrogen would begin coming out of those tissues in the form of bubbles in the person's liquid blood. It is like when you take the cap off a bottle of Diet Coke. The bubbles then flow around the bloodstream and can land in the brain, causing a stroke, or damage to many other organs into which they may enter. The only treatment is to get the victim into a hyperbaric chamber and apply pressure to force those nitrogen bubbles back into the liquid and tissues from which they came. All my space shuttle medical response teams had a listing of all of the hyperbaric and dive chambers around the world and could quickly mobilize an aircraft in a moment's notice to get the shuttle crew to one of them.

Weight loss: Astronauts in space tend to lose weight while on a mission. Their muscles begin the process of wasting away because those muscles have no gravity to work against. Their muscles simply are not needed to hold their bodies up against the constant pull of gravity we all experience on Earth. As a result, an astronaut's body mass will decrease during any even modestly extended time in space. In fact, if an astronaut, chosen in part because of his or her robust health and physical development, were to stay in space for a really long time they very well might become too physically weak to get out of their space vehicle on their own.

Heart function impairment: Heart arrhythmias were noted in many of the Gemini and Apollo missions in the 1960s. It is thought to be due to the redistribution of body fluids that occurs in zero gravity.

Orthostatic intolerance: This is the fancy medical name for a condition in which a person cannot tolerate standing up because, whenever they do, their blood pressure drops significantly. This has happened, to varying degrees, to many astronauts, at least for a time after their return to Earth. They eventually get over it, but it's a dangerous condition for an astronaut because it might render them unable to rescue themself in an emergency situation. If you can't stand up, how are you going to escape from a spacecraft, especially one that requires you to unbuckle your safety harness and climb out of your seat, and may require you to climb or slide down a ladder or slide, jump off a wing, or even jump into the water or a life raft?

Thickened blood: As mentioned, fluids in the human body typically get redistributed around that body when it stays in a zero-gravity environment. As part of that redistribution, red blood cells tend to get concentrated, causing the astronaut's blood to become thicker than it normally would be on Earth, and therefore much harder for the heart to pump. That is especially the case when the heart, which is, after all, a muscle prone to wasting in zero gravity conditions, has been deconditioned by prolonged time in space.

Decreased exercise ability: Because of all these metabolic changes astronauts gradually lose their ability to physically exert themselves. Essentially, they can get very badly out of shape even though, because of the typical space-related weight loss, they continue to look quite fit – at least until they get back on the ground and discover that a flight of stairs is a challenge, and that walking from their office to their car out in the parking lot feels like running a marathon.

Decreased bone density: In zero gravity, the bones have nothing to work against, and so calcium begins to leach out of the bones and back into the blood system. As a result, astronauts' bones become measurably weaker during long missions. It has not happened yet, probably because no one has gone more than 438 straight days in space, but, in theory, astronauts would begin to suffer bone fractures if they were to remain in a zero-gravity environment long enough.

Space motion sickness: Space travel causes people to puke. Literally. The Aerospace Medicine world thinks that is because of how the human inner ear works to help us maintain our balance. People have been born and raised for millennia in a gravity environment. But we think when gravity is absent, the brain begins receiving unusual sensations like those that would occur if a person was being poisoned. And that triggers a vomiting response. Space vomiting tends to occur at least in the first few days of a novice's exposure to outer space, though it may continue constantly or on an off-and-on basis for much longer. And it further contributes to an astronaut's potential inability to aid himself or herself during an emergency upon return to a gravity environment.

Interestingly, all of these changes that occur to humans in space flight have led to the idea that if eventually astronauts stay in space for long periods of time without at least some form of artificial gravity their bodies may adjust to life without gravity so thoroughly that they wouldn't EVER be able return to a gravity environment. The thought of NEVER being able to return to Earth is mind-blowing. But it would mean a new species - Homo Spacialis - would evolve. How this new species would procreate in space is another area of aerospace medicine questioning. Remember— every physical action has an equal and opposite reaction. So, humans would have to figure out some way to engage in intimate but physically vigorous activity without sending their partner - and themselves - flying through the cabin. Obviously, people would have to be strapped down, or anchored to hard points in the vehicle to procreate.

All of this, of course, seems like a big digression from our story about saving airline passengers who suffer a sudden cardiac arrest while on a plane. But this is the kind of thinking an aerospace medicine/public health specialist goes through in designing mass programs. And I think my particular professional background in dealing with these subjects made the creation of American Airlines' in-flight defibrillator program appear easy by comparison. In fact, during my time with NASA, I faced much bigger challenges than figuring out how to get defibrillators on board commercial flights.

One of those challenges dealt with figuring out how the astronauts might have avoided being killed in the horrifying explosion on, and the crash of shuttle Challenger in January 1986, if such was even possible. The NASA team studied the idea of installing a telescoping pole that would explode out the side of the cabin door and away from the orbiter as a possible escape path in flight. The astronauts aboard an orbiter involved in an accident bad enough to require they bail out would deploy that extendable pole, tether themselves to it by a carabiner, and then slide down that pole until they cleared the orbiter's body and wings. Upon reaching the end, the astronauts' parachutes would deploy to gently lower them to safety below. But to pull off that kind of escape, the shuttle first would have to slow to less than 200 mph so the astronauts' bodies wouldn't be torn apart by the high speed wind stream to which they would be subjected, or blown back into the vehicle's body, wing or huge vertical tail the moment they stepped outside. The idea also assumed they would survive a blast like that which happened aboard Challenger or some other catastrophic failure. It also meant they would have to wait inside the doomed vehicle long enough – potentially several minutes - for it to slow down and under that 200-mph safety limit. After studying possible escape route very carefully, senior program leaders determined that it simply was not a viable alternative.

The second tough challenge I and my team worked on was the Assured Crew Return Vehicle (known as the ACRV) for the new Space Station project. We had a big role in the ACRV because potential medical emergencies, like a serious injury to, or illness of a station crew member would be one of, if not the most likely reason for an unplanned, unscheduled return to earth. Complicating such a situation would be the need to either abandon the Station entirely in order to get one astronaut back to Earth, or to leave crew members on the station with no way of escaping it later after the ill astronaut and perhaps one or two others took the only re-entry vehicle docked at the Station back to Earth.

Remember in the very first Star Wars movie when an escape pod carrying droids C3PO and R2D2 (who was carrying the stolen plans to the Death Star in his memory banks) was jettisoned? It was, for all practical purposes, just a round ball-shaped capsule designed to survive the stress of re-entry. Well, the idea I and my team worked on was very much like that. The ACRV was a simple a ballistic re-entry vehicle, meaning it would return to earth like the way the old Apollo and Gemini spacecraft did. It would simply fall to earth, through the intense heat of re-entering the atmosphere, and then would be slowed by parachutes before making a relatively gentle water splashdown. And if an ARCV survived all that, our Operations team overseen by the DDMS unit would have naval ships on station near the splash down point ready retrieve both it and its human occupants. Of course, the G-forces experienced by anyone inside the Assured Crew Return Vehicle would be tremendous, and multi-directional. And it was unknown whether an ill or seriously injured crew member could even survive those. But, the thinking went, it would be better to try getting that astronaut back than letting him or her die up in space. But, as with the telescoping escape pole idea, the situation presented was so complex, with so many potential failure points, that the ARCV idea, too, was dropped.

Perhaps then it's rather amazing that, despite all that I knew about what could go wrong, and what could happen to the human body in any number of emergency circumstances involving the shuttle program, I myself applied to be a mission specialist – a non-pilot astronaut - that same year, 1991. Col. Martin Victor, the head of the Patrick AFB Hospital at the time and my boss, told me the huge amount of work that I'd done related to medical issues in space flight had made me the Air Force's number one candidate to be an Aeromedical Specialist astronaut. Unfortunately for me, but fortunately for potentially millions of Americans in the years ahead whose lives would be saved by defibrillators placed on board commercial airplanes and in tens of thousands of public buildings across America and beyond, NASA that year selected exclusively Navy people for that and other specialist slots reserved for members of the military. As a consolation prize, I guess, I did win the "prestigious" Silver Snoopy award from the NASA Astronaut Corps for my dynamic support of the space shuttle program and the emergency medical aspects of space programs. Few people know about that particular award, but because the honoree is chosen by the astronauts themselves, I value it greatly.

Even as I worked with and, essentially for NASA through DDMS, next door at Patrick Air Force Base I was also the flight surgeon for both a helicopter squadron and a Pararescue Jumper unit. The PJs were the most fit men (at the time, they were all men) you could ever encounter. They were also trained medically. As noted, they were the heart and soul of our emergency response program for the shuttle emergency response operations, not only for the launch site at the Kennedy Space Center but wherever the shuttle might land after an aborted mission. They were the reason I had to stay current in helicopter egress and water survival techniques. They also trained me on hoist work, meaning I had to practice descending from, and ascending back to massive helicopters on a cable. That put me in position to experience hurricane force winds stirred up by the helicopters whirling rotors above while suspended 30, 40 or even 50 feet in the air.

Sometimes my fun-loving PJs and helicopter crews would have a little fun at my expense. Under the guise of "training" they would drop me into the wilds and marshes of Cape Canaveral, where hungry, fearsome feral hogs reigned supreme. Sometimes I got the feeling my PJs and flight crews left me there on the ground a little bit longer than was necessary, just for laughs. I grew to welcome the experience of being lifted up through the hurricane-force winds generated by the helicopters' rotors, especially when I look down as I was being hoisted up and see a herd of snarling, slobbering, hungry hogs congregated at the very spot where I'd been standing moments earlier. I would shout over the noise of the engine, rotors, and wing at my crewmates, who typically were doubled over in laughter. "Don't worry, I'll get you in the end," I would say. And since I would be the doc performing their annual physical exams, they all got my meaning.

In my role as the unit medical officer for those PJs at the Cape I also got my first taste of using defibrillators in flight. Typically, our team had a pretty impressive array of medical supplies and equipment on board the Sikorsky HH-53 "Jolly Green Giant" helicopters that our unit flew. That medical payload sometimes included a large portable defibrillator that the EMERGENCY! paramedics used on TV back in the '70s.

A couple of Kennedy Space Center managers, Don Doerr and Art Mapes, graciously provided one of those defibrillators to the Air Force PJs unit. And the helicopter squadron itself had one of its own. Sometimes I and the PJs would be called upon to rescue cardiac arrest victims out at sea east of Florida. We often had to hoist those patients up straight from their boats to our helicopter. Those patients typically would reach the big heavy metal chopper drenched in salt water from the spray churned up by the helicopter's rotors. They also would be tied into the metal basket stretcher, which itself was attached to the electric hoist by a thick steel cable. By the time the crew got such a patient secure inside the helicopter, I and all the crew members assisting with providing medical care also would be drenched in salt water. Then, because the patients we rescued typically were in cardiac arrest they usually needed a good, high-voltage shock from one of those huge defibrillators.

Think about that for a second. If there is a situation on the planet in which you would not advise administering a big blast of electricity to someone in cardiac arrest that would be it. You could generate bolts of lightning between the paddles of a defibrillator just by holding them a certain distance apart, and that was in pristine conditions. On the wet floor of a metal helicopter in which everyone is drenched by salt water, the danger factor was off the charts. Still medical necessity ruled. Whenever I or anyone else who happened to be wielding those paddles, shouted "All Clear," every crew member braced for what was about to happen. When the shock was administered to the patient, not only would he or she bounce up in reaction like a basketball, the doc, and the PJs all felt the power of the electrical current surging through their own bodies, too. I thought I was OK after many such shocks. But over the years, as my daughters learned about my adventures shocking wet patients in metal helicopters, they began teasing me about the effects of all those shocks on my mind. They went from joking that "M.D." (for Medical Doctor) really stood for "My Daddy," to actually meaning "Mentally Deranged" by all those shocks.

But it was only a few years later that those experiences in the Jolly Green Giants and a change of career started me to thinking there must be a better way of using defibrillators in an airborne environment. I also drew on that experience to determine that a stethoscope – a basic medical tool that can be valuable in nearly all situations – was pretty much useless in an aviation environment. I had tucked those little lessons away in my memory, then drew on them later in the development of the defibrillator and enhanced medical kit programs at American Airlines.

In December 1991 Laurie gave birth to our second daughter, Catherine, in Florida. She also announced that she was henceforth out of the baby business. "If you want more, you need to find another wife," she told me. I thought it wise not to take her up on that offer. But Catherine's birth and the realization we were moving into a new phase in our life as a family began setting the stage for the biggest change ever in my improbable path toward impacting the world.

Operation Desert Storm was going on the Middle East, and soon was to be followed by Operation Desert Shield, the full military assault to take back Kuwait from Iraq and its dictator Saddam Hussein and to take the fight deep into Iraq. I was working with the Air Force and NASA in northeast Florida but knew I was due for a transfer and suspected it might be to the Middle East. But by that time I also had paid back all the time that I owed to the Air Force in exchange for my medical education. Meanwhile, I had been promoted to Lt. Colonel ahead of schedule (or below the zone, in Military lingo]. That was a high honor unheard of in military medical circles, and it put me on track toward becoming, potentially, a high-ranking and very influential leader within the Air Force's Medical Service. But to get to that level I knew I would have to serve some time in a combat zone, and obviously at that time, the Middle East. So, I was beginning to wrestle with the question: "Do I stay and risk deployment to the Middle East war zone, or do I leave the Air Force?"

It was during that time that my friend and civilian medical colleague at NASA, Dr. Jeff Davis, left to become the medical director for American Airlines. And he asked me to join him on the medical staff there. So, we planned to leave Cape Canaveral, the Air Force and NASA with a wealth - perhaps even an unrivalled-for-a-doctor amount - of experience in real-time, operational flight environments. And as I left that life behind, I could not help but wonder what applying all my aerospace medicine skills and experience to the world's largest airline might bring about?

CHAPTER IV

Just the Numbers...

So, Laurie and I, and our two young girls loaded up the cars and moved to Texas, where I began work at the American Airlines' headquarters in Fort Worth, on the south end of the huge Dallas-Fort Worth International Airport.

Initially we did not have a house to live in, so we started life in Texas in a two-bedroom apartment in the old (for Texas, where pretty much everything is new) town of Grapevine. Grapevine was not far from American's headquarters. In fact, the town lies just north of DFW Airport, and the airport's terminals are in Grapevine as well. Indeed, if you ever get a parking or speeding ticket around the terminals or the hotels in the center of the airport, your fine money goes to the city of Grapevine. While I was busy working, Laurie slowly went insane – well, almost - staring at the walls of our little apartment and tending to two young children while they searched for a place we could call home[5].

---

[5] One day while Laurie was at the pool at the apartment complex, she met another young mother, Kathy Schaefer. She had a young child, named B.J. B.J. and Erin became good friends and played the day away in the pool in those first few weeks.

American Airlines! The very name stirred up excitement deep in my inner being. For an Aerospace Medicine specialist, this was where it was at. Thousands of pilots and flight personnel to tend to, and hundreds of millions of passengers a year. That gave me a huge pool of "patients" about which I could think. How could they best be helped? How could their safety be guarded more effectively? How could I bring my public health knowledge and skills, learned at Harvard, and honed when I worked on the space shuttle program, to bear on this enormous and enormously complex mass of people?

This, of course, probably sounds weird to you. But that is because a tiny fraction of a percentage of people who will ever read this book are Public Health professionals. So, what is it, you ask, that is so special about commercial airline travel that makes an Aerospace Medicine doctor's heart beat faster when he contemplates working with such a population? Well, contrary to what most people think, the commercial flight environment, though safe for the most part, is NOT innocuous. Although flying commercially is not nearly as hazardous as flying (or working) on the space shuttle or in high performance military aircraft, there still are many potential health hazards that have to be considered, even if the vast majority of airline passengers never give a second's thought to any of them.

Kathy and Laurie also became -and remain to this day - dear friends. Kathy's husband Bob was, at the time, a new pilot for American. And the McKenas and Schaefer families had more in common than being American Airlines families. Kathy and Bob were both graduates of the U.S. Air Force Academy in Colorado, while I'd just ended my 10-year career in the Air Force. The Schaefers helped the McKenas greatly to get established in Texas. Laurie especially left many dear and good friends in Florida, and missed them dearly, so Kathy was a Godsend

The Health Hazards of Air Travel

So, as a prelude to placing advanced medical equipment on board airplanes let's familiarize you with what goes on in ordinary commercial airplanes from a health perspective. There are medical hazards and risks you likely have never considered. I and my colleague at American, Dr. Tom Bettes, captured these hazards in a September 1999 article in American Family Physician, a publication aimed at family practice doctors.

The article noted several environmental and physiological stresses may be encountered when consumers determine to fly commercially. These include activities that occur even before the traveler boards his or her plane. Think: "running to catch a flight" or other physical or mental stress-inducing activities (running late; fighting heavy traffic in route to the airport or not knowing the way there; being unable to find a parking spot; being unfamiliar with the airport's layout; suddenly remembering you left something important back home or in your office; waiting in long, slow-moving security lines, and so many more things). It remains unknown to us just how many cases of in-flight heart attacks or other health events that seemingly crop up without prompting while the traveler is on a plane actually are triggered by events that took place before they ever set foot on that plane.

Then there are the actual physiological effects of flying, which most of us simply ignore. First, as you ascend in an airplane, the air pressure gets lower and lower. Literally, each cubic meter of air weighs progressively less against your body for every 1,000 feet of altitude you gain. That is what causes your ears to "pop" as you go up into the sky. Because it is being pressed less and less as you rise, the air inside your middle ear expands. That is, the same number of molecules of air inside your head gradually spread out and take up more space in there. But this change does not take place as fast inside your head as it does outside your head because various structures in your inner ear, mouth, nose, and throat are not designed to support rapid pressure changes. And that creates a pressure imbalance between the air inside your head, and that which is on the outside, pressing against your ear drum. As you ascend the body's natural way of dealing with that pressure imbalance is to bleed off some of that expanding, lower-pressure air in your ears via a tube between the middle ear and the throat called the Eustachian tube. That tube is like a one-way valve, to a certain degree. The popping you feel sometimes as you ascend is just part of the balancing out of the rapidly changing pressure inside your head. It normally happens smoothly, and when it does you will not hear any popping. But sometimes the pressure gradient –the invisible barrier between the lower and higher-pressure air in your Eustachian tube builds up more on one side than the other. At that point, the air under higher pressure inside your ear will push through that gradient and shove the lower pressure air out. That is the popping noise you hear - and feel.

Normally, going up is fine (beyond the popping sound). But as you descend, the Eustachian tube can sometimes snap shut, especially if you have a cold or lots of fluid in there as the result of active sinus drainage or an infection. In such situations the pressure difference between the air inside your Eustachian tube and the air outside cannot be easily balanced. That pressure imbalance can cause a painful ear blockage that can last for minutes, hours or occasionally even days.

Of course, pretty much the same thing can happen anywhere within the body where air can get trapped. That includes places like the sinus passages, the bowels, or any number of other locations in the body. It is not entirely uncommon for this to cause painful sinus or bowel blockages, and the like.

While such situations are little more than a nuisance to most air travelers, this issue of fluctuating pressures as planes ascend and descend has some potentially serious medical ramifications for certain people. If a passenger is travelling with an air tube placed into his or her lungs, the person or someone traveling with them must be sure that the air in that air tube is replaced by liquid. Otherwise as a plane descends the air flowing through that tube and into the lungs can expand and rupture the person's windpipe.

Also, if a passenger is wearing an air splint (to stabilize a broken bone, injured knee or something similar) the air in that splint will expand as the plane gains altitude as each molecule of air enlarges because it is under less pressure. In reaction, the air cast will get tighter and tighter and could begin to choke off the blood supply to the leg, the arm, or other appendage. Thus, if you ever must fly with an air splint on be sure you know how to release some air from it as you ascend. If that is not possible, ask your doctor for a different cast.

Not only is the loss or gain of absolute air pressure a potential medical issue when flying, the various gases that combine to make up the air molecules we breath (oxygen and nitrogen mostly, plus other trace gases) are themselves under more or less pressure as a plane descends or ascends. The effect of that as you ascend is a drop in the concentration of those gases within any given volume of air. Thus, the body gets less and less oxygen as one ascends even if they feel like they are breathing in the same amount of air with each breath. That is because there is less oxygen in each of those otherwise consistent breaths.

It is just like trying to breath as you hike up a tall mountain in the Rockies. You get less oxygen per breath of air than you take in than when you are walking at sea level. Most people tolerate this relatively well. But some people with anemia, lung disease, chronic obstructive airway disease, heart disease, and certain other conditions can become symptomatic, faint, or develop other, worse reactions because they already have a reduced ability to carry blood oxygen. Such people are particularly vulnerable to rapid pressure loss when a plane climbs to cruising altitude.

People with medical conditions that can leave them vulnerable to rapid air pressure loss should consult with their doctor before flying. Airlines are generally able to provide supplemental oxygen, but carriers typically require passengers to coordinate through a doctor and to get a prescription before they will allow a passenger to use bottled oxygen on board a plane. Also, to ensure safety, that bottled oxygen must be procured through the airline.

As we discussed previously, most people are used to and comfortable in an environment here on the ground. When you are flying, however, commercial jets maintain a relative altitude between 5,000 and 8,000 feet during routine flight. Since they typically fly above 30,000 feet, where the air is too thin to survive, modern airplanes have an internal atmospheric control system that lowers the pressure inside to reduce the amount of air pressure on the outside of the hull. But those systems rarely, if ever, allow the interior air pressure to go under what would be experienced by a hiker at 8,000 feet. Thus, in effect, every time you fly it is like driving up an 8,000-foot tall mountain. How high is that? Well, if you have ever driven the Blue Ridge Parkway in western North Carolina, you likely have seen and been to the top of Mt. Mitchell. And if you have hiked around at the top of the mountain you no doubt felt a bit winded because of the thin air up there. Well, Mt. Mitchell, which is the tallest mountain in the eastern half of North America, is about 6,600 feet tall. So, no matter how high your plane actually flies, the air inside will be more-or-less like the moderately thin air atop Mt. Mitchell. (but nothing close to the ridiculously thin air at Mt. Everest, which at 29,029 feet is the world's tallest, and where extraordinarily fit climbers typically cannot survive more than a few minutes without supplemental oxygen).

Obviously, as the air gets thinner, less oxygen gets into your lungs. And the medical consequence is that a normal baseline blood oxygen of 98%, which is about what the average person's blood oxygen would be while reading a book, can drop to 60 or 70%. These numeric readings may mean nothing to you. But at a blood oxygen level of between 60 and 70, blood molecules lose some of their oxygen-carrying efficiency. At that level they carry around 10% less oxygen than normal. For people with no medical issues, this drop in blood oxygen efficiency is not a big problem, though they likely will notice it. But throw in some congestive heart failure, anemia or chronic obstructive airway disease and this loss of oxygen-carrying efficiency in the blood can become a big issue. For people with these conditions, it is important for them to have a preflight sea level oxygen level in the 68 to 70 range to be sure you can safely fly without supplemental or additional oxygen. If it is lower than that, then special arrangements must be made with the airline for bottled oxygen to be used in flight.

Most airlines have a "Special Assistance Coordinator" or some similarly titled person or office that is available to handle the medical needs for customers who need supplemental oxygen, wheelchairs, or other assistance. Some people with particularly acute lung disease may need pulmonary function testing, high-altitude simulation testing that measures their arterial concentration of oxygen, or simple observation of their ability to walk and climb stairs before they can be cleared by their doctor to fly.

Another potential health concern related to flying is probably something you have not heard about. Sorry. That's a pun, because the problem is literally related to passengers' hearing. We all know about – and have experienced - noise in aircraft. For most people it is an annoyance, but not a real medical issue. But prolonged exposure to even lower levels of noise can cause hearing damage. So wearing hearing protection, or for the wealthier among us, noise reduction headsets, is a smart move (and merely wearing earbuds or headphones blasting out loud music to cover the sounds of flying isn't "just as good" because you could be causing as much or more hearing damage that way). Wearing ear protection can make commercial flights a bit less stressful. But there are, of course, additional noises on some flights, such as crying babies that even ear protection will not fully block out. Babies crying is an unpredictable and unavoidable fact of air travel. And there is only so much we can do to help the poor mother and/or father to deal with that situation.

Another risk issue for passengers is clear air turbulence. Despite what you may assume, air turbulence severe enough to bounce a heavy jet around occurs most often without a warning. The plane will suddenly drop a few thousand feet, and whatever is not secured [including you] will immediately fly up to the ceiling of the cabin – before falling hard back to the floor as the plane levels out again. Meanwhile, that bin above your head with four or five 25-pound carry-ons stowed in it might pop open because of the big bump, and then some or all those bags can fall out onto the passengers below.

We all read or see news reports several times a year about some plane flying somewhere in the world being involved in a case of severe clear air turbulence. In most such cases, multiple passengers are injured while nearly always crew members – particularly flight attendants, who usually are up and working in the aisles – suffer broken bones, head traumas or serious back injuries. That's why veteran travelers know to always wear their seatbelts whenever they are seated – even when the "Fasten Seatbelts" sign is NOT illuminated. And passengers should be prepared to throw their arms over their heads, and to lay their bodies over those of children seated next to them, to protect against falling bags.

Another physiological issue with flight is the very low moisture content of the air in the passenger cabin. That is why your mouth and mucus membranes tend to dry out when you fly. And it is why it is important to drink lots of water to stay well-hydrated, especially on long-duration flights. And no, booze is not just as good as water for this purpose. In fact, alcohol can dehydrate you even faster and more thoroughly than drinking nothing at all. Alcohol causes you to pee (diurese) more than otherwise would be the case. And that accelerates the rate at which you lose the fluids that you desperately need to stay in your body when you are flying.

Jet lag is another physiological problem with air travel. And it is the bane of the global traveler. 'East is Least' and West is Best' is the aphorism they taught us in our aerospace medicine residency. In other words, when you travel Eastward (opposite the direction in which the sun moves), you feel the jet lag more. When you travel Westward (or with the sun, which, in effect, lengthens your day) your body can compensate for the jet leg more easily. It also appears that exposing yourself to the outdoor light in the new location at which you have just arrived helps you get over jet lag a bit faster. Exposure to natural light is a key factor in resetting your internal clocks, also known as your circadian rhythm. So, getting outdoors and experiencing the daylight cycle in your new time zone is one of the best ways to reduce the effects of jet lag.

Another rather obvious but still not widely-recognized health issue related to air travel is the result of doing nothing – literally – for extended periods of time. Being immobile for a prolonged time in ANY location, be it a plane, a train, a long movie (like Gone with the Wind, regardless of where you see it) can lead to what is called Deep Vein Thrombosis, or DVT. Put more simply, that means you can develop blood clots in your legs from being seated for long periods of time, especially if your legs are uncomfortably compressed by tight quarters like those increasingly found in coach sections of airliners. That, in fact, has given rise to another name for the problem: Economy Class Syndrome. So, it is a good idea to talk with your doctor prior to any long trips. Leg and calf exercises, walking occasionally when the seat belt sign is off (but re-read the section on clear air turbulence!), taking aspirin if your doctor directs it (it thins your blood a bit), or using leg compression stockings might be what he or she recommends for your situation.

In addition to being folded up and locked into tight seating arrangements, you are also exposed to radiation when you fly. When you are flying at 30,000 to 45,000 feet, as you are on nearly all commercial flights, there is simply less atmosphere between you and the sun than when you are standing on the ground. One of the atmosphere's primary jobs is to 'soak up' the incoming radiation from the sun. But when you are five to eight miles high your exposure to solar radiation is significantly higher. This is hardly a concern for even most regular air travelers. Airplanes skins themselves offer a bit of protection and the amount of time you spend at such heights is still pretty small. However, flight attendants, and especially pregnant flight attendants or those planning to get pregnant should discuss the matter with their OB-GYN doctor. Setting a date for when the flight attendant should stop flying to reduce the fetus' exposure to high altitude radiation is a good idea. That is because rapidly dividing cells like those in a developing fetus are particularly vulnerable to such radiation.

Sometimes your travel destination can be a key health factor, too. We all know that near the North and South poles radiation from the sun penetrates to the Earth more readily. But there are also transoceanic locations such as the South Atlantic Anomaly (off the East Coast of South America and extending west to cover most of central Brazil, Peru and a bit of the Pacific Ocean) where the inner Van Allen Radiation Belt comes closest to the Earth's surface. It gets as close as 125 miles to the surface (vs. a normal distance of more than 3,000 miles high). This "dip" in the belt leads to an increased flux of energetic particles in this region and exposes orbiting satellites to higher-than-usual levels of radiation. So, if you repeatedly fly from, say, Sao Paulo to Paris, Madrid, or Lisbon, you will be flying through the anomaly area a lot and will get much higher-than-normal total exposure to radiation. This may or may not produce any noticeable medical issues in your lifetime. But given the choice, you would prefer to get less exposure to radiation just to be safe.

When you are the chief medical officer of a major airline, these are all issues that have to be addressed when your "patients' are the tens of thousands of employees and the hundreds of millions of passengers who fly annually on your carrier's planes. Again, in aerospace medicine it is the environment that so very adverse, so it is the responsibility of aerospace medicine experts to be aware of that and to monitor and, to the extent possible, limit individuals' exposure to that adverse environment.

But there is an even bigger complicating factor with commercial air travel than just the inherently adverse environment of air travel itself. And that is the health status of each and every passenger or crew member who boards a plane. Most people who get on planes are reasonably healthy. But if even only 10% of travelers a year board with some sort of health problem – whether it's chronic, post-operative complications, breathing issues, or even just an ordinary, run-of-the-mill cold, that still translates into something like 85 million passengers a year on U.S. airline's planes – and nearly 460 million passengers a year globally – who already are sick or ailing when they begin their journeys by air.

Though some of those sick travelers won't feel any sicker as a result of flying while ill, it's safe to say that in nearly all cases, the flight environment makes their illnesses and symptoms worse (if they're taking prescription meds they may actually get better during a flight, but that would be in spite of the adverse effects of flying – they likely would have gotten better even faster had they not chosen to fly). Any way you look at it, flying while sick makes you more vulnerable to the adverse environmental impacts of air travel.

We aerospace medicine docs can control this problem well with military pilots and crews. We know them individually. We monitor their health very closely. And if we see any evidence of illness among this small pool of otherwise extremely healthy people, we can ground them temporarily, or permanently if necessary, for health reasons. And in the case of astronauts, not only are we able to build in effective medical protection protocols, we are able to reduce their health risks greatly by carefully selecting astronauts based on their superior health and fitness histories. Plus, we keep the space vehicles shielded from outside contaminants. Even ground crew members and program leaders are not allowed around a space vehicle or the astronauts themselves in the final days before a launch if those ground crew members or program leaders exhibit any signs of a potential illness, even if it is only a cold.

Commercial airlines have nothing close to that kind of selective discretion. They pretty much fly anyone who presents himself or herself at the gate and have only the thinnest legal ability to turn away travelers, and only for the most extreme health reasons – assuming the airline is even aware of such health concerns.

Indeed, in the United States one issue is that under the laws meant to protect people with disabilities who want to fly airlines cannot ask travelers about their health conditions; people must voluntarily tell the airline they have a medical issue. Even if the passenger knows they have a highly infectious, deadly disease – and chances are, they do not know – they do not have to disclose that to their airline. And the airline cannot ask about it even if there was reason to suspect a passenger had such a medical issue. The heart of the problem is that in most cases people do not disclose they have an ongoing health issue because they do not know they should and/or because they do not want to disclose it. And in most cases, they do not even know they have a health issue[6].

Thus, a subset – a surprisingly large subset – of people who fly have medical conditions that can be aggravated or set off by air travel. That means they are more prone to medical events, like fainting,

---

[6] In very rare situations, such a U.S. airliner departing a country with experiencing an outbreak of a very deadly and highly contagious disease like Ebola, the FAA, the State Department and the Centers for Disease Control can cooperatively issue temporary rules requiring airlines to inquire about travelers' potential exposures to such a disease but that is an extremely rare circumstance.

or even heart attacks or sudden cardiac arrest, on board. But, as noted, in most cases, they are not aware of the potential dangers.

How dangerous can it be?

Well, when someone with cardiovascular disease, or who recently has had a heart attack flies, the stresses of the flight environment can kill them. When someone has a heart attack, part of the heart muscle dies. That area then becomes quite irritable and it can be a focus point that can cause the heart to beat in bad (fast or irregular) rhythms. And that can be lethal. When such a person is exposed to the stresses of flight such as those explained previously – especially lower oxygen levels – really bad things sometimes do begin to happen. Further, heart muscle damage can result, with even greater tendency to create irregular and/or rapid heartbeat rhythms, which again can lead quickly to death. The risk of these bad things happening is highest in the first two weeks following a heart attack. To be safe, aviation specialist doctors recommend against air travel for at least four weeks following a heart attack. A treadmill test prior to flight can help the doctor clearing the person for flight to be sure there are no areas of the heart that are prone to further damage if exposed to the low oxygen levels in flight.

People who have had procedures like percutaneous angioplasty, where the doctor uses a balloon to open up clogged arteries, or coronary artery bypass surgery, where the doctor puts into place new vessels that will bypass, or go around a clog in the patient's arteries, normally can fly within a week or two of the procedure. But that is assuming all goes well with that procedure and the recovery process. Such people still should check with their cardiologist before flying the first time after bypass surgery.

Sometimes after ANY operation, pockets of air can be trapped inside the body. Since the air expands when the plane goes up into the air, bad things can happen. This is called barotrauma. Expanded air presses on internal tissues and organs and can cause damage, or at least severe pain. So, air travel should be delayed for at least two weeks after virtually any type of surgery, to be sure the body absorbs that free air.

Pregnant women generally are advised not to travel when approaching their expected delivery date. Partly this is so these mothers – and their newborns - will be near their own doctors and hospitals should those babies arrive early. Of course, having a baby in your own city is a big matter of convenience and, sometimes, an important factor in your insurance coverage. But there are serious health considerations behind the advice to mothers-to-be that they should curtail their air travels as the anticipated date of birth approaches. Because of the incidence of superficial and deep thrombophlebitis – blood clots forming in the veins, usually in the lower legs - associated with increased levels of clotting factors and vein dilatation common in pregnant air travelers, these ladies should request an aisle seat whenever they do fly, no matter how early or late they are in their pregnancies. And they should get up and walk around the cabin some when it is possible and reasonably safe to do so. They also should stretch and perform isometric leg exercises, especially during long flights. Pregnant patients with a history of significant anemia, prematurity, cervical incompetence, bleeding, or other increased risks should be advised not to fly all. And most OB-GYNs these days strongly warn their patients against flying after their 36th week of pregnancy, or at about the eight-month mark. Many doctors issue such instructions even earlier in the pregnancy.

Traveling long distances by air also can be challenging for diabetic people; especially if the travel is across several times zones. Adjustments to mealtimes, glucose self-monitoring and timing of medicines must be considered. People with diabetes should carry all medicines with them during the flight as well as supplies of needles, syringes, blood glucose monitoring equipment, a glucagon emergency, and sugared snacks. On most airlines special diabetic meals can be requested in advance of travel. That typically can be done by calling your airline and asking to speak to the Special Assistance Coordinator.

Because of rapid cabin pressure changes normally encountered on commercial flights any medical condition affecting how wide open or closed the eustachian tube or sinus openings will be could lead to complications during flight. Remember, eustachian tubes manage the equilibrium of pressure in the middle ear. Surgical procedures involving the inner or middle ear may be affected by pressure changes, so people who have recently had such procedures should not fly until cleared by the doctor.

Passengers with recent abdominal, central nervous system, ophthalmologic or thoracic surgery are susceptible to problems with the expansion of gases trapped inside their bodies as planes ascend. So, they should not fly until cleared by their doctor.

And, of course, passengers with communicable diseases including tuberculosis and measles should delay travel until the period of communicability is over.

For orthopedic injuries, passengers should use bivalve air casts to prevent circulatory problems. If the passenger is wearing a pneumatic splint it is important for some air to be released prior to flight so the limb is not strangled when the air inside the cast expands upon ascent.

Passengers with epilepsy should see their doctor before flying to ensure they are taking truly therapeutic levels of antiepileptic medicines and are carrying their medications with them in the cabin.

Where did the Idea of On-Board Defibrillators Come From?

As long as there have been airlines, there has been the notion that the airline needs to tend to passengers' medical needs. Don't forget, the very first flight attendants were required to be nurses because people feared the harsh environment of flight – which in the early days included flying in non-pressurized airplanes – could cause physical injuries, trigger seizures, or otherwise set off spasms or acute health events among passengers who had underlying illnesses or conditions. And, indeed, though we long ago gave up the require-ment that flight attendants be trained as nurses, there are, indeed, many, often complex factors related to air travel that can cause great embarrassment, discomfort, pain, injury or even serious illness and death for people who have the medical conditions listed above. But what if all the wise prevention steps fail and a serious health event still happens in flight... like when your heart suddenly stops?

I was not unique, or even the first, to think about placing defibril-lators on planes, but I and my team were the ones who made it hap-pen on such a large scale. For me, the notion of putting defibrillators on American Airlines' flights dated to about 1992, when I first came to American's headquarters, just south of the Dallas Fort Worth airport. I had just arrived at American as a staff doctor from Cape Canaveral Air Force Station and Patrick Air Force Base, where I ran the med-ical aspects of the space shuttle contingency program, and from NASA where I was a key member of the astronauts' medical man-agement team. Shortly after arriving at American, I wrote a memo to the Medical Director at the time, my old colleague at NASA, Dr. Jeff Davis, noting that Qantas Airlines had the devices. Furthermore, I asked, what precluded American from doing the same thing? I was naïve, and asked questions like that, often to Jeff's dismay.

He had recruited me to follow him to American, which I great-ly appreciated. But we did have different approaches. He was an experienced corporate manager type of doctor. I was fairly aggressive and sometimes pushed bureaucratic limits. In a sort of professorially way, Dr. Davis' view was that Qantas already had tried it and defibrillators' use was so very low, and the maintenance requirements for the huge devices they used was extremely high, so he was not convinced at that time that it was a good idea. He also was concerned, like several others, that because of the metal frame of the airplanes, the huge shocks generated by defibrillators might do more harm to others on the plane than whatever good they did for the individuals being defibrillated. I remember Jeff telling me once that "People just want to get from one city to another and did not pay to be electrocuted."

It is true that other international airlines – Qantas most prominently among them - had tried placing defibrillators on board, but their fleets were very, very small. Air Zimbabwe for example had only a handful of planes at the time. Virgin Atlantic had them, but the usage again was so low, and the required maintenance so high it raised the obvious question: "Is this an appropriate piece of equipment to have on the planes of the world's largest airline?"

At that time, American Airlines had about 400 big jets in its fleet flying not only in the United States, but also all over the world (it has more than 950 today). American also owned and operated the various companies that flew under the American Eagle name, between major airports served by American's big jets and smaller destinations where limited demand required the use of smaller, less expensive planes. Those nearly 300 additional planes also had to be considered in any plan to equip American's fleet with defibrillators.

The actual use of the devices on those international air carriers that had them at the time was very low. That primarily was because those other carriers flew a lot fewer passengers than did American.

They were all focused almost entirely on long-haul routes. Yes, they used very large wide-body planes, but only flew them once a day, typically. So the total number of passengers didn't come close to matching the totals racked up by American, which despite its international expansion beginning in the 1980s, was still mostly a domestic airline with lots of planes assigned to operate four, five or even six flights a day across a duty period of 16 to 18 hours.

All those things put together created a set of very daunting obstacles to any request for funding that one might want to present to any CEO, and especially to American's hard-nosed, suffer-no-fools CEO, Bob Crandall. He was a legendary cost-cutter who had once fired a guard dog to save a few hundred dollars a year. And he famously had saved the airline several million dollars annually by ordering olives to be removed from the salads it served on its planes.

Only a couple of years after I came to American with Dr. Davis Jeff moved back to NASA. I was named as his replacement. Of course, the promotion came with a huge challenge. I became Corporate Medical Director for the world's largest air carrier at the time when American was going through a program called "Added Value Analysis." That is a euphemism for downsizing, layoffs, and restructuring. Jeff likely saw what he interpreted to be the handwriting on the wall regarding the Corporate Medical Department's future. Was it a dinosaur headed for quick extinction? It is easy to see how one could come to that conclusion in those days. So, he decided to take NASA up on its offer to come back and run the agency's Life Sciences division, and their Space Medicine program.

American's management, however, concluded – surprisingly during the first round of restructuring cuts - that they still needed some form of an internal Corporate Medicine Department. American, after all, did fly around 100,000 people daily in those days, and the public health implications of such a large traveling population were enormous. At any second, a moderately sized "city" of people was in the air on American's planes. And all those people were having the same kind of health issues up there as they would be having if they had remained on the ground, perhaps even more so because of the added complexity of the adverse flight environment.

Also, many of American's employees, like pilots, had to meet government-mandated health standards, and many others were subject to drug testing and workplace safety rules and requirements, including attending various health and safety training programs. Taken together, all that drove a need for American to have some sort of medical presence. So, thankfully for me and my team in the medical department, our presence at American was still required (though eventually, years after I left, the medical department was eliminated and its work outsourced).

Still, the times were tough. I had to defend my department regularly at annual budget reviews conducted by the airlines' then-CFO, Gerard Arpey (a fast-rising young executive who eventually would become American's CEO in the 2000s). The boyish-looking and otherwise congenial Arpey would always begin these budget reviews with the question: "So why the hell do we have doctors on staff anyway, Dave?" Gerard was nice but, like Crandall, always direct and to the point. It was almost as if every year I had to go through an excruciatingly detailed "zero based budgeting" review to justify the existence of my department to my bosses. If it was not Gerard, it was Tom Horton, who not only followed Arpey as CFO but in the late 2000s would follow him again as CEO of American. I dutifully would explain the regulatory requirements, such as FAA/DOT drug testing, OSHA hearing requirements, and other essential programs that an airline was required to maintain. Then I would have to explain why it was more cost effective to have in-house staff do that kind of work rather than contracting it out. I never lost one of these annual fights to save our department. But I always felt the existence of American's internal Medical Department was tenuous, to say the least, and it always was in danger of being outsourced.

But, interestingly, it was within that perpetually never-quite-comfortable corporate environment, and within that milieu of circumstances, with the very real possibility of the medical department's work being outsourced, that American's defibrillator program was birthed. As it turned out, American Airlines Medical was one of the last great corporate medical departments in the airline industry. There was a staff of about 150, and clinics at each of the major hubs. And its existence within the airlines' organizational structure probably was the only way an ambitious new program relying on out-of-the-box thinking, could have been implemented. Our competitors, United and Delta also at the time had large in-house corporate medical departments led by corporate medical directors at that time. Gary Kohn was the medical director for United, and Chris Biscard was Delta's medical director during my tenure at American. Early on after taking over as head of the department I determined that I would not lead a dinosaur of a medical department, one resigned to merely functioning the way it always had, down the road to extinction. I determined my medical department would always be pushing for ways to innovate and improve the standard of care it provided to the airline's employees – and to its passengers.

So, as the new Corporate Medical Director, I took a different management approach. I was told repeatedly that the mission of the airline was to get people safely from point A to point B, and all else was fluff and extra. But what caught my eye – and my managerial attention - was the adverb "safely." As I focused ever more intently on that one word other questions kept coming to mind.

How does the airline care for this enormous traveling population?

What happens if someone gets ill on board?

What happens if a passenger gets on board overseas with Ebola or Meningitis and puts himself or herself in a position to spread such a deadly disease around the world?

How should the airline track it?

How would the airline notify other nearby passengers, and employees who encountered that passenger of the new, terrible risk they faced?

The passage of the Americans with Disabilities Act in 1990 meant that an older, more disabled pool of customers was flying on commercial airlines much more than ever before. But, as you would expect, they were bringing all their medical issues – some of which were pretty severe - with them. Because of this and other elevated health risks I quickly came to believe there was a real and important medical niche market for the services provided by airline medical departments. We were, I believed, absolutely essential cogs in American's ability to meet its own standard of delivering people "safely" to their destinations.

I drove home that point to my department, and, whenever I could, to American's top management. I argued, gently but with persistence, that the prime role of a Corporate Medical Director and his department should be to attend to those medical issues, plus manage all the many required, complex and demanding health and safety programs that agencies including the Department of Transportation, the Federal Aviation Administration and the Occupational Safety and Health Administration imposed on all big companies and, especially on high-profile airlines like American.

In effect, I sought to tie my department's purpose directly to the airline's primary safety mission in expectation that doing so would make it bullet proof during American's grueling annual department review and budgeting process.

Not long after I took over as corporate medical directory, Linda Campbell, the registered nurse on whom I frequently relied to implement new or changing aeromedical programs across the entire company, briefed me on some new developments she had recently heard about at a nursing convention. Advances were being made with defibrillators, she told me, knowing of my previous interest in finding a way to treat passengers who experience sudden cardiac arrest in flight.

My boss at the time, Tom Kiernan, American's Senior Vice President of Corporate Services, happened to be a voracious reader, and had, on his own, read about a new device the size of a laptop computer, that could deliver the kind of enormous jolts needed to restart a heart. And, it did not need the kind of huge electrical power requirements conventional defibrillators in those days required, and which, among other reasons, made installing them on planes a non-starter of an idea. He shared that article with me.

Susie Wallace, a flight attendant who also worked as a paramedic based in New York, had heard of these new devices, too, and even had used them.

What I brought to the equation, in addition to my tenacious pit-bull dogged determination, was my ability to use numbers to support new medical program ideas. That Harvard Master's Degree, it turns out, made me almost uniquely qualified to make the argument in support of deploying new, miniaturized defibrillators on American's planes. Airlines are now, were then, and always have been very data-driven enterprises. And under Crandall, who is renowned for his quantitative approach to management, American was, by a wide margin, the most data-driven of all carriers. And unlike most doctors, I, thanks to my Harvard training as a Public Health professional, was both highly skilled at, and comfortable with using numbers to drive medical – and business – decisions. I was a case of being the perfect person, working at the absolutely perfect moment, and for the absolutely perfect company for such an undertaking.

Of course, at American the language of debate was "Finance," with a capital "F." Bob Crandall, Don Carty, Bob Baker, Gerard Arpey, Tom Horton and every other senior officer there in those days were all finance guys, meaning they came out of their respective graduate schools of business as financially-focused managers. Though all of them at one time or another held operational, marketing or technology positions in their careers, they were at base, financial guys. Even Bob Baker, who as President of the airline actually managed American's day-to-day operations, was a finance guy at heart. But, thanks to my Harvard training I had learned the language of math and could speak it fluently, persuasively, but with a different twist. Naturally, I could talk to top executives about complex health and medical subjects and make that somewhat foreign language understandable to them. But I could also cross over and talk to them in their own language – finance, which is math-based – and make compelling arguments that relied on both medical and financial information.

Epidemiology. Public health analysis. Cost/benefit analysis. Supply chain understanding. Employee training. Legal liability. I had an almost unique educational background that made me well-suited to make the case for placing defibrillators on American's fleet of planes. And, thanks to all those years I spent performing on stage as a musician, I also had the self-confidence and stage presence necessary to sell my idea to tough, no-nonsense business decision makers on the sixth floor at American's headquarters, where sentimentality was strictly forbidden. So, when it came time for me to pitch American's brain trust on my idea, I was able to deliver a detailed and convincing, statistics-laden report on my research into what was happening medically in flight to American's (and all airlines') customers. After all, I was not just an expert in the medical issues, but also was a trained analyst of medical data and of data regarding standards of medical treatment and disease prevention. I often described himself in those days as the "new geek" in the Corporate Medical Director department. I had a large staff working for me, and a marvelous secretary, Bettye Harris, who kept me organized and in check. As a geek, I took all the learning I had picked up at Harvard and tried to find large pools of data that I could study in order to "diagnose" what was happening to my "patient" - the enormous body of travelers who flew on American. For me, the fun was in the study itself. What could I find out? No one before me had studied all the medical factors at play among the millions of people who flew on American Airlines. For that matter, as far as I knew, no one had ever studied the medical factors affecting all passengers on any airline.

I took the view that my medical and safety counterparts at all three of the unions at American in those days (pilots, flight attendants, and mechanics and other non-customer-facing ground workers at the airports) were just as serious about protecting the health and safety of their members as I was about protecting the health and safety of all employees and the airlines' passengers. The health care and wellbeing of the employees was to me not an adversarial issue, I reasoned, because everyone at the company ultimately wanted what was best for the employees in terms of their health and safety. So I stayed away from hot button issues like employee compensation, duty hours and other business relationship matters between management and employees, and sought to form collegial partner-ships with my union counterparts dealing almost exclusively around the issues of employee health and safety – and that of the passengers, too. So, I first became friends and established professional relation-ships with the various Union health coordinators. At the Association of Professional Flight Attendants union (or APFA), I got to know Emily Carter and Debbie Luhr, who led the union's Health department, and Kathy Lord-Jones who led APFA's safety office.

These union hall staff liaisons talked with flight attendants all the time, and they heard many things from the flight attendants that I likely never would have heard directly. In some conversations there were mentions of what was called a "drop dead" zone on the 767 air-craft. This was a seating zone on American's "small" wide body jet, the Boeing 767, where flight attendants reported that customers would simply stand up and then faint. They wondered if it could have been some cabin oxygen flow issue. At last, I had a problem to look at. I pulled all the flight passenger incident data (and did the analytical work under the auspices of American's Legal department at first).

The data was readily available. American was an analytical com-pany to say the least, with lots of reporting. If a passenger takes ill, the flight attendant must file a report, which comes to headquar-ters and enters a database. I noticed that the 767s were being used principally, for overseas flights, with long stage lengths[7]. Using the

---

[7] "Stage length" is the industry term for the distance between point of depar-ture and the destination, or to the place where the plane lands next in the case of flights that require an intermediate stop. It's a term right out the 18th and 19th Centuries, when inter-city travel often was accomplished in horse drawn coaches that traveled in "stages" between "stations" where fresh teams of horses could be hitched to the coach and where the passengers could get some food and/or relieve themselves.

data I pulled and analyzed, I rather quickly was able to show that given the length of the routes on which 767s typically were deployed, the longer the stage length of the flight the more likely one was to experience a fainting event or, for that matter, any medical event. Statistically speaking, those events were very rare. But they were easily explained by the numbers. It was logical there would be increased fainting events and other events, even non-medical ones, in 767s flying long routes. The finding simply is that the longer you fly, the higher your risk of something happening. It is sort of like—the more you drive, the greater the odds that you will get into an accident. It turns out it did not require rocket science – or medical science – to figure out the 767 'drop-dead zone' anomaly, just data collection and data analysis.

Medical Diversions

But, in a great example of the old researcher's category of "things I learned while looking up other things," I noticed several other peculiar things in the data while working on that 767 drop-dead zone question. There were changes – and not necessarily positive ones – in the number of flights each year that American had to divert from their original destination because of medical issues on board. The number of such medical diversions was growing every year. Worse, while the sheer number of medical diversions might be explained purely by American's growth as airline in that era, the rate of diversions - meaning the number of medical diversions per 10,000 passengers, or whatever, was rising. So, more was going on than just the airline's operational growth.

A medical diversion usually represents a serious medical event so bad the flight's captain decides to land the airplane at the closest, safest airport to get the customer the significant medical care he or she needs. These numbers on the chart are per revenue passenger mile, the number of such events annually divided by the total number of miles that paying customers fly in one year.

First, I noticed that medical diversions, at least for American, were increasing. These were the numbers for medical diversions per million revenue passenger miles [RPM] per year based on our own data and that of the FAA and the Department of Transportations' statistics:

	1991	1992	1993	1994	1995
American *	1.29	0.77	0.92	1.30	1.52
Air Canada*	0.59	1.60	1.38	0.87	0.90
Air Alaska	-	-	-	1.57	-
America West	-	-	-	1.48	-
Canadian*	-	0.64	0.70	0.27	0.65
Continental	-	-	0.60	0.93	-
Delta*	1.55	1.89	1.63	1.33	-
Northwest	-	-	-	1.40	-
United *	0.31	0.26	0.21	0.42	-

Medical Diversions Per 1 Million Revenue Passenger Miles Flown
(1 paying passenger flown 1 mile = 1 RPM)

I also noted that by the end of 1995, the medical diversions were still increasing:

Alarmingly, the number of apparent deaths on board the flights were also increasing. Remember, as a matter of practice, no one is declared dead on an airplane—the flight attendants do not have that kind or ability and authority. But these were the cases where a flight attendant began and reported beginning CPR on a customer—and it had to be someone with no pulse, no breathing, and unresponsive, because that was how we trained them to know to start CPR.

But remember, those symptoms that the flight attendants were trained to understand as signals to begin applying CPR techniques also are the hallmarks of that silent assassin, sudden cardiac arrest. So the line between a passenger who needed CPR to be performed on them and a passenger who no longer was alive and could not be revived via CPR was a thin one – and, at least early on in the CPR process, a very fuzzy and hard-to-discern one, too.

So, I put two and two together, and it equaled Sudden Cardiac Arrest. This is that condition that could only be treated with a defibrillator. Nothing else will do the trick. Not a shot of epinephrine to the heart. Not a nitroglycerin tablet being tucked under their tongue. And not even perfectly performed CPR by the most well-intentioned flight attendant, regular passenger or even an acclaimed cardiac surgeon who happens to be aboard the flight. I looked at those simple numbers and thought: "It is time to get defibrillators onto American Airlines flights."

Once I arrived at that conclusion, which I determined was statistically valid and morally imperative, I started asking various vendors for actual devices and mockups of these new-fangled Automatic External Defibrillators, also known as AEDs. Linda Campbell also got several models. Soon, my office was full of them, and my secretary, Bettye Harris, had to be very careful wading her way to my desk. She had to tiptoe through a minefield of defibrillator models laid out across the floor. At one point, Gary Kohn, the then-medical director for United Airlines, and, as such, my professional rival, called, as he often did, and asked: "Are you looking at defibrillators?" I told him, tongue in cheek, staring intently at several models on the floor in front of me, "Yes, I am 'looking' hard at defibrillators".

I took one of the devices from my office floor a couple of miles over to the flight attendants union's headquarters and spoke with Denise Hedges, the President of the Association of Professional Flight Attendants. I did this even before I approached American's upper management with the idea. Hedges was a respected woman whose stern presence had a way of creating a bit fear in those who first met her. As head of the APFA, she had led her 21,000 members on an 11-day strike in November of 1993. That strike lasted until President Bill Clinton used little-known powers uniquely granted to the president by the Railway Labor Act that governs management-labor relations in the rail and airline industries to end it and send the parties back into federal mediation. An agreement was reached six months later, although the terms of the deal were little different than what management had been offering just prior to the strike. Still, had Clinton not stepped in, and had the strike continued another week or two, it could have pushed the world's largest air carrier into bankruptcy. That showed that even the attendants, commonly viewed as the weakest of the three unions at American, by far, had political muscle enough to bring the airline to its knees. Well, at least it did under a strong-willed leader who could hold the notoriously fractious group together through the strength of her personality. As a result, Hedges had immense personal power in the days when I first approached her about defibrillators. Despite the hard-exterior vibe that she could give off, Hedges was quite open with me. We could talk freely with one another about a variety of attendant work and health related subjects. When we first met, I shared with her my views on how difficult it was for me, or any doctor to medically disqualify flight attendants under the then-new Americans with Disabilities Act. That is because under that law, a doctor had to be able to prove "direct, imminent, non-speculative threat of harm to self or to the travelling public" to succeed in grounding an attendant.

I told Denise Hedges my approach had been, and would continue to be to address each potential case of health disqualification individually. I told her I absolutely had to have hard, indisputable medical facts to show the attendant in question was a "direct and imminent threat" to safety, and the attendant's medical issues simply could not be reasonably accommodated by American via medication, a health improvement program or some other kind of intervention. "At last, a medical director not out to needlessly disqualify my people" she exclaimed in that first meeting. So, Denise Hedges, the fearful head of the Flight Attendant's Union, began to warm up to me during our initial meeting. I showed Hedges and the leaders of the APFA's medical and safety offices a model of a new automatic external defibrillator. I asked them if they thought flight attendants could handle those devices and the task of hooking them up to ill passengers in flight. After Hedges saw how simple the device was to use, and how it would speak to the person rendering aid, and walk them step-by-step through the process, she and her colleagues quickly piped up: "Yes...yes they can."

Flight Attendants and Cabin Safety

It was a novel idea to let flight attendants shock customers. But flight attendants have a long history in commercial aviation and played a significant role in cabin safety over many years.[8] The outstanding book, *Femininity in Flight* by Kathleen M. Barry is an excellent resource capturing this marvelous safety history. As that book explained, Flight Attendants, originally known as stewardesses or stewards, took their role almost directly from sea-faring travel attendant positions. At the airlines they took on primarily a safety-focused role. And that made sense because of the nature of flying, especially in the early days when the design, manufacture and operation of airplanes was, shall we say, less than mature. Planes were not pressurized. Engines tended to be under-powered for the tasks assigned. Pilots were making up operational and safety procedures as they went. And customer safety service standards were still being experimented with. Even the federal regulatory requirements were in flux as the industry went through an extended period of what can be likened to a baby taking his or her first, unsteady steps. It was obvious from the start that aviation can be an unforgiving environment, so the flight attendant, instead of just being a waitress in the sky as so many people mistakenly see them, was there to save your skin whenever things took a turn for the worse.

The very first flight attendant, or steward, was a German,

---

[8] *Femininity in Flight: A History of Flight Attendants.* Kathleen M. Barry. Duke University Press, Durham and London 1957.

Heinrich Kubis in 1912.[9] He was first an attendant for customer care on the Zeppelin LZ to Schwaben and was also on the ill-fated Hindenburg. Thankfully, during the Hindenburg incident, he was able to jump out of a window to safety as the flaming lighter-than-air craft neared the ground.

Then, Imperial Airways of Britain in the 1920s had "cabin boys" or stewards.[10] Stout Airways in the United States was the first in this country to employ stewards in 1926, working on flights in Michigan. Western Airlines followed in 1928, and Pan Am in 1929 employed male stewards to serve food.

The first female flight attendant started an early tradition of flight attendants being medically trained nurses. Nurse Ellen Church was hired by United Airlines in 1930. Then, as World War II grew into the huge international conflagration that it became the demand for nurses to work with the military overseas and at home became so great the requirement flight attendants also be nurses was dropped over time. As more airlines were created from scratch or from mergers, they followed the pattern of employing non-nurse "air hostesses" or "stewardesses." Dr. Barry explains in her book that this was one of the few jobs during the Great Depression for which women were eligible. That helps explain why the initial corps attendants was predominantly female. And, to be sure, those jobs were highly competitive, with innumerable applicants for just a few positions.

The requirements for these ladies, as noted in a 1936 *New York*

---

[9] Airships: The Hindenburg and other Zeppelins. http://www.airships.net/blog/worlds-first-flight attendant.

[10] "Before the Stewardess, the Steward: When Flight Attendants Were Men. Thesocietypages.org, retrieved December 3, 2018.

Times article, now are anachronistic and somewhat humorous. They included a requirement that they be:

Petite (weight - 100 to 118 pounds)
Not too tall (height - 5' to 5'4" to 5' 4")
Between the ages of 20 and 26
Subject to a rigid physical exam four times a year (some long argued that this was a back-door way of making sure no attendant tried to hide a pregnancy, at least for a while)

In the prim-and-proper – and euphemistic - language of the day, able to move and carry themselves as one who is "assured of the bloom that goes with perfect health."[11]

I certainly would not have met those requirements, which are laughable now. But in the cultural and business context of that day, appearance was considered an important factor. That is because in those days the knowing exploitation of female sexuality was viewed as a way to attract more businessmen to flights, not as something sexist or culturally insensitive (though it clearly was those things, at least to the modern mind). Attendants' uniforms became sexier as time progressed. They became formfitting, with stylish heels and gloves. In the U.S. "stewardesses" had to be unmarried and were fired if they decided to wed. In fact, that policy persisted at some airlines well into the 1960s, as did age limits, although some carriers had gradually raised the "age out" age into the low 30s over time.

In the '60s and '70s, advertising became racier, including National Airlines' provocative "Fly Me" program. They would outlandishly and sensually suggest flying, for example, 'Candy' to

_____

[11] *The New York Times*, April 12, 1936, page N1.

Orlando, or some other exotic destination. Braniff, in fact, hosted an advertising campaign called the "Air Strip" with allusions to flight attendants doing strip teases as they changed uniforms in flight. The "strip" itself was not anything that we today would think of as sexually exciting. The "girls" just removed outer layers of their uniform (coats, vests, longer outer skirts), to reveal name designer inner uniforms that were easier to move and work in and, perhaps, revealed a little more leg. Sometimes they donned sweaters or aprons (planes can be a little cold at altitude and serving drinks and dinner can be a little messy). But they did all that changing of clothes in a choreographed, flirtatious manner, sometimes with one attendant doing a mini-fashion show presentation over the in-cabin PA, explaining the design details of each grouping of uniform pieces. Still, the mere idea of male passengers watching a woman change at least some of her clothes was seen by airline managers and their Madison Avenue ad gurus as a way to increase passenger traffic. Now a wellspring of diversity, the flight attendant corps was not always such. Ruth Carol Taylor was the first African American flight attendant, hired in 1957.[12] The corps is now a broad spectrum of female, male, wed, unwed, straight, gay, and all races colors and creeds.

There still are some minimum height requirements that remain because flight attendants must be able to physically reach safety equipment. There also must be some strength requirements. The emergency egress doors are heavy, and airlines cannot risk having a flight attendant be the cause of cabin deaths during evacuation because the attendant is physically too weak to get a door opened.

---

[12] Conrard, Don, November 15, 2005. Promoting Diversity. Alaska's World from Alaska Airlines.

Part of the great diversity now enjoyed in the flight attendant ranks arose out of the U.S. Equal Employment Opportunity Commission. Some of the first complaints involved age discrimination, weight requirements, and bans on marriage. In 1968, the EEOC declared age restrictions to be illegal sex discrimination.

The number for flight attendants required on board is driven by safety regulations. The FAA requires at least one flight attendant be aboard per 50 seats, occupied or not. Thus, a plane with 51 seats requires a minimum of two attendants while one with 151 seats requires at least four. That requirement figures prominently in the design of aircraft. If an airline is going to have to have four attendants in either case, it's better to offer say, 185 seats than it is to offer 151seats, though other factors including engine capabilities, total weight, pilot contract factors governing their pay, and market demand also figure into the aircraft design equation.

While many travelers still view flight attendants as waiters and waitresses in the sky, they are really there for safety reasons. Outside the view of passengers, attendants go through safety briefings with the flight crew before every flight. They review safety and emergency checklists, check of all the emergency equipment, including the oxygen and defibrillator, make sure they have what they need to assist special needs passengers and unaccompanied minors, and get a weather briefing, primarily to be aware of and prepared for unusual conditions, like possible turbulence, during the upcoming flight.

Then there are the actual inflight safety duties they must be ready to perform during an emergency. Attendants need to open heavy doors in an emergency and direct the evacuation of the passengers. Attendants at American Airlines are well trained in first aid, caring for injuries, and dealing with intoxicated passengers or those showing signs of mental disorder or otherwise aggressive behaviors. They are trained to fight in-flight fires and to deal with smoke in the cabin, depressurization events, a passenger giving birth, a passenger having a seizure or other acute medical event. None of this, of course, is pleasant to deal with but somebody must be prepared to help in those and other nasty situations. Flight attendants fill that role. And, in the event of a crash or other significant event that forces an emergency evacuation, they are trained how to get everyone onboard out in less than 90 seconds while using only half of the available doors

Flight attendants have proven many times to be a very capable bunch. In fact, there is a long history of attendants around the world performing masterfully and heroically under intense pressure to protect and save lives. Here are just a few:

In April of 1936, Nellie Granger aided survivors after the crash of TWA Flight 1, then walked 4 miles in snow to find help.

In 1986 Pan Am Flight 73 was hijacked on the ground at Karachi, Pakistan. Senior purser Neerja Bhanot was killed while shielding children from terrorists.

In 1968 British Overseas Air Corporation (a predecessor to British Airways) Flight 712 crashed trying to return to Heathrow Airport near London after losing an engine on takeoff minutes earlier. Flight attendant Barbara Jane Harrison died while trying to save passengers from an on-board fire.

TWA Flight 847 from Athens to Rome was hijacked by terrorists associated with a faction of Hezbollah in June of 1985. Lead attendant Uli Derickson served as a translator between the terrorists (one of whom spoke her native German) and the captain. She shrewdly negotiated the merciful release of 17 older women and children from the plane during a fuel stop in Beirut. And she sought to protect the identities of Jewish passengers by hiding their passports from the hijackers.

In 1988 Aloha Airlines Flight 243 suffered a catastrophic structural failure that caused the top portion of the airplane's skin over the first-class section to be ripped away at 24,00 feet. Attendant Michelle Honda, who was standing in the aisle at the moment the roof came off, was thrown violently to the floor and almost sucked out by the resulting decompression forces. But she held on to seats and the arms of passengers and, though injured herself, was able to crawl up and down aisles to assist passengers, more than 60 of whom were injured, too.

In December 2001 American Airlines attendants Hermis Moutardier and Christina Jones, working aboard Flight 63 from Paris to New York, fought with now-infamous "shoe bomber" Richard Reid to keep him from lighting a fuse to detonate explosives concealed in his shoes. Reid, 6' 4" and well-built, successfully fought off the two women, but their actions gave other passengers enough time to pounce on and subdue the would-be bomber just three months after the 9-11 terrorist attacks.

Flight Attendants on US Airways Flight 1549, the famous "Miracle on The Hudson" flight in January 2009, successfully evacuated in 90 seconds all passengers from the aircraft that crash landed in the Hudson River, even as the cabin filled with icy cold water from the river.

So, our unlikely crew: me, Denise Hedges and the three other union health and safety officers agreed professional flight attendants were up to the job. After all, they are FAA-required safety officials on every plane; and are already trained to basic first aid standards. This, the small group determined, would help flight attendants more than it might hinder them. Armed with the statistics and the resolve of Hedges and her team, I began studying how I might pitch the idea to American's senior management. But, as it turned out, I got my unexpected opportunity to bring it up with CEO Bob Crandall before I was completely ready. And the second time I had a chance to pitch him my idea about defibrillators I had him stripped down to his underwear.

Robert Crandall, CEO

One person at American struck more fear into my heart than even Denise Hedges, the imposing flight attendant union president: Robert Crandall. He was deeply respected and, yes, feared by pretty much everyone at American's headquarters in northeast Fort Worth (plus most 114,000 others who worked for American or its sister companies under the AMR corporate umbrella). To all but the most senior employees who were closest to him, he was "Mr. Crandall." And even those who felt free to call him "Bob," in casual conversation or meetings with him, reverted to "Mr. Crandall" when referring to him in conversation with others lower on the corporate ladder or people outside American. He was President, CEO and/or Chairman – or all three at once – of American and AMR for nearly 20 years until his retirement in 1997. He is credited with:

The creation of AAdvantage, the first and enormously successful frequent flier program

The rapid modernization and expansion of the airline's SABRE internal reservations system into the industry-leading seller of airline tickets via travel agents and, eventually directly to the public via the Internet

The world-changing use of data and systems to maximize revenue with sophisticated, computerized variable seat pricing tools

And directing American's financing of its rapid fleet growth in the 1980s and 1990s through innovative and aggressive deal making on Wall Street and elsewhere.

Crandall also was widely known for being very tough on his staff, employees, union leaders, and airline competitors alike. His drive to make American the very best airline he possibly could on behalf of the airline's passengers and shareholders compelled him to lead aggressively and to accept nothing but top-notch performance from all those around him.

The first time I was called into Mr. Crandall's office in late December 1995, I had just been appointed Corporate Medical Director, an event that itself occurred only on the heels of one of American's "Added Value Analysis" projects. I met Mr. Crandall at 6 a.m.[13]. The meeting also included Tim Doke, American's head of Corporate Communications. Though crashes are rare at American, the airline sadly had lost one of its planes and all but four of the 163 souls onboard in the mountains near Cali, Columbia, only a few days earlier. A local pathologist in Columbia was claiming via the news media that there was alcohol in the deceased captain's blood. Crandall and Doke were concerned such a claim could make an already horrible situation for the airline much, much worse. So, they sought counsel from me because, as an

---

[13] With Crandall, 6 a.m. meetings were almost a daily occurrence because he liked to get office work done early before flying off in mid-morning for meetings elsewhere, or before plowing into long strategy meetings with his top officers or deep discussions of strategic or other complex issues all afternoon.

aerospace medicine expert with a decade of experience monitoring the health of Air Force pilots and astronauts, I possessed all the credentials necessary to be regarded by the courts as an expert witness. Crandall and Doke did not want me to go on the witness stand. But they very much wanted to know what the medical and physiological facts were, and therefore what American's additional liability exposure might be if those claims about the pilot's blood alcohol content were true. I quickly fell back on my aviation pathology training and my experience working on the recovery and analysis of the bodies of the astronauts killed in the explosion of shuttle Challenger. And I began to answer their questions.

"Alcohol is a decomposition product from human bodies in decay," I said, sounding very professional and proficient in my use of "Doctor-speak."

"One must measure the alcohol contained in a separate, protected space in the human body, like the vitreous fluid in the eye itself before one can draw any conclusion about what is causing the alcohol in the blood."

I eventually was able to make it clear that just taking a BAC sample from blood on or near the body of the dead pilot proved nothing. Even drawing a sample from within one of the pilot's crash-caused wounds was not helpful. Only blood drawn from a small, isolated part of the body could yield anything close to conclusive evidence as whether there really was alcohol from drink in the pilot's body as opposed to alcohol appearing as the by-product of the decomposition that began taking place within that pilot's body the moment he died. As it turns out, the human eye is a very good place to find any stored alcohol from drink as opposed to alcohol created by the natural chemical processes of decomposition.

I felt like I earned my pay that day. I also hoped that maybe

Crandall, Doke and, through them, other top American brass, would feel like they had made the correct decision in keeping American's aeromedical expertise in-house rather than contracting it out. It turned out the alcohol level in the deceased pilot's eyeball was, in fact negative. That pretty much proved the pilot had not been drinking in those critical hours before going on duty, when FAA and company rules forbid it. Once that bit of information was nailed down, Doke, who as the head Corporate Communications had the unenviable task of trying to protect the airline's image in the days after that crash, exclaimed, "There is a Corporate Communications god!" The information I provided then could be used by American to explain why testing of the pilot's blood had led to a false-positive initial report. Thus, my first serious business encounter with Crandall had gone well, at least from my perspective. And I think it probably helped form in the boss's mind an early, positive assessment of me.

Robert Crandall is a tall man, with impeccably combed hair and glasses. In those days he was pretty much always seen in a tie and full suit. Even in his office, where he took off the suit jacket and usually rolled up his shirt sleeves his tie always remained pushed tightly up into his shirt collar. Crandall set the appearance standard for all of them, both literally (there was a dress code, and he pretty much dictated it) and figuratively by the way he himself dressed and presented himself.

"Men think better in ties" he used to say.

At one point, the Human Resources department spent months preparing a presentation for Crandall and his executive team, known as the Planning Committee, regarding the launch of a relaxed "casual Friday" dress code as many other big, traditional companies had begun to do in those days. After months of research and bench marking of companies' policies both in the airline industry and other businesses, they were more-than-ready to present it. But Crandall took one look at the cover page of the paper presentation at this Planning Committee meeting and tossed it aside. "Not in my lifetime. Next presentation," he said. (Well, he was wrong in that shortly after his retirement in 1998, his successor Don Carty, allowed some relaxing of the dress code, but he was right in that it certainly did not happen when he was running the company.)

For employees, even fairly senior ones like me, encountering Crandall in the elevator could be quite awkward. Thanks to his renowned success as a manager and leader, his official title, his legendary managerial intensity and his big personality, the man had quite an aura about him. He always seemed to know who everyone that worked there was by just one look of his striking, steely blue eyes. While I thought – or hoped – that I had made a very positive impression on Crandall at our "alcohol in the eyeball' meeting, I was no different than any other mid- or senior-level manager at American in those days. We all had our "elevator pitches" ready to go in case we ever had a moment with Mr. Crandall – in an elevator or anywhere else.

One day, I was on my way up to the 6th floor to attend the weekly staff meeting of my direct boss, Tom Kiernan, American's senior vice president of corporate services. In addition to the medical department Kiernan oversaw functions like Safety, Corporate Communications, Human Resources, Corporate Real Estate and Purchasing. And I thought he was the best boss ever. Tom knew he did not know the medical/occupational field and gave me a fair amount of leeway to do my job. In return, I always briefed Tom and kept him well informed through regular one-on-one meetings, staff meetings, and weekly reports.

On my way up to Tom's staff meeting, Mr. Crandall walked into the elevator. We were alone. "Good morning Dave!'" Crandall said in his standard, chipper, clipped New Englander's accent (Crandall grew up mostly in Rhode Island). "Oh my gosh, he remembers my name," I remembered thinking at that moment as I returned the greeting. I was surprised and a little taken aback by the chance in encounter. I paused for a few seconds before gathering myself enough to begin, awkwardly, something of an elevator pitch. I was not yet fully-prepared to deliver a complete presentation on the subject, but by the fourth floor I knew I was running out of time and would be losing my chance in just two more floors. I was like Ralphie in the movie, A *Christmas Story*, blowing it in front of Santa, whom he had come to tell he wanted a "Red Rider carbine-action 200-shot model BB rifle with a compass in the stock." As we passed the fourth floor I finally blurted out: "Sir, do you know we are losing at least 50 customers a year to what appears to be sudden cardiac arrest? There is a new device we can put on planes that can save many of their lives." To my surprise, Crandall did not kick me down the slide with his boot like Santa did to Ralphie. Instead, Crandall said, "I want to hear more," Then the door opened on the 6th floor and he got out of the elevator, leaving me pleasantly stunned.

So, the stage was set. Now I had to think very carefully about what would be the best way to tell Mr. Crandall more; and not just more, but more in such a way as to win his support for spending money on a program that I instinctively knew would never even cover its own costs, let alone increase revenue for the airline. One part of my job gave me truly unique access to every one of American's senior leadership, and to interact with them on both a professional and very personal basis. American had in place an Executive Physical program. Once a year all of the company's elected corporate officers had to come to my clinic for physical exams. Then I would have follow up meetings with each one of them to debrief them on all their clinical results.

The American Airlines Medical Department, at that time, was renowned for our medical assessment facilities. The department had an in-house laboratory, x-ray facilities and a staff of doctors and nurses right there at headquarters across the freeway from Dallas-Fort Worth Airport, the airline's biggest hub, and just a few hundred yards from the airline's training center and System Operations Control center, where experts in every aspect of operations managed the giant carriers' operations in real time the way NASA engineers monitored space flight from "Mission Control." Only American's SOC, as it was known, was a huge room into which you could probably stuff 20 "Mission Controls."

A couple of years earlier, the medical department actually had been housed inside the Learning Center. The department's lab was outfitted with observation windows that allowed tourists visiting the learning center and Company Museum, known as the C.R. Smith Museum after the man who originally built the airline and ran it for 40 years, to look down and observe the busy medical lab. At that point in the tour the guides would always tout that we only selected the best, most physically fit candidates to serve as pilots and attendants. The lab ran 40,000 specimens a year from about 15,000 job candidates who made it that far into the hiring process. The medical department also brought serious job candidates in for treadmill heart exams. In fact, it used to be said that the American Airlines physical for prospective pilots was even tougher than the physical done on astronaut candidates. And as one of the few people to be able to make such a comparison, I agreed that it just might have been. I saw the Executive Physical program as an opportunity to get to know the company's top leaders and, hopefully to get an "in" with some of them.

Seeing your executive team naked each year (one at a time, not as a group) gives one a lot of power as a Corporate Medical Director. I probably got treated with far more respect than I deserved, almost certainly because of that unique doctor-patient relationship no other department head at American had any hope of developing with the top bosses. They liked the 'doctor' part of my job as Corporate Medical Director, which otherwise was far more of an administrative, program management and policy role than it was a real hands-on medical job. I also had that prescription pad, which allowed me to prescribe medicines for them, and for their families, if the need arose. I became 'their" doctor, available 24/7 to keep the enormously busy executive team going. In fact, part of the reason I had my office right on the first floor of the headquarters building, with a small clinic, was to give them quick and easy access to medical care so they didn't have to waste hours visiting a private doctor's office, or risk getting really sick by deciding not to take time off to see a doctor when they were feeling ill.

Tracy Nelson was the registered nurse who ran the clinic, and she was on a first name basis with all the executives. Smart as a whip, she had insights into situations that worldly geniuses do not have. Plus, she did not hold back, and was very direct and forthright and told you precisely what she thought... no holds barred.

One day, not too long after their brief encounter in the elevator, Mr. Crandall was in my office, stripped down to his skivvies for the exam portion of his physical examination. Here was this legendary CEO, who was feared by all, sitting in front of me, almost naked. I told him: "As I shared, Sir, we are losing about 50 people a year to what appears to be sudden cardiac arrest. That is an electrical anomaly of the heart that causes sudden death. Without a lifesaving shock, they will assuredly die. The technology has since evolved where there is a book-sized device that we can have on board to save a good percentage of their lives. It talks the user through how to do it, and very little training is required. Flight attendants can easily be trained to use them."

"Flight attendants?" was Crandall's first response. But he was very interested. He asked me to prepare a presentation to the entire senior management planning committee.

The dreaded senior management presentation!

My heart rate instantly went through the roof. That sounded like Ralphie from A Christmas Story going up to 10 Santas all at once, knowing that any one of whom could boot him down that slide. I also thought, in a "turnabout is fair play" sort of way, that meant I would soon be the one who would be, metaphorically, turning my head and coughing. Choking is a better word, I thought.

After several weeks, the presentation was ready. By this point, Susie Wallace, the paramedic/flight attendant had also mentioned these devices to Mr. Crandall. Her timing was impeccable. I started talking with her about my plan and presentation and included her in my initial teleconference planning meetings. Linda Campbell, my top aeromedical nurse, as always, served as a sounding board, making sure the points were airtight. Nobody in our then very small team wanted to see me shot down in burning flames before their very eyes.

The morning of the presentation I gathered four of what I considered to be the best examples of these new defibrillators and took them up to the presentation in what looked like a shopping cart. Somehow, that "shopping cart" made it into the Chicago Tribune. John Crewdson was a reporter there, and at that time he was looking very intently into what airlines were doing regarding defibrillators. Based on his questions and understanding of the subject, I always thought Crewdson must have had 'moles' at American's Headquarters. I was well aware Crewdson mentioned me repeatedly in his Chicago Tribune stories. And I was flattered, though I tried hard not to show it, both out of respect for my team putting the plan together and out of concern the program could fail, leaving me looking like Don Quixote, tilting madly at some medical windmill. I and my team knew we were well ahead of other airlines in the effort to provide AEDs to airline passengers. But we purposely were being very coy about what we were up to. After all, none of us were sure it could work or be done on a fleet as large as American's, and we did not want to look foolish if our plan came up short. Somehow, though Crewdson learned about my presentation to the senior management and started pressing hard for more information. He even asked John Hotard, the Corporate Communications team member assigned to stay abreast of what Corporate Medical was doing, "Where'd Dr. Dave get a shopping cart?"

Before going into Crandall's Planning Committee meeting to make my presentation I made sure the examples of AEDs I was bringing with me were all turned to "Training" mode. It probably would have been poor form to deliver a high voltage shock to one of my senior executives, regardless of how cantankerous some of them could be. So, I did not want any of them around a real, live defibrillator. I could only imagine what Crewdson would write had something like that had gone wrong. Linda Campbell, that astute aeromedical nurse, accompanied me into the presentation. I liked having Linda present for any major presentation. When I would get to the point of being like a deer in headlights from executive cross fire, Linda would jump in with more detail, and to give me a chance to mentally regroup.

I also had learned from that legendarily failed Human Resources presentation about introducing "casual Fridays." Rather than provide each of the executives with a hard copy presentation that they could toss in the round file, or shred, I used PowerPoint, which was in those days a pretty new and neat presentation tool. They loved the color and the pizazz. I shared all the statistical analysis and epidemiology of what our customers were experiencing in flight, and I did so using beautifully colored graphs. To ignore or dismiss this presentation out-of-hand they would have had to toss me and the projector and my laptop out of the room physically. So, I figured I had a somewhat captive audience.

As I moved methodically through the presentation, addressing both the medical and the statistical facts, I was aware the most critical portion of my presentation was coming up toward the end. The most important page in any American Airlines senior management presentation is the page – or the entire section – covering the cost-benefit analysis of the proposed program. American, famously, did nothing and implemented no new programs or services unless top management believed it would drive more market share, more revenue, and more profits. That was very much the center of American's DNA in the Crandall era.

But once I flashed my one-page – yes ONE PAGE - cost benefit analysis up on the screen, you could hear the crickets chirp.

That single slide said simply: "There is no cost benefit for the program."

For very obvious reasons, this was the most dangerous and worrisome part of that presentation. American simply did not do stuff for free. Nor did it do stuff that would cost it millions of dollars and considerable time investment from some of its people with the expectation that it would generate $0 in additional revenue.

Then the next –and last - slide in my presentation followed, saying:

"Because the life-saving shock would be given quickly, we esti-mate saving perhaps 30 customer lives a year. It is simply the right thing to do for our customers."

Keenly aware of how shockingly unusual this part of my pre-sentation would be, I had thought ahead and had set up my own portable speakers in the meeting room ahead of time. I was de-termined to play a recording of a thunderous round of applause, whatever the executives' response. And so, I did, adding a bit of cornball comedic relief to break up the stunned, silent response.

The executives at first looked at each other, not having heard anything like that before. Then they all looked at Crandall. After what seemed to be an eternity to me, Crandall thankfully broke into his hearty guffaw, and they all heartily guffawed following his lead. I too heartily guffawed, but nervously. Again, it could have been a very short medical director career for me. But, like Sally Field at the Oscars, I also quietly felt like I could say "You like me... you really like me!" Having seen all the executives naked at one point or another, I cashed in a lot of those "doctor respect" points that day. They approved the program, authorized several million for the initial purchase, and to do a trial implementation of training the first round of flight attendants, known as the overseas pursers.

By the time I made my presentation, my family had been hearing about defibrillators day in and day out for weeks. They were prob-ably tired of it. Certainly, Laurie was. Our youngest, Catherine, was now 5 at that time. She used the defibrillator training models I had brought home to run mock codes on her Beanie Babies (another craze of the day). If one was bad, they would get an extra (pretend) shock. Thankfully, she did not turn into a masochist, but completed a Ph. D in Analytical Chemistry at the University of North Carolina at Chapel Hill and is now a research engineer at the Duke University Shared Materials Instrumentation Facility [or SMIF for short]. I had always been a bit of a goof ball in the family and at work, cracking jokes and then laughing hysterically at them. Catherine started to laugh too at them at an early age. The poor girl inherited both my sense of humor, and my workaholic tendencies. It was like we had the temperament. Meanwhile, Laurie and our older daughter, Erin, would just groan at my goofy jokes.

One day, Laurie was alone in the kitchen, and she did not know one of the defibrillator training models was in the adjacent room. For some reason, she could hear a deep, male voice coming from the other room.

"PLACE THE PADS ON THE BARE CHEST."

She panicked, though only for a moment before realizing that the device was announcing a self-check. Still, it was a bit unnerving.

Erin, who was about nine at that point, became a fan of Bob Crandall. Based on what she'd heard her dad and mom talking about as I was doing my research and preparing for my presentation, Erin came to see "Mr. Crandall" as being as powerful as Santa Claus—a very powerful being who could bring about good things. So, she wrote him a letter, and gave him some of her favorite Halloween candy that she recently had collected doing "Trick-or-Treating." Crandall's secretaries – yes, he had multiple ones - brought Erin's gift into his office—and again, out rolled that tremendous, loud guffaw. He loved it. He loved the candy too—it was one of his favorites—Willy Wonka Bottle Caps. He even wrote her back, thanking her. And he sent her back a photo of him signed in golden ink. Now 32, with a master's in education, and teaching at an inner-city school in Dallas, Erin still has that letter and photo.

At dinner with the Crandall's at their house, I was honored though to get to talk at length with both Bob and his wife Jan, and with many of the other executives. What impressed me was what good, kind hearted people both of the Crandalls were. Mrs. Crandall especially was tireless in charity work. And what I experienced that night was not the ruthless, hard-charging, and demanding Robert Crandall frequently described in the nation's largest newspapers and magazines, and on the television news. That night Crandall's relaxed and gracious side, a side of his personality that rarely was on display publicly, was on display. It struck me the Crandalls were real and sincere people who constantly strived to do good and to be the best in whatever they undertook.

Crandall, over his last few years at American, began to call me a "true renaissance man," because I could play piano so very well. Each Christmas, I would wheel a piano into the headquarters building's large six-story atrium and start singing carols. The team from the medical department joined me, as did folks from other departments. The tradition became known each year as "The Holiday Songfest." Hundreds and hundreds of staff on every floor would hear the music wafting up the atrium and through the building's wide corridors and office bays and stroll out to the atrium rails. There they would look down on the music makers, often joining in with the singing. Over time, Carol Harris, a vivacious clinic nurse with a heart of gold and a voice of an angel began leading everyone in the singing. I would play Christmas carols, and songs from other faiths. And all of the hard-working headquarters staff would have a grand time during the lunch hour.

Mr. Crandall would graciously join the festivities and offer the best holiday greetings to the employees and their families. He never played Santa Claus for us, but in later years one of his senior vice presidents, Dan Garton, and his secretary would dress up as Mr. and Mrs. Claus. They would ride down the glass elevators, smiling and waving in their costumes for all to see, after "landing" Santa's sleigh on the roof of the headquarters building. People began bringing their children. Dan/Santa would listen to their wishes, while Mrs. Claus would pass out candy to the crowd. I loved music, and I loved Christmas, so I was in my glory during those moments.

Crandall also gave me, indirectly, what I consider to be the greatest compliment I ever got in the workplace. Each year the senior executives reviewed the performance of potentially promotable people. And, according to my boss, Tom Kiernan, during one of those reviews Crandall, upon getting to my name, said, " ... then there is Dave McKenas. He is a shining light on how departments should be run."

That is a very different picture of Crandall than what many others have painted. But those were my true interactions with him. I cherished him and his leadership greatly. I still do.

CHAPTER V

First Do No Harm

Wow! I was elated! Just like that, my idea of placing defibrillators on-board our planes, as well as enhancing the on-board medical kits on our fleet, was approved by American Airlines' very top management. Well, at least they had approved placing those new tools on some of our planes. I suppose you could say they did it as a pilot, or test program. But I think it's fair to say their intention was to extend the program to the entire American fleet of big jets, and then perhaps even to the American Eagle fleet of "regional jets" and turboprop planes, unless some unexpected and very adverse events forced the company to stop or even abandon the program.

That very day, I could not stop thinking of the 50 lives being lost per year, or more than one person per week on American Airlines alone, who died from sudden cardiac arrest. I felt like a missionary. I was zealous to get the program implemented as fast as possible. Although sudden cardiac arrest was happening everywhere, and on all other air carriers, this was the corner of the world I and my team and my team could make a significant impact, and I could not wait to get started. But my zeal quickly was tempered by the blank canvas right in front of me. "How the heck do we implement this?" I wondered.

No one had ever created a life-saving program like this one; certainly not on a scale this large. Never. So, we could not look to other industries for guidance or some sort of road map. Our small team – which would be growing a bit larger pretty soon, at American Airlines were going to be pioneers; not just for a huge airline, but for all public entities in the deployment of automatic external defibrillators on such a grand scale. We, in effect, would have to invent this particular wheel. However we did it, one thing was clear from the start. It was going to be a huge logistical challenge. Remember, American had 400 big jets scattered all around the world at any given time. We also were looking at training nearly 25,000 flight attendants to use these devices. And, by the way, each attendant to be trained would be certified to use these devices under the authority, medical license and oversight of one man: ME! – and whoever eventually followed me in the job. So, I – and very soon thereafter the core of our team – became keenly aware we had no clue, yet, about how we would design such a huge program for the world's largest air carrier.

Thankfully, among the few of us on my crew we had enough good sense to recognize the first thing we needed to do was to sketch out in broad brush strokes the philosophy of the program. That then would provide us a baseline for thinking about what steps did – and just as importantly, did not – needed to be taken, and in what order. As Glinda said to Dorothy on her trek to Oz, "It's always best to start at the beginning." So, on that very first day that Mr. Crandall and his top lieutenants gave us the go-ahead we on my little team put on our ruby slippers and stepped onto the first brick in our own personal Yellow Brick Road.

The Bob, Carol, Ted and Alice Task Force

In 1969, there was a movie called *Bob, Carol, Ted and Alice*, staring Natalie Wood, Dyan Cannon, Elliott Gould, Robert Culp and others. The movie, which was controversial at the time, was about, at least on the surface, "wife swapping." But it really was more about how different people have different skill sets and strengths that, when properly aligned with other people's skills and experiences, life works much better. The ultimate message was that the creation of teams out of random and merely casual relationships really does not work well, whether we are talking about marriages, sports teams, performers, or teams at work. While we certainly were not going to be doing any wife swapping, the idea of finding all the pieces of the puzzle and putting them together the right way certainly was applicable to our task. So, we adopted the movie's title as the name we gave to our multi-departmental project Task Force. I chaired the team, though there's no "Dave" in the Task Force name.

"TED" was our code for The Emergency Defibrillator itself. ALICE stood for the Advanced Life and Cardiac Emergency kit. And, to make the theme work, we also noted that we did have both a "Bob" and a "Carol" on our team. But that all turned out to be a mouthful to say, and annoying to have to type out multiple times in memos and reports (and even emails, which we were beginning to use quite a bit in those days). So, eventually we boiled it down to just "The TED Task Force," and began referring to the actual defibrillators themselves singularly as "Ted."

Members of our Medical Department were TED Task Force members not only out of default but out of our real need for all their skills and insights. But we also included members from a number of other departments, each of whom eventually would be responsible for guiding the implementation of the various aspects the program but who first would play pivotal roles in creating the many detailed steps in that program.

Julie Bourke Suchman came from Flight Service (the flight attendants' department). She was a marvelous, wise flight attendant with vast experience who oversaw the training of American's attendants. She at first was queasy at the prospect of re-training all existing attendants when her department primarily was focused on training newly-hired attendants. The prospect of training 1,300 pursers (lead attendants), let alone the entire roster of around 25,000 flight attendants, and doing so in quick order, was daunting. But she took on the task, then promptly was promoted and had to pass her TED responsibilities on to Melanie Wahrmund. Dayle Culhane, a lead flight attendant known as a purser[14], came on board too, to work on the task of planning and executing the training of all those pursers, who we recognized would play key roles in the success or failure of American's defibrillator program.

Linda Campbell, my principal aeromedicine nurse, and right arm, and I already were working with Dr. Richard Cummings from

[14] Pursers, at American anyway, essentially run the cabin operation. When the Captain needs to communicate with passengers or other attendants the Purser is their representative and leader. And the Purser holds the most authority in the cabin for dealing problems of the mechanical, service supplies or human variety. So, while every attendant would be trained to use defibrillators, we anticipated that the Pursers likely would play the key role in any significant health issue that occurred on any of their flights.

the American Heart Association, conveniently based in Dallas, when we got approval to formally launch TED. He was the Chair of the American Heart Association's Emergency Cardiac Care Community. He helped us understand one of our first tasks was to come up with new material to train flight attendants on a large scale. Nothing like that really existed at the time. That, in fact, is really why we needed the AHA on board with us. They were – and continue to be - the national authority on cardiac rescue techniques.

Barbara Rice, a nurse who led the "army" of nurses who worked for the Medical department not only at headquarters but at all of our hubs and certain other really big non-hub airports and crew bases, as well as at our maintenance facilities around the world, played a key role. Her nurses were the ones who would "chase planes" around the nation so that they could install and maintain all those defibrillators. Martha Seiler led our logistics team in pro-curing all those defibrillators, keeping them in stock, maintaining them, and keep them functioning. Peter Sode, our own financial guru, made sure funds for this big project were properly secured and dispersed, and that those of us who maybe weren't the best at keeping track of what company money was spent for what, kept us on our toes and on budget throughout the process.

Also, on the Task Force were representatives from American's Avionics department and from the airline's huge Maintenance and Engineering department. Why? Well, for starters we all had to know what would happen if we shocked someone onboard on a metal air frame. We also had to fully understand what, if anything, using a defibrillator would do to an airplane's guidance system, its commu-nications gear, and other systems. Would anything really important to flying the plane go haywire as a result? Based on my experience with defibrillator use in helicopters flown by the Air Force and NASA, we did not think so. But we had to know for certain. We also needed to find out where on the various types of planes in American's fleet, was the best place to store AEDs. We needed the technical airplane and avionics experts' input on those and other matters.

The team also had Christa Hinkley, head of Corporate Insurance, and a representative from the Legal Department. Before we could deploy AEDs, the company needed to know with a high degree of certainty what insurance issues and legal liability issues did or did not exist, and how big those issues were. We also had to figure out what federal and state laws applied, or even whether any state laws applied to us. Thanks to the legal principle of "federal exemption" airlines operating in many different states are in many, but not all ways, relieved from having to comply with up to 50 different sets of requirements. So, we needed to make sure defibrillator deployment and use fit under the federal exemption, and if not, how we would have to proceed. We also needed to figure out what our legal and insurance issues might come up if we ever had to use a defibrillator in the air above any of the dozens of nations over which our planes flew. We even needed to review our policies regarding whether we ever formally declare a person on board one of our flights to be deceased?

Our TED Task Force also had to study what the effects of vibration, dry air and constantly changing atmospheric pressures would be on the AEDs themselves. Since we were the first to put AEDs in any such environment, we did not know. But we had to know before we could put them onboard our planes. We addressed sundry issues such as these. For example, early on no one knew if the lithium batteries in the AEDS were even safe to use on airplanes that repetitively changed altitudes, ambient pressures, and atmospheric content? How, when, and where should American refurbish the devices? And how much would that cost? To be safe, our project leadership group, backed up by our technical experts on the TED Task Force, decided to err on the conservative side by replacing our AED's lithium batteries yearly even though we were pretty sure they would last much longer than that.

We then had to determine whose job it would be to manage the logistical nightmare of tracking at the time all 400 or more of American's planes in order to refurbish, without fail, 100% of the AEDs on each of those planes annually? Originally it was those nurses from AA Medical that I mentioned. They were not necessarily happy about it because it was not fun duty. If you ever were unfortunate enough to be at an airport where several of our planes spent the slow over-night period docked at the terminal you probably would see only the terminal and the aircraft cleaning staff members doing their normally unseen but important jobs. But every once in a while, you also might see a couple of ladies in white pushing rickety carts from gate to gate, where they boarded the planes to check on the medical equipment and the kits. That is when AED batteries got replaced, if that was needed, and where the medical kits were checked and, if necessary, replenished.

Our Task Force worked feverishly to address these issues, each of which was absolutely critical to creating this brand-new program without precedent. People's lives were dependent on the work of this noble group. So our team worked with a sense of purpose because of all those challenges, and with urgency because we knew well that each month that passed before we could get AEDs and the enhanced medical kits placed on board our planes meant that more lives were being lost that we might otherwise have been able to save.

As we began our TED Task Force work in earnest, we were about 18 months away from Mr. Giggey's historic in-flight cardiac arrest event. In NASA-speak, the time was T-minus-18 months to program lift off. Only, we had no way of knowing that at that moment. All we knew was there was so much to be done while people continued to die on our planes on a statistically-small but still heart-wrenchingly regular basis. Everyone on our team was painfully conscious of their obligation to those people.

Primum Non Nocere

In medical school, and again at Harvard, I learned the first principle of any medical service provided, and of any public health program was summed up in the Latin medical aphorism: *primum non nocere*, or "First, do no harm." And in practice it means that before you can set out to do good for the public one must be sure no one is harmed (at least not significantly) because of unintended consequences. Admittedly, surgeons must "harm" patients by cutting them open to perform surgery, but in context such harm is minor and is necessary to complete the larger healing task. Similarly, defibrillators sometimes can leave small burn marks or irritations on the patient's skin, but again the harm is both insignificant and absolutely necessary to prevent a far, far worse outcome. Still, it was important for us to know before launching the defibrillator program we would not be doing any significant or unexpected harm to our in-flight heart patients with those defibrillators. We all can think of circumstances in our lives in which something unexpected went wrong with, or happened as an unintended consequence of a procedure or process that had been put into place with the best of intentions. We knew that as a public transportation company whose customers must have absolute trust in the airline American could not afford to have any such mistakes or unintended consequences. And, therefore, our program could not afford such mistakes or unintended consequences either because if any such things happened it quickly would bring an end to the defibrillator program.

"So, what could possibly go wrong," you ask, using the popular cliché.

Well, if the AED's battery was low several things could go horribly wrong. For one, it could force the user to administer multiple shocks to a patient, inflicting pain, and more significant damage to the skin or internal organs than is acceptable. Or, obviously, the patient might die when a fully-charged battery would have been sufficient to save their life.

What about a short in the AED? It is not likely, but that would expose the user, the patient and others nearby to unexpected, unregulated powerful shocks. In theory such a shock could transfer into the plane's metal frame or other metal parts and cause damage. Or, if the short existed because of chaffed wiring between the AED and the shocking probes, anyone touching the device or the chaffed wire could be in for a very painful jolt.

Primum non nocere is a tough standard, indeed. It is, in fact, central to the Hippocratic oath to which all doctors swear upon graduation from medical school. And it was the standard we were compelled by our ethics, our legal and practical concerns and, most of all, by our honor to apply to the creation of American's defibrillator program.

At the first team meeting I told the group: "We need to structure this program so there can be no unintended harm to our employees, to the customers, or to air travel itself. It would be poor form if one of the batteries in the defibrillators exploded, for example, causing a plane crash. We must think of and plan for any unexpected consequence of such a program."

My first thoughts about the program can be found in an editorial written at the request of Dr. Russ Rayman, who was at that time the President of the Aerospace Medical Association. The Aerospace Medical Association is a wonderful organization of doctors, nurses, physiologists, and all sorts of other medical pros who take care of people in aviation and space flight settings. I confided to Dr. Rayman candidly what I had done right after we got approval from American senior management to begin work on our program. Dr. Rayman's quick response was that what we were doing was medical history in the making! He then asked me to write an article regarding about this then-controversial program for his group's journal, Aviation, Space and Environmental Medicine.

Of course, I was glad to do it. He wanted my team's thinking on this program out there in front of world's top aviation medicine experts to get their insights into and critiques of our program. In the medical arena, doctors do this all the time. I even had a name for it: "medical collaborative speak." I often would drive my wife crazy with this "collaborative speak." When you get physicians together in a room to talk about a patient or plan very often, they will start by stating the obvious. That is to get team consensus they are doing the right thing for the patient. They then build from there. If anyone sees a down side to the care plan being established, they say so at that point. And from that point on, the group goes to work brainstorming and researching to come up with a better or refined plan or approach.

This practical methodology works well when you have one doctor saying something like "I think Gentamicin would be the antibiotic of choice in this case of resistant bacterial infection," and another counters with "But you will blow out their kidneys, as she is already in renal failure." That approach does not, however, work so well when the doctor's spouse says, "I think you should reboot your iPad to fix that error," and the doctor's argumentative response is "Do you think I am stupid? Of course, I have already done that."

Still, I actually wanted some "collaborative speak" input on our program from my Aerospace Medicine colleagues. Getting such feedback, it turns out, was not as easy as I had hoped it would be. I discovered the downside of being chief medical officer at the world's largest airline, and of having worked before that as a medical officer in the space shuttle program and in the Air Force, and of having earned credentials as an aerospace and public health doctor was that others in the field looked up to me – too greatly in my opinion – and were reluctant to speak up with questions about or challenges of any work with which I was associated. But I really did need their help and insight. Nobody is infallible, and certainly not me, just because of whatever credentials they might possess. I had to make it clear to my colleagues on my team not only what our initial thinking and plans for the defibrillator program were but also, we truly were interested in hearing any concerns, doubts, or suggestions from them BEFORE we actually implemented it.

Our plan, on the surface was straightforward:

We had definitively established via historical and statistical review of the data that sudden cardiac events were the most common in-flight medical event and were a major cause of medical diversions – at least they were on American, and that such likely was the case on other carriers, too

Our "captive" population of passengers both permits and compels an immediate response to any customer who experiences this life-threatening condition on one of our planes. People on a plane are not going anywhere, (unless they are invited to see *Gone with the Wind* in the special unruly passenger section—out on the wing)

The environment is controlled; there's built-in crowd control in the form of seat rows and skinny aisles, plus good lighting and climate control

Delivering a life-saving shock from an AED so quickly will greatly enhance a customer's chances of survival

So, our plan was to purchase and deploy defibrillators on our planes.

I explained so much more still had to be incorporated into our planning. I told them every one of our team members had to be mentally engaged and prepared to bring up new thoughts and challenge ideas that somehow did not seem quite right to them. We could not overlook any question, issue, or aspect of our plan

Obviously, American Airlines had a big fleet—400-plus at the time (and nearly 900 today) - roving all over the world. And that did not include all the smaller turboprop and "regional jet" planes in the affiliated American Eagle fleet. But we quickly determined it was both natural and appropriate that the program should start with our over-water aircraft, and that we use that as a kind of test of our plan to equip all American jets with AEDs.

Over-water aircraft are those assigned to fly international routes, such as Europe, Latin America, and Japan, as well as certain domestic flight that cross over water – big water, like oceans, not mere lakes and streams. The plan was to have the defibrillators on these planes by the Summer of 1997. The team thought we should train just 2,300 flight attendants on when and how to use the defibrillators by the start of that summer. That sounds like a lot of people. And it is. But it is far fewer than the entire cohort of approximately 25,000 flight attendants. We could not train them all at once, so to us not only did putting the defibrillators on over-water planes make sense because those planes typically were hours away from the nearest hospital but also because it made the early training challenge a bit more manageable.

On top of training, eventually, all 25,000 or attendants, we had to figure out a way to incorporate refresher training into our attendants' annual re-training regimens. So, in our early, rough planning we determined that by the end of 1998, American would place the devices and our enhanced medical kits on all our mainline aircraft. In the meantime, even if not all of our attendants were yet trained in the use of the defibrillators, at least any physicians or paramedics who happened to be on board a plane with a stricken passenger – and which was equipped with a defibrillator and the new kits - could handle the critical first hour of most emergencies. Then, by the year's end 1998, all our attendants would be trained and ready to handle those events themselves. Beginning in 1999, they were to start getting defibrillator refresher training in their yearly emergency procedures training classes

In my article in Aviation, Space and Environmental Medicine, I also reminded the entire medical community as to why American was making this move. In such situations people tend to confuse medical facts and needs with corporate ulterior motives. But the simple medical facts were, according to the American Heart Association:

- More than 1,000 people per day in the United States suffer from Sudden Cardiac Arrest, the lethal condition we were aiming to fight with our innovative onboard program
- In most cases, it is all but impossible to predict who will have a sudden cardiac arrest, or where it will happen
- The chances of surviving sudden cardiac arrest are less than one in ten, with most victims dying before reaching a hospital

• Those who do survive a cardiac arrest have a good chance of living many more years; approximately 80% are alive one year later, and as many as 57% are alive five years later.

As I had told Mr. Crandall and his executive team at their "Planning Committee" meeting, in the case of sudden cardiac arrest the life-saving shock from a defibrillator must be given within minutes, or the person most assuredly will die. I stressed this point of "medical gospel" to my aviation medicine colleagues both inside and outside American. While this is common knowledge not only among physicians but the general public today, it is important to keep in mind that in the mid-1990s most physicians were not familiar with AEDs. They still thought of defibrillators as a huge piece of machinery that only ER and heart docs used. In fact, it is a safe bet that most physicians back then, had they been on-board a plane when a passenger went into Sudden Cardiac Arrest, would have resorted automatically to simple chest compressions and mouth-to-mouth breathing. That was the protocol they knew at the time, so that is what they would have done. The thought of stepping aside to let a mere flight attendant work their "voodoo" with this new little box-with-wires contraption would have been anathema to them.

So, what we were bringing not only to the airline industry but to the medical world was the "new" truth that the chance of survival decreases about 10% for each minute that defibrillation is delayed. What we were saying was, to many medical people back then, a dramatic departure from past practices. We were, in effect, telling them to forget CPR in such cases, at least initially. Instead, they were to apply the AED's probes, turn it on and watch it work its magic, and to do whatever it told them to do. Even, for example, in a case involving a passenger who experienced a sudden cardiac arrest immediately after a plane pulled away from the gate, we were telling trained, veteran doctors that the time it would take to get the plane back to the gate and paramedics to them could kill the patient, so the best approach was to use one of these new-fangled mini-defibrillators right there on the plane. It was, by any calculation, a radical change in medical procedures that we were preparing to introduce to the world.

Horrors! Not start with CPR? Not start with chest compressions and mouth-to-mouth? Many of our well-meaning colleagues around the airline and medical industries did, in fact, respond with shock, like someone just shouted out an obscenity in church. I and my team countered such responses by noting there were still times and places for those older protocols and techniques, such as when someone experienced sudden cardiac arrest and a defibrillator was not readily available. But we were going against the tide of established thinking and practice. Thankfully, through our coordination with the American Heart Association we quickly realized they, too, were already moving toward this major procedural change. We were running down parallel tracks in that regard, which provided us a great deal more intellectual comfort that we were, indeed, on the right track with our plan.

Many in the chorus of critics would ask: Why now? Why could you not have put these devices on planes earlier? We heard this on many occasions, most often on the witness stand from opposing counsel in litigation stemming from the death of a passenger on one of our flights before we deployed the AEDs. But the hard fact was that AEDs were not authorized for use on board commercial airplanes until just prior to American's decision to move forward with them. Further, the technology for an automatic external defibrillator with a more effective yet less powerful charge (and one that created a more effective "biphasic" wave form) simply was not available on the market until around the time we began looking into ways to lower the number of sudden cardiac arrest-related deaths on our flights. In reality, the reason why American moved forward with AEDs when it did was because the technology had just advanced to the point we could actually do so safely. In fact, we first had to prove it could be done safely with these new devices before we were allowed to put them on our planes.

Many physicians, nurses and paramedics had used the large defibrillators, and others had seen them in movies and on television in hospital emergency room setting. Those units though are cumbersome and required a physician or trained medical person to use it. That is because they required a trained expert to interpret the patient's heart rhythms. AEDs, on the other hand, were smaller, lighter, more durable, and easier to operate. And, as I often shared with the media, and at conferences: "These devices have the wisdom of 100 cardiologists in a box, studying the heart rhythm in a matter of seconds". I was purposely bold in making these assertions: "The device will never falsely shock anyone," I said repeatedly. "It will only shock that one deadly rhythm behind sudden cardiac arrest: ventricular fibrillation."

In the article I wrote for Dr. Rayman's journal, I said American had been watching the development of the automatic external defibrillator technology over several years, which by the time it appeared in print was true. Our process did not happen overnight. Finally, the U.S. Food and Drug Administration approved the use of the devices for commercial air travel. And American responded almost immediately with their plan to get them on board as soon as humanly possible. From my perspective, and that of my TED teammates, even that was not soon enough. We were eager and motivated to push this life-saving technology into cabins of our planes. Remember, too, that this was about the time when airlines were told by the FAA they could no longer use cell phones or other electronic devices below 10,000 feet for fear the radio emissions would interfere with the planes' avionics and guidance systems. Given those concerns, some thought we were crazy to even ask the FAA for permission to release a small bolt of lightning inside of a commercial flight cabin (which is, in effect, what happens when a defibrillator delivers a shock). Thus, American needed, at the very least, the FDA's approval of AEDs in the treatment of humans onboard an airplane before we dared to approach the FAA about releasing 'lightning' inside an airplane. So, the decision to place defibrillators on planes actually grew out of one of the very tenets of medicine itself. It was the right thing to do for the travelling public. The company's senior management realized the program was not inexpensive. More importantly, they freely acknowledged there was no cost benefit. But we were going to do it anyway because it was the right thing to do for our customers, who were and continue to be of paramount importance to American – and, to be fair, of any properly and ethically managed airline.

At the time, American was lucky to have a Corporate Medical Department with enough people of talent and with the resources available to undertake the medical oversight of this gargantuan logistical complex program. The physicians and nurses of American at each of the major hubs could monitor the program and devices. The "standing orders" to the flight attendants on when and how to use the device would fall under my personal medical license and, eventually, under the license of the doctors who someday would follow me as chief medical officer of the airline. Because the AEDs keep an internal record, the precise clinical events of each case in which they are used, our team devised a way to "chase" the plane on which any AED was used, so we could retrieve the device and its internal data card, and replace the device with a fresh one. The data from those AED cards would be transmitted immediately to the hospital where the afflicted passenger was taken for treatment. That data would be added to the hospital's own tracking data on that patient to give doctors there a more complete view over time of what their patient had experienced and, hopefully, enable them to make better, more informed diagnosis and treatment plans. The same data from the AED's cards also would be analyzed by our team of experts as a way of doing continuous quality assurance monitoring on our AED program. Along with that data, American staff physicians were on call 24 hours a day, seven days a week to assist, by radio, flight attendants, pilots and responding on-board physicians through any in-flight medical event. Information gathered through such radio calls also would be fed to the hospitals on the ground and into our quality control program as a way of cross-checking our AEDs' performance.

Another challenge for our team was to create not only the initial flight attendant defibrillator training course we'd put our active attendants through at the start, but also to figure out how to integrate that new training into the already jam-packed medical and cardiopulmonary resuscitation training course work through which we would put all of American's newly-hired attendants going forward. That was much bigger than just tacking on an extra 30 minutes or hour of instruction to the existing plan. The new defibrillator training would have to fit smoothly and cohesively into the other medical training new attendants would get, but do so within roughly the same amount of time. Simply adding an extra day to the weeks-long training program would not work because with the airline growing rapidly in those days there were no off days in the training academy. The day one group of attendants received their wings and left for their initial work assignments, a new class of attendant trainees moved in behind them.

There also was the small problem of where on our various models of aircraft would we put these things? Space on commercial air carriers is, as you can imagine, very limited. Overhead bin space is precious, even in those days before bag check fees prompted lots more people to carry their bags with them into the cabin. Passengers want space for their things, so on-board real estate is valuable. Some customers, in fact, might prefer space on board for the fine bottle of liqueur they just purchased. But our important, life-saving equipment, as relatively small as it was, took up space that somebody's bag or liqueur bottle, or gift, or coat otherwise would have occupied. Then there was a more practical but unseemly concern: American did not want their defibrillators – which while not hugely expensive were far from cheap – to be pilfered by passengers (especially ones who could be a part of some potential criminal enterprise focused on stealing the devices and re-selling them on the black market). So, we had to invent some way of securing our defibrillators so they would not "grow legs" and exit our planes along with the passengers at the next stop. The planning team determined that we could mount the devices in an overhead bin, or on a bulkhead toward the front of the aircraft. The device would need to be locked in a specially-designed mount. Only cockpit and cabin crewmembers would be able to unlock the device and remove it from its mount.

In my journal article, I also discussed the criticisms we anticipated we might get because of our defibrillator program. One such potential criticism we thought we might get was that American would end up carrying an out-sized percentage of high-risk passengers, like those with known and even severe heart disease. Rather quickly we determined our answer to any such criticism would be "so be it." American was committed to carrying all passengers, even those with disabilities and known serious medical conditions so long as we could accommodate their special medical requirements and so long as they were medically stable enough for air travel. In fact, one customer wrote to me after we launched our program publicly saying that because her husband's heart stopped frequently that they henceforth would fly only on American because they knew he could be resuscitated should it happen while he was flying. Attracting such passengers certainly was not our purpose in equipping our planes with defibrillators, but doing so helped give passengers greater peace of mind or security when traveling with us we were glad to be able to help.

Another concern was the potential liability the airline might incur as a result of training our flight attendants how to shoot bolts of lightning through the bodies of our customers. But, thankfully, American's management was not overly concerned about the legal liability related to having non-traditional first responders like flight attendants use our defibrillators. First, our attendants were to be trained by, and operate under the direction and authority of physicians like me and our large in-house medical staff of American. Beyond that, attendants and pilots on our planes had – and continue to have - immediate access via radio to the airline's medical staff in the event of any and all in-flight emergencies. Even when planes are halfway across the Pacific Ocean, they can contact our systems operations control center located on our headquarters campus in Fort Worth, which can then switch the radio call to our medical staff.

But we were concerned that American might need to pay huge amounts of money to indemnify all its attendants and pilots – plus its entire medical department and any other employees who conceivably might get involved in a situation involving the use and care of defibrillators against potential lawsuits and damages claims. I, in particular, might become a huge legal target since any American employee who used a defibrillator would be doing so under authority tied directly to my personal medical license. I believed, as did pretty much our entire team that although we live in a litigious society there would be no ill will, in the form of a lawsuit, directed toward anyone who tried to save a customer's life. Maybe that was a naïve position to take, but it is what we believed. Yet we also recognized the liability concern was real and we need to be aware of, and certain about it before we launched.

Thankfully, we were pleased to learn through Christa Hinkley, American's Director of Corporate Insurance, and a member of the TED Task Force, that as a corporate officer and chief medical officer I was, in fact, covered by American's huge insurance policy. In the event of any adverse outcomes stemming from the use of a defibrillator (or from the improper use or failure to use such a device) I, personally, was protected from liability claims and, therefore, so was any defibrillator-trained American employee. In fact, I rather quickly came to believe liability concern actually was greater for those airlines, airports and other public places and service providers who were not prepared to respond to serious in-flight, pre-flight, or post-flight medical crises. Once American launched our program, our competitors, along with airports and other public facilities quickly lost their ability to claim they were unaware of, or unsure whether the use of such devices would be available or effective.

Interestingly, many of our competitors negatively critiqued our defibrillator program, and did so openly. Obviously, I thought they were wrong morally and ethically, and also based on the medical facts. But I also thought they were wrong from a legal liability perspective. A medical director at one competing airline told me he thought I had lost my marbles. In response I made the point his and his carrier's liability was now greater than mine/ours. Then I closed the conversation with "Have a nice day" and a passive-aggressive smile that I must admit I am rather expert at.

People often asked: Why not leave this equipment to be used by a responding physician? Indeed, our team thought through that question a lot. We knew better than anyone that physicians as a group travel a lot. American's internal data showed that in those days, at least one doctor was aboard our flights about 85% of the time. That meant that 85% of the time we would be able to call for the help of doctor who happened to be a passenger on a flight and turn over a case of sudden cardiac arrest – or any other medical emergency – to them. Still, my team and I agreed that we did not want to place such serious situations in the hands of a doctor who may, or may not be expert in treating patients with major heart issues, and who may or may not have been drinking just prior to the emergency. In fact, as we learned very early on after launching our defibrillator program, lots of doctors in those days were quite unfamiliar with the use of AEDs and many did not trust them. Instead, they relied on older, less effective medical response protocols even if it meant the chances of losing the patient were demonstrably much greater under such an approach.

Plus, while 85 of 100 flights had a doctor aboard, at least statistically speaking, that meant 15 other flights did not and that a decision to rely solely on passenger physicians responding to calls for help pretty much doomed anyone suffering a cardiac arrest aboard the 15% of our flights on which we knew there would be no doctors available. Flight attendants, however, were absolutely certain to be aboard each and every American flight. And if we trained them to use defibrillators and the other tools in our enhanced medical kits, we knew we would have a trained and competent first responder on every flight operated by our airline. Additionally, because attendants are authority figures in flight, and because they typically are up and about in the cabin and are trained to look for signs that passengers need assistance – with anything, not just medical issues – they would be perfectly positioned to take charge during in-flight medical emergencies and to quickly organize the correct and most effective medical response possible.

Besides, do not forget that flight attendants are on board American's aircraft – and all commercial airlines' planes - primarily for passenger safety reasons. Yes, they served drinks and food and provide various services aimed at making travel more comfortable for our customers. But the days of "coffee, tea or me" were by then long gone. Attendants always have been trained in first aid and in handling emergencies, even in the days when airlines played up their sex appeal as a way of attracting a predominately male clientele.

Thus, it was a natural choice for us to rely on our attendants as our frontline troops in our defibrillator program. Indeed, almost from the outset we coordinated with the flight attendants' union, the APFA, and with the top leaders of the airline's Flight Service department (that is the name of the attendants' department). Neither group expressed any significant reservations about attendants taking on this critical new responsibility for trying to save the lives of passengers stricken by sudden cardiac arrest. That is not to say they did not have questions and concerns. But from the start both the union and the flight attendants' corporate managers bought into the concept and were eager to work with us in creating the proper response protocols and training programs. They did not know the medical facts at first. And at first, we on the TED Task Force did not know all we would need to know about how and why attendants to all that they do onboard planes. But we quickly formed a great working relationship and learned from each other on our way to making the defibrillator program work in the real world at 35,000 feet.

Automated external defibrillators were something of a new technology in the mid-'90s. And the company was entering new territory by putting them on our planes and training our people how to use them. We determined that despite our eagerness to push the AEDs out onto our planes and into public use, we would take a very measured approach to studying various issues like product reliability, maintenance, and training in the aircraft environment. We did not want to overlook potential problems because of our eagerness to get the defibrillator show on the road. And we recognized that by choosing to start with overwater flights – which by their very nature are international flights – that the stakes were higher than on domestic flights. During an international flight the chances are much higher that a cardiac arrest victim is much farther away from proper care at a hospital than is a person with the same issue flying within our domestic system. That made starting the program on international flights the right decision, but it also meant if something really went wrong with our program the fallout – both medically and in public relations terms – would be greater.

I remember writing in that first aerospace medicine journal article that the device American selected was neither the lightest nor the lowest priced device available despite American's widely-known reputation for watching costs (in addition to the cost of the devices themselves, weight was a factor because each pound of weight onboard increases the amount of expensive fuel burned in flight). American is famed for always looking for the best deals it can cut with vendors. But in this case we simply chose the best product from the standpoint of performing its medical mission, its ease of use and its reliability.

Finally – and we could not say this enough to convince the cynics and American's many critics – ours was not a marketing ploy. I heard many, many snide comments to the effect that Bob Crandall and Mike Gunn, our senior vice president of marketing who was in charge of generating nearly all of American's revenue through the tickets we sold and the strategies and tactics we used to attract customers, did this just to make more money for American. Nothing could have been further from reality. And I found it insulting to even think that it was. It was a decision based on what would be best for our customers. Remember, I was the guy who told Mr. Crandall and his top lieutenants in that fateful Planning Committee meeting, that the defibrillator program I was recommending we launch would never, ever make American one extra dime of revenue. Still, they signed on to the idea at once.

Now, it was fortuitous that after each person saved in the first few years after the defibrillators were placed on our planes there would be a joyous media frenzy. As a result, our defibrillator became a minor, unintentional marketing coup within our industry. As a result, my mug was on more TV sets around the nation than I ever wanted it to be! But marketing was never our intent. It was not even a secondary or tertiary consideration in our thinking. So, like the Marines and their battle cry, Semper Fi, our team came up with our own geeky Latin battle cry - *primum non nocere*: First, do no harm. This was our secret greeting as we met each other in the halls We had, indeed, started down the yellow brick road.

Physicians, of course, hear that phrase – *primum non nocere* – all the time. But our TED Task Force, and eventually our roll out team, knew what it meant it. American's executive team embraced the philosophy, too. Like those of us on the medical team, they did not want to put one more passenger in harm's way because we did not have available the proper tools that could save a life aboard one of our planes whenever the need arose. And the company's top leaders, while not involved in the details of creating and implementing the defibrillator program, were concerned from the outset that once we deployed the defibrillators on board our jets they would be safely used and maintained and they would not inadvertently harm others. So, yes, the go-ahead decision was a business decision made at the highest levels of American Airlines and its parent, AMR Corp. But the folks at those highest levels really did keep the welfare of our customer at the fore. And if nothing else proved it, this particular decision certainly did.

Our TED Task Force, the roll out team and the company's top leaders all believed American's introduction of defibrillators on our planes would, most assuredly, save lives. And we believed if our program proved successful the ripple effect would lead other commercial airlines to do much the same thing. In that case we knew American's reward would be great; we would be the pioneers in the use of a new life-saving technology in an important new way across an entire industry and, eventually throughout society.

Of course, once we made all those decisions, we still had to actually buy hundreds of new defibrillators.

In the Dead of the Night

Tom Kiernan, my boss at American, happened to be reading an article on this very subject, and learned of the brand new "Heartstream Forerunner." He passed that article down to me and, after reading it, I obtained a sample device and added it to my already impressive collection of defibrillators strewn across the floor of my office. My secretary, Bettye Harris, was by that point threatening to put me on one of the "Hoarders" shows on TV! She had had to clear a narrow path just to reach my desk. And that path was the portion of my floor not covered by different models of defibrillators. Minette Rich in American's purchasing department was a wizard at procurement, and at negotiating great deals for American (she had to be or Mr. Crandall would have replaced her with someone else in a heartbeat). She and our team carefully studied the pros and cons of each device.

The Heartstream (now called Philips HeartStart) was a new type of defibrillator. It was very elegant in design. Most defibrillators shock the chest from point A to point B, with a much larger charge. The Heartstream instead used "biphasic" technology. That means the shock it delivered traveled from point A to B and then back to A, all in a microsecond. As a result, the person's heart receives a smaller jolt of electricity, but receives it twice in quick succession. As we were first learning at the time, that approach gives the heart a much better chance of righting itself. The Heartstream device also measured the resistance of the chest wall through which it had to deliver its shock, then calculated the exact right amount of electricity that it needed to administer to restart the person's heart. Like in the story of the Three Bears it delivers not too much electricity, not too little electricity, but just the right amount.

The vendors that our team dealt with seemed ruthless. There was much maligning of the competition and lots of untrue allegations lodged against competing defibrillator makers and suppliers. They all wanted to close a big deal with a huge, high-profile customer like American, and they were not the least bit hesitant about trashing their competitors to win the competition.

All except Heartstream, that is.

As the chief medical person on our team I carefully studied the technical medical literature on biphasic defibrillation. All my Harvard training kicked back into gear. Some articles I read poo-pooed it. But then I would look at who sponsored the article and, sure enough, in many cases, the sponsor was a company with a financial or business interest in defibrillators that used a different approach and technology.

After much private debate amongst our team, with many outside experts, and with Emily Carter, Kathy Lord Jones, Linda Campbell, and Debbie Luhr from the attendants' union, we determined the device from Heartstream would be the way to go. But Minette, our purchasing guru, astutely advised "This is a new company. We really need to go out and see their operation to make sure they aren't making them in their garage." So, Minette, Linda, Emily and John Hotard from Corporate Communications joined me in travelling to Seattle, Washington, to visit the folks from Heartstream and their facilities. When we arrived there, it was typical Seattle weather—foggy, and drizzling. We arrived in the evening, and the Heartstream team took us straight to their facility. By the time we got there, it was the dead of night. But we quickly could see that it was no garage. Far from it.

Heartstream had an elaborate set up and a large team of technicians. There were numerous testing stations where defibrillators would be subjected to all sorts of physical abuse and mechanical trauma. For example, there were test chambers that simulated repetitive vibration, stations that simulated high altitudes, and stations that repeatedly inflicted hard thumping, high heat, and intense humidity on defibrillators just to make sure they would hold up under those and other conditions that they likely would be exposed to onboard airplanes. There was from the outset of our meeting there with the Heartstream people a sense of history. They knew if we selected them it would put their upstart company on the map. Their CEO actually said, rather prophetically, "If you do this, it will be big news. The notion of putting defibrillators in the hands of 25,000 flight attendants is earth shattering."

The next day, our group watched several demonstrations of the device. Some of the Heartstream executives demonstrated the devices with the pads (the business ends of the device) attached to their bare chest, how there would be no interference with the device even when there was lots of movement, as one would expect there to be if it was used on an airplane in flight. I have to say that seeing grown men, shirtless, dancing with defibrillator leads on, was a bit of an odd sight. And pretty darn funny. Then they asked me to do it, too. I declined. I did not want to make people more ill than they already were from jet lag and fatigue because that would have been just too much flesh for the world to see.

Our group then returned to Dallas-Fort Worth. It was long flight, but there was very much to ponder and it gave us time to sort through our thoughts individually. After getting back to the office, I reached out to a Dr. Rick Page, a renowned electro cardiologist at the University of Texas Southwestern Medical Center, which was also a renowned teaching and research hospital and medical school in Dallas. My big concern was the biphasic technology. Did it really work? Based the discussions and debate with Rick and the other members on the TED task force I made the final decision to choose this new upstart company, Heartstream and picked their Forerunner model to place on American's entire fleet.

Announcing the Program

Once our program philosophy and approach were established, the next instruction from Bob Crandall was scrawled on a weekly report that I had sent to my boss Tom Kiernan. Tom always read my reports and passed them along to Mr. Crandall with any comments he wanted to include. After making the critical decisions on how and implement the program I received one of my weekly reports back from Mr. Crandall's office. He had scrawled across the top of it a simple, but clear instruction: "If we are the first, then we should make it known."

At that point, John Hotard, a veteran Associated Press reporter and editor who had joined American's Corporate Communications team more than a decade earlier, became even more involved in the program because we were about to have a press conference. Being the former newsman and clever corporate communications man he was, John started calling our defibrillator program "The story that never dies." Indeed, he continued to get press inquiries about it even long after I left American. John Hotard and Will Ris, who as senior vice president for government affairs was American's man in Washington, D.C., planned a trip for me to the National Press Club in Washington, where I was to make the announcement of ground-breaking defibrillator program. A press release was also prepared for release at the same time, on November 19, 1996. Incredibly, that investigative reporter who had been snooping around the whole defibrillators issue for a year or so, John Crewdson from the Chicago Tribune, somehow got word and beat American to the punch. He wrote about our plan in his paper on November 17, 1996, two days before our announcement.

"American Airlines is expected to announce Tuesday that it will become the first US airline to equip its planes with automatic defibrillators, the portable battery powered machines that can reverse an otherwise fatal cardiac arrest with a jolt of electricity to the heart," he wrote. It was in that story where he also added the surprising – to me anyway – detail that "the defibrillator issue gained momentum in early August when the American Airlines medical Director, Dr. David McKenas, wheeled a shopping cart filled with portable defibrillators into chairman Crandall's office. Senior managers agreed to get the appropriate departments and disciplines together. A task force representing the Airlines' medical, maintenance and field operation departments was established to resolve a lot of minutia." After Crewdson's early report, I began to think that I should get a sweep for electronic "bugs" performed in my office. His story was right on all the details.

In my capacity of as Corporate Medical Director I had received a considerable amount of media training from the Corporate Communications team. And I had previously performed as a piano soloist in front of thousands of people at a time. So, you would think I would be at ease at a news conference. But addressing a news conference is a unique thing, and very different from playing piano on stage or practicing answering questions from the friendly guys from our top-notch Corporate Communications team. At a real, live news conference, if I made a mistake, or said something really wrong I knew, or at least I believed, it would reflect poorly on American Airlines. And though I had a good relationship with Mr. Crandall, I still was aware of his reputation for expecting, or demanding, top notch performance from his people. So, I went to the news conference with John Hotard, whose supportive efforts to keep me calm were only partially successful.

To my surprise and delight, upon entering the room before the news conference began, I saw Denise Hedges, the fearsome woman who lead our flight attendants union and who had first assured me her members could handle the responsibility of using defibrillators on ill passengers. She was there to stand by my side during the news conference and gave a positive statement of her own, representing the union. I also learned she would be issuing a supportive news release from APFA once we had formally made our announcement. Denise also noticed – how could she not have noticed? - that I was sweating like a pig in the bright lights set up for the TV cameras. I am of partial Italian descent, so my skin generated more oil than a french fry deep fryer under those lights. In response, Denise gave me a one-minute lesson on using foundation, and even let me have her powder puff to knock the shine off my forehead and cheeks. Having shared makeup, she and I became unlikely buddies forever.

Once the news conference began I dutifully read a prepared statement that had been written for me as the news release was handed to reporters (and simultaneously issued by the corporate communications department to the Associated Press, all the major news outlets and airline trade publications that regularly covered American, and to a number of medical publications that we anticipated also would be interested in the news we were make. The room was filled with reporters. Following my statement, I dutifully addressed many questions. Overall, I did not think it too stunning of an event. But the news from American's press conference spread throughout the media like electricity. Though a relatively small item in the grand scheme of the airline business, something about it captivated the media. The notion of flight attendants, formerly serving coffee and tea, now potentially shocking the bejesus out of customers, was on all the major news channels. I started giving regular interviews, and even did an entire program for the Discovery Channel. A week would not go by that year in which I did not talk to someone on the air about American's new defibrillator program. AMR stock even went up two points the day of the announcement. While I cannot fairly claim credit for that bump in the stock price since so many other factors go into stock price movements, but I like to think I had something to do with that nice little jump. In fact, I jokingly pointed that out to my boss Tom Kiernan, who then told Gerard Arpey, our CFO at the time. Gerard, who a few years later would become American's president and then CEO, chuckled at my apparent financial naiveté.

Sometime after the defibrillator program's announcement, I was eating dinner with my family at a Saltgrass restaurant near our home in the suburban DFW area, when my daughter Erin looked up and said, "Daddy, you are on TV!" Sure enough, it was a CNN interview about the defibrillator program. About that time, I turned to our waiter and pointed his attention to the TV. "Look! That's me!" I told him. I guess he was not very impressed. My new-found "celebrity" certainly did not earn us any free appetizers or desserts that night. I guess the clock on my Warhol-ian 15 minutes of fame were already ticking down.

Meanwhile, back at the office, the calls of dismay began rolling in once again. "Who do you think you are, teaching flight attendants to use defibrillators?" That came from an esteemed colleague and medical director of a competitor airline. A member of our Airline Medical Director's Association called, complaining "You didn't tell any of us about this. You do not come to our meetings. We are supposed to coordinate on stuff like this. The whole thing is going to fail anyway." Another called me and snarled, "You are a stupid, obnoxious, corporate geek and an idiot for doing this." I calmly replied to that caller, "I am not obnoxious... but the other adjectives may be true."

I could only guess as to why they were calling me and expressing such great frustration, or even hostility. But I suppose they all had gotten an earful from their CEOs or other high-ranking executives about how they had let American jump so far out in front of them and reap such a big marketing and public relations benefit out of it. But, as I have explained previously, we never gave a minute's thought to the marketing benefits such a program might produce (in fact, we were more concerned it might blow up in our faces). And other than Mr. Crandall's instruction to me to make sure we make it known publicly if we were going to be the first to put defibrillators on our planes, we never gave much thought to the PR aspects of the program, either.

I also got several calls from physicians in the Aerospace Medical Association who thought I had lost my mind. Only Dr. Russell Rayman, the highly regarded head of the Aerospace Medical Association, gave me his candid support. People again accused me and American of orchestrating a publicity stunt, and scoffed that American would never save anyone with its defibrillators. All I could do considering such commentary from fellow medical professionals was to be very clear about what I told our Planning Committee executives to get approval to launch the program.

"There is no financial return on this program. It is simply the right thing to do. If we save one life through this program, it is worth it."

That, essentially, was the script I used over and over and over in defense of American's decision to move ahead with its defibrillator program. It had nothing to do with marketing or public relations. Still, many of my medical colleagues simply did not believe this. They assumed it could not be true because they believed at American Airlines it is always about cutting costs and making money. They just could not believe that American, in this case, actually willingly increased its costs and expected to take in zero additional revenue because of our defibrillator program. Whenever I got tired of such the accusations, I would change my tone and get a little tougher with one response that put the onus on our competitor airlines. "The liability," I'd say, "is now greater for YOUR airline, because you are not planning to have this life saving equipment on board." Sure enough, I was proved prophetic on that score. One of American's competitors was slapped with a large lawsuit after a passenger died on board one of their planes, which, of course, were not equipped with defibrillators.

I shared all of that with our TED Task Force at a meeting after our deployment. One of our members, who happened to be a big fan of the *Wizard of Oz* and was forever referencing scenes and lines from the movie, said "Ignore the flying monkeys trying to trounce us. When the Wicked Witch of the West tries to stop us on our quest, we need to plow ahead, on through thick and thin, forest and plains, and just stop to enjoy the opiates in the poppies!" As the company's Chief Medical Review officer in charge of the airline's drug testing program I jokingly warned that particular team member to be careful about using that line in front of others. "Don't enjoy the opiates too much," I added.

CHAPTER VI

THE DOCTOR GOES TO WASHINGTON

American Airlines had barely announced its plan to put automatic external defibrillators at that Washington D.C. news conference when Bettye Harris, my secretary, walked into my office and announced: "They want you to testify before a Congressional Subcommittee regarding the defibrillator program." Immediately I felt a rush of absolute panic. I knew the program was right for us at American, but it was new and untested. I could not yet verify our AED program had saved any lives. Yet Congress already wanted to learn about the program. I was already worried about being a fool in front of my senior executives. Now, however, I catastrophized that I was being set up to play the fool in front of Congress, too. I was, to say the least, facing that, um, "opportunity" with considerable trepidation. Nevertheless, I accepted the invitation. After all, how does one turn down a request from Congress to appear before members at a hearing?

I decided to take my then 10-year-old daughter Erin with me to see the Capitol and some of the great historical sites in Washington. I also figured having her along might keep me from focusing on, and fretting too much about my time in the famous hot seat in front of a Congressional panel. I thought, "Surely they won't slaughter me in front of my own offspring!" My wife is not fond of traveling and decided to stay home with our younger daughter, Catherine. So Erin and I packed our bags and went to Washington D.C., accompanied by John Hotard, the corporate communications pro who'd been assigned to manage all communications about our program, and Linda Campbell, my top aeromedical nurse and, truth be told, a real force in keeping the TED Task Force moving swiftly and efficiently toward our goal. We met Will Ris, American's vice president of governmental affairs once we got to Washington, where he lived and worked.

On the evening of Tuesday, May 20, 1997, the day before I was to testify, Erin and I walked around some of the historic sites in Washington. We visited the Lincoln Memorial where I told her about Abraham Lincoln. Always a lover of animals of any sort, she admired the huge statue, but was more interested in the pigeons that were marble Abe's companions. I also showed her the beautiful reflection pool and told her about the famous "I have a dream" speech that Martin Luther King delivered there. Alas, once again she seemed more fascinated by the pigeons, whose fallen feathers she set about collecting. So much for learning some history, which was my stated reason/cover story for bringing her along to D.C.[15]

---

[15] As a proud aside, Erin eventually earned a master's degree in history with an emphasis on teaching, you guessed it, History, at Austin College, a hidden pearl of a college in Sherman TX, about an hour north of Dallas. Today my now-married daughter teaches history, social science, psychology and statistics at an inner-city Dallas school, H. Grady Spruce High School. Erin would not want to be anywhere else. "They need us here, Dad," she tells me. So maybe taking her along on that Washington trip paid off after all.

The Halls of Congress

My Congressional testimony was scheduled for Wednesday, May 21, 1997. It was a sunny, beautiful day. I awoke with a sense of optimism, but also a hefty dose of fear and trembling. But, thankfully, all of my performance training and experience let me hide my fear fairly well. I was to testify in the House of Representatives' Subcommittee on Aviation, a unit of the larger Committee on Transportation and Infrastructure. Rep. John Duncan, a Republican from Tennessee who served in Congress for 31 years until his retirement in 2019, was the subcommittee's chairman.

Erin sat dutifully in the back of the subcommittee room with Linda Campbell and John Hotard. Thankfully Erin had brought her Game Boy – remember those? - with her just in case she got bored (and she got bored very quickly once the hearing began). I, meanwhile, sat up front in the hot seats with several very impressive experts invited to testify at the same hearing. I was ready to take incoming fire from the congressmen and women.

I could not help but think to myself as I waited for the hearing to begin, "Would this committee even have assembled if American Airlines had not taken its initiative?" Certainly American was not the only cause of the hearing, but it clearly was the catalyst that got the subject bumped up to the level of importance and interest that necessitated the hearing. The notion of on-board defibrillators, devices that could shock people, and placing enhanced medical kits on board and in the hands of flight attendants seemed to be on everyone's mind the days before the hearing. To my surprise it actually had become a topic of some considerable national importance.

The lineup of speakers included two ladies who testified about the loss of their husbands to cardiac arrests suffered on board commercial flights. Their stories wrenched my heart the most because I so firmly believed they would not have become widows had our program been launched earlier and had other carriers followed suit earlier. Indeed, our program was designed to prevent there ever having to be more widows, or widowers, created because of inflight cardiac arrests. (Of course, I knew that we likely would never bat 1000 in our efforts to resuscitate passengers, but our goal always was to save every single passenger who in the future would experience a cardiac arrest aboard one our flights).

There were also two union representatives on my panel. One, of course, was my fearsome friend from the Association of Professional Flight Attendants, Denise Hedges. The other was Mary Kay Hanke, a Vice President with the Association of Flight Attendants, an even larger union that represented attendants at several other airlines, including United. Denise and I met in the hallway prior to the hearing. I assured her I did not need to borrow her makeup again and sheepishly reached into my pocket and pulled out my own powderpuff and foundation. We both laughed hard at that.

Another speaker on my panel was my esteemed colleague, friend and early outside support of American's AED plan, Dr. Russ Rayman. He was appearing under his title as President of the Aerospace Medical Association. Dr. Rayman knew our program was controversial. Indeed, he had been the one who had asked me to write an article for his journal about why American Airlines decided to put AEDs aboard all its planes. He did that specifically to address the uproar American's AED plan had created within the Aerospace Medicine community. So, it was good and comforting to have Dr. Rayman with us during the hearing, especially since I knew he was so supportive of our program and its potential proliferation throughout our industry and beyond.

Aerospace Medicine specialists are a small group, but avidly interested in such innovations. Many airlines had gone apoplectic over American's decision, so I saw this hearing as a great chance to explain our view to them. I planned to base my explanation on the article I wrote for Dr. Rayman: First Do No Harm! The Role of Defibrillators in Commercial Airlines. In fact, that article was published in the Journal of Aviation, Space and Environmental Medicine in the very same month that this congressional hearing took place.

During the hearing itself I explained there was no cost benefit to American from placing the defibrillators and enhanced medical kits on board our planes. I made it crystal clear that our CEO, Bob Crandall, and all of his top executives and I believed that putting those AEDs on all our planes was simply the right thing to do now that the technology had advanced enough to make it possible. Our task as a company was to get people to their destinations without harm, I testified. And given that sudden cardiac arrest on a plane can be a death sentence, we all believed that we could not, in good conscience, do anything other than to equip our planes with AEDs. I'd already said many times in interviews, "It is the right thing to do. If we save one life through this program, it is worth it." And I said it again that day before the Congressional subcommittee. I never stopped trying to convince people, including those in Congress, of that simple, straightforward truth.

The panel the subcommittee had assembled was huge. It also was funny, in a way, because except for those already mentioned, most of those panelists, particularly the doctors, felt they were the drivers behind American's pioneering decision. That was strange since I had never even met most of them before that day, I knew exactly how it went down, and it did not include them.

One who I had met previously was the FAA's top medical officer, Dr. Jon Jordan. His group bore the regulatory responsibility for determining what kind of medical and first aid equipment should be on board commercial air carriers in the United States. But I found it especially odd he sought to make it appear he played an important role in getting American to place AEDs on all our planes since he initially had been rather resistant to the idea when I'd first brought it up with him. I sat next to Dr. Jordan, from the FAA. Every aerospace medicine specialist in the country admired and respected him. And he was smart, both medically and politically. Of course, he had to be to hold such a high-ranking, highly political, job in Washington. American, with our AED program, had leapt out ahead of anything the FAA had actively considered enacting in our industry. But American had done so voluntarily, and with no regulatory, legal, or Congressional prompting. Of course, that was my usual M.O.: act first; handle questions and challenges later. To be fair, American probably should have coordinated our move with the FAA's medical department. But we did not. And I came to realize that meant I had, however unintentionally, put Dr. Jordan on the hot seat.

After we at American announced our AED plan publicly Dr. Jordan directed his top doctor in the FAA's Southwest Region (based in Fort Worth and responsible for over-seeing American and other carriers based in Texas and surrounding states), Dr. Guillermo Salazar, to track our every move, from training to implementation. As a result, Dr. Salazar spent a lot of time at America's headquarters just south of DFW airport. I saw Guillermo everywhere. At times it seemed as though when I went to the men's room, Dr. Salazar was there. My team and I, of course, had nothing to hide from him or the FAA. In fact, we were delighted the FAA was so interested in our AED program. We also hoped that would lead to more rapid adoption of our plan across the entire industry.

Once the Congressional subcommittee meeting began, the members noted they had not reviewed the issue of medical supplies and equipment on aircraft for some 13 years. They noted that in 1984, a little over 300 million people took commercial flights in the United States. By the time we met for the hearing in 1997, there were roughly twice as many people flying annually at around 600 million passengers. Yet the FAA had not made any changes or addition to the mandated inflight medical kit airlines were required to carry since 1986. My assessment of the requirements for the medical kit prior to our AED program's introduction of enhanced medical kits had been that those old kits were pretty pathetic. So, given that, I was left to wonder how poorly equipped those medical kits must have been prior to 1986. Rep. William Lapinski, a Democrat from Chicago, was the ranking member of the committee and noted that some members had worked the previous night until the wee hours of the morning. He mentioned that a Rep. Don Pease, an Ohio Democrat, was barely awake, let alone coherent. Chuckles erupted across the room.

Here is what each witness had to share:

The Widows

First, several widows spoke about losing their husbands to sudden cardiac arrest. These presentations were, as you can imagine, quite tearful. Many people in the hearing room that day were touched, including me. I had tears in his eyes during each of these ladies' presentations. My goal, and the goal of everyone involved in our AED program at American, always had been pretty simple and straightforward. We wanted to do whatever we reasonably could to keep more people from becoming widows or widowers due to sudden cardiac arrest at 35,000 feet. And those ladies' sad testimonies confirmed for me that what we were doing at American was right.

The Union Leaders

My colleague and friend from the Association of Professional Flight Attendants, Denise Hedges, who had taught me earlier how to put on makeup, spoke on behalf of her 25,000 American Airlines flight attendants. Denise began by telling the story of how aviation history was made at 8 a.m. on May 15, 1930. That is when Helen Church, a trained nurse, boarded a flight operated by Boeing Air Transport, a predecessor of United Airlines. It was a Ford Tri-Motor airplane assigned to fly from Oakland to Chicago. Her job title? Stewardess. And her responsibility was to take care of the passengers, but not in the way we think of today when we think about attendants serving drinks and food. Rather, because planes in those days were not pressurized and flew at lower altitudes where the ride could fairly often be pretty rough, there were legitimate concerns about passengers experiencing motion sickness, nose bleeds and perhaps other symptoms related to rapid three-dimensional movement in thin air. The fact that the first "stewardess" was also a nurse was supposed to provide reassurance to concerned air travelers and those considering taking their first trip via airplanes. And, as a result, she pioneered the tradition of hiring attendants primarily to work as safety professionals, not waitresses or waiters in the sky. And that remained the case pretty much until World War II's growing demand for nurses to serve the troops made it impossible for the airlines to continue hiring enough of them to meet their needs.

Denise went on to tell the subcommittee members that American's flight attendants were already trained how to render basic first aid during onboard emergencies such as epileptic seizures, burns, choking, broken bones and other health events. During the attendant's six weeks of initial training, they spend most of their time learning how to perform their aircraft and passenger safety procedures and how properly to deliver medical emergency aid for a wide variety of health events that might occur in flight. On top of that, every attendant at American (and other carriers) is required to attend recurring training annually where they get refresher courses or training on new or updated procedures – and where they must demonstrate their continuing proficiency on various procedures. But Denise also made it clear that at that point in time cardiopulmonary resuscitation (CPR) was the only tool flight attendants had to address cardiac arrests. That was a critical problem, she told Congress, because on long, international flights, landing the plane to get a passenger medical help was not even an option, and even landing a domestic flight to get a passenger to advanced medical care was a crapshoot. Not only might it take too long for a plane to get all the way to the ground and to paramedics for the passenger to survive a cardiac arrest, there was in those days no guarantee a defibrillator would be available at many smaller airports, or even at some bigger ones.

She told the subcommittee she had learned from me that an airplane actually could become the perfect place for someone to suffer a cardiac arrest – but only if each airplane was equipped with an AED. No one wants to have a cardiac arrest, but if you're going to have one what better place for it happen than in a confined space equipped with a defibrillator and at least three people (the minimum compliment of flight attendants on big jetliners) trained to use it? The attendants, and the plane's defibrillator would be able to respond to a person suffering a cardiac arrest in seconds, and to have the machine hooked up to the patient in easily less than a minute. And because the length of time between the onset of such an arrest and the delivery of the proper amount of voltage needed to restart it is the single more critical factor in surviving such an event, there may not be a better place, outside of a hospital emergency room or surgical suite, to have a cardiac arrest. But again, she emphasized, that could only be the case if all planes were equipped with AEDs, as American's were.

Finally, she addressed the members of the subcommittee's concerns about responsibility and liability issues related to attendants' treating cardiac arrest patients onboard commercial flights. Denise told them American's attendants were, in such cases, acting as agents of American's medical department and that the company's liability coverage covered them in relation to the use of defibrillators. And legally they operated as agents under my personal medical license (or the license of anyone who subsequently held my title as the airline's chief medical officer). In short, for these limited purposes our flight attendants, in effect, were all members of American's medical department. As I listened to Denise, it brought a point home to me. Although I had had approved that liability arrangement, the truth of it never really had sunk in. But at that moment I thought, for the first time, "Oh boy. If anything goes wrong with any one of 25,000 flight attendants my medical licensing boards would hear about it." Then my defensive sense of humor kicked as I followed up that silent, sobering realization with this thought: "Note to self—ask my doctor to place me on a Valium prescription!"

Denise was followed by Mary Kay Hanke, an International Vice President at the Association of Flight Attendants. She represented a much larger population of flight attendants than Denise--- 40,000 flight attendance at 26 different US carriers. And, like Denise, she noted that FAA at the time required every newly hired flight attendant to receive 40 hours of safety instruction before being assigned to actual flight duty. But she also included the important detail that the FAA only required airlines to instruct flight attendants on where the first aid kits are located on their various airplane types, how those kits functioned, and when to use them. Furthermore, attendants were instructed that those medical kits could only be used by a physician or other confirmed medical professional who might be on board. And, Mary Kay said, there were wide differences in the training standards and quality among the 26 carriers whose attendants were represented by her union.

The Vendor

The next person to testify was the CEO of medical services vendor MedAire, Joan Sullivan Garrett. Then, as today, MedAire provided on-call physician teleconference services for airlines. When a pilot learned of a medical crisis onboard his or her flight, they could make a radio call down to their operations center and ask to speak with a doctor. Many carriers contracted with MedAire to handle those calls for help either on a 24/7 basis or whenever the airline's own corporate doctors were all off duty, such as during the late overnight time periods when few airliners actually are in flight. One of the wonderful aspects of this group was they had an extensive database that provided them great historical insight into whatever might be going on medically onboard commercial airplanes. I knew Joan as an interesting and dynamic lady and a shrewd business woman. In many discussions with my former boss, Jeff Davis, and me, she would try to convince American to use their "on call physician" services. However, we in the American Airlines medical department already provided 24/7 physician on call service. We had doctors on our own staff who took turns on duty as the on-call flight physician. So, we did not need MedAire's services. But Joan was a hardy business woman and continued to try to win our business. For a Corporate Medical Director who was trying to sell his management on why our company needed an internal medical department, Jeff was not about to outsource a key medical function to a group like MedAire. I further believed our trained aerospace medicine doctors would do as well, if not better than Joan's trained emergency room doctors in handling medical calls from our planes. And the truth is, all the pilot needs to find out when they make a call like that to a ground-based doctor is whether the medical event happening onboard warrants diverting the plane to the nearest airport so the patient can get to a hospital quickly. The doctor on the ground is not going to coach a flight attendant through any surgical or invasive diagnostic procedures. And the AED will handle the actual decision to shock or not shock a patient experiencing a heart issue. Therefore, the doc on the ground just needs to learn what symptoms are being presented by the passenger-patient so that he or she can decide if it's okay for the plane to continue flying to its planned destination or that it needs to land pronto. While important, that is the only "prescription" the doctor on the ground can "write" in such cases. Still, Joan's group did have excellent data on in-flight events from their client airlines. And that gave her valuable insights, which she shared that day with members of Congress. MedAire had dealt with more than 3,000 in-flight medical incidents over 10 years via their 24-hour medical emergency hotline called MedLink. MedLink's 16 board-certified ER docs had access to a worldwide medical services database that helped them make those critical "land-or-keep flying" decisions. But that database also allowed her to categorize those cases by specific medical events or illnesses, and she had determined that 80% of all in-flight medical situations can be attributed to just 105 medical causes. That may sound like a lot, but given the huge number of potential illnesses and injuries the human body can suffer, that greatly narrowed the area of focus for MedAire's doctors handling medical calls from 35,000 feet. The highpoints of her research in the nature of those medical calls showed that:

36% were neurological events such as strokes or seizures

19% were related to cardiac issues, but that number was steadily climbing and stood at 23% through the first four months of that year, 1997

11% were respiratory in nature, involving such things as asthma and allergic reactions

10% were gastrointestinal issues

4% were related primarily to passengers' issues with diabetes

Joan said the physicians in her group were experiencing a recurring need for better airway management tools, IV equipment and emergency drugs such as injectable epinephrine and atropine, and medicines to calm asthma attacks to treat passengers-patients but emergency kits often or never had such basic and essential medical supplies in them. She also noted the use of some of those needed supplies would require the use of monitors and qualified medical professionals onboard

And, she explained her company was discovering that more and more medical professionals were becoming more fearful of responding to calls for doctor assistance on flights on which they happened to be traveling. Big legal liability concerns were the primary cause of their growing reluctance to volunteer to help in such cases. Joan was able to show through MedAire's statistics that historically 80% of their calls involved a medical professional who had volunteered their services, but that in 1996 – the previous year – the rate of medical professional volunteer response had dropped to less than 50% of MedAire's calls from the sky.

I also felt that problem was becoming a big issue. "How do you get physicians to come forward to help?" Without any grand plan or anything, I'd started a "Thank You Letter" program in which I would send a nice thank you note and 50,000 AAdvantage miles to any of our passenger-doctors (or other medical pros) who did respond to a captain's or an attendant's call for medical volunteers. I told the sub-committee members that those were the kind of doctors American would love to see continue as loyal customers of our airline. But I also expressed my concerns about the great and growing need for some form of more clearly stated liability protection for our "Good Samaritan" physicians and other medical professionals who responded to an on-board crisis. In talking about this in front of that Congressional subcommittee Joan and I had planted the seeds that later became the Aviation Assistance Act. More on that later!

The American College of Cardiology

A Dr. James Atkins was the next speaker. He represented the American College of Cardiology. He also had been medical director of the paramedic program at DFW international Airport and Love Field for over 20 years. Dr. Atkins noted an emergency diversion and landing required at least 20 minutes with another 10-20 minutes to get the plane to where the victim could be removed from the plane by appropriate medical personnel, assuming that any such personnel were even available (especially at small airports where traffic was too light to support having paramedics stations there full time). Jim noted that Qantas (the Australian flag carrier) data in April 1997, estimated that the rate of cardiac arrest events per year would reach about 311 worldwide, with between 70 and 80 per year happening aboard U.S.-based carriers.

But as he said that, I thought to myself that the estimates for American alone were that we would see about 60 cardiac arrest events per year just on our own planes. So, I had reason to believe the Qantas numbers Dr. Atkins referenced were out-of-date or unrealistic. American's flying population, though large, represented only around 20% of all passengers who traveled in any one year aboard all U.S. airlines, and a much smaller percentage still of all passengers in a year globally. Still, even based on the much more conservative – and likely wrong – numbers he used in his presentation, Dr. Atkins said he believed defibrillators onboard planes, used by trained responders, would save 10-20 lives per year. Furthermore, he suggested if defibrillators were placed in all terminals, about 60-80 lives might be saved in the U.S. annually. So even if his numbers were low, I agreed and whole-heartedly supported his conclusion that access to defibrillators and training our people to use them was the right way to go.

Dr. Atkins thought it best to have at least four trained crew members aboard each flight. American's model, however called for ALL flight attendants to be trained how to use AEDs. We knew that in some cases, especially on smaller planes, we would never have 4 flight attendants in the crew. The FAA requires one attendant per 50 available seats, so on our American Eagle regional airline affiliates' flights there might be only one or two of them assigned to those planes (one for planes with 50 or fewer seats, two for those with 51 to 76 seats, with 76 being the upper seating limit before our labor contracts required flights to be operated by mainline American rather than American Eagle). Our large fleet of domestic planes was dominated at the time by the McDonnell Douglas (now

Boeing) MD-80, which typically offered just under 150 seats. So, there were only three attendants assigned to most of our MD-80 flights. In fact, very few of our flights in those days, like today, had more attendants assigned than the FAA's rules required. The only exceptions to speak of were long-haul international flights that took hours and hours to complete. American, compelled both by language in its labor contracts and the practical need for additional hands to prepare food and drink for, and to serve large numbers of passengers would assign more-than-minimum cabin crews to work such flights. Plus, having some, but not all of our attendants trained to use AEDs would have introduced a lot more complexity to our flight attendant staffing task, which already was enormously complex because every one of our 25,000 attendants had strict Federal limits on how many hours they could fly each month and each one of them was on a slightly different hourly count. Adding the need to always have at least four AED-trained attendants on each flight held lots of potential for forcing us to cancel many flights, especially late in each month, because we lacked enough available AED-trained attendants.

Dr. Atkins also believed the idea of placing defibrillators on small aircraft like those used in our American Eagle regional operations must be evaluated carefully, and separately from the idea of putting them on big commercial jets. I and American's TED Task Force and senior management, however, had already made commitments to put AEDs on our regional aircraft flown by American Eagle. We did that because of the irrefutable statistic that the odds of surviving a cardiac arrest drop 10% for every minute of delay until the patient gets that lifesaving shock; and that was true regardless of the type or size of the plane involved. That's because it takes a significant amount of time for small planes to get to the ground, and to a gate;

about as much time as it takes for that to happen with a big jet, even though some regional aircraft don't fly at quite as high altitudes as big jets. Therefore, pretty early on in our planning, we and Peter Bowling, then the CEO of our Eagle operation, and our team decided that AEDS had to be placed on all our Eagle planes, too. A plane is a plane is a plane, we thought, and the time until receiving that lifesaving shock was just as critical on those planes as it was on American's giant 777s. As was the case throughout our TED Task Force planning and implementation periods, our approach was to implement and answer questions later. We were going to put AEDs on our small planes and if anyone wanted to second-guess us thereafter, we would be glad to talk with them about it. Actually I found it somewhat gratifying that other people on my panel, and some of the subcommittee members, were speculating about what might be needed to make the idea of AEDs onboard airline flights work. But we at American already were way ahead of them, and we had already made what was more clear all the right decisions – at least for our airline.

The Federal Air Surgeon

The next speaker to face this Congressional subcommittee was Dr. Jon Jordan who at the time was the Federal Air Surgeon for the FAA. Dr. Jordan first presented the history of aircraft medical kit development that involved the FAA rule making. His presentations included extensive commentary as to what should and should not be included. In 1995, he recalled, the FAA had convened a working group to coordinate their efforts with the industry and the medical community so well-informed decisions regarding potential improvements to the standard aircraft medical kit. That group was to report its conclusions to the FAA's Civil Aeronautical Medical Institute, which then would publish recommendations at the start of 1996. It was kind of a yawn-inducing, meaningless march through bureaucratic history. But the fireworks would come later!

The Aerospace Medical Association

My colleague Dr. Russell Rayman, President of the Aerospace Medical Association, began his testimony by reiterating some of the history of the advancement of in-flight medical care over the years. The American Aerospace Medical Association also strongly recommended that airlines be required to report, on an anonymous basis, all in-flight medical events and deaths for a period of just 12 months to some designated central repository. Then a medical kit could be designed based on the analysis of all that real world data about the nature and frequencies of various health issues that crop up onboard airliners. That, he suggested, would be a better approach to making decisions about the contents of medical kits rather than using partial data and guesswork. He was not aware, however, that I and my department already had studied several years of American Airlines data and had already come to conclusions about what we believed our enhanced medical kits needed to include. Others would have been welcome to look at our data and come up with own suggestions or simply adopt our conclusions, based on the assumption that American was big enough an operator to be a reliable proxy for the kind of medical issues that crop up on all airlines.

The Air Transportation Association

Edward Merlis was a vice president at the Air Transport Association of America. That was/is the principle Washington trade group and lobbying organization for this nation's big airlines (though today it is called Airlines for America. He testified that historically medical professionals or medical rescue workers flying as passengers respond to about 80% to 85% of in-flight emergencies. He said American's experience with its AED program would be key in the overall industry's evaluation of the efficacy of having AEDs on commercial flights.

The Qantas Medical Director

Dr. Eric Donaldson was my counterpart at Qantas. His airline is something of a unique bird, and that made it an interesting carrier to watch. Australia, as everyone knows, is a very large nation geographically, but its population is relatively small in comparison with all the world's other major air travel markets (North America, Europe, Asia, South America, the Middle East, and Africa). And, obviously, it is a heck of a long way from everyplace else in the world. So, it has a relatively small domestic air travel operation, and a remarkably far flung international air travel market with lots of very large, very long-range aircraft. And all those long flights aboard really big planes made Qantas especially vulnerable to cases of passengers experiencing major health events. It is a derivative factor of the very long flights that dominate Qantas' schedule.

Dr. Donaldson noted that four years prior to our hearing, Qantas had looked at the reasons why they were having so many medical emergencies onboard their aircraft. It was losing about four passengers per year to an unexpected cardiac death, which for a carrier so small relative to, say American, was a very concerning number. Dr. Donaldson noted all Air Attendants (their equivalent of Flight Attendants), are trained in CPR and they all got refresher training every year. He also noted there was an ambulance company in New South Wales – Australia's most populous state and home to Sydney, the nation's largest city and biggest air hub, whose vehicles were equipped with semiautomatic defibrillators. Furthermore, the employees who used those defibrillators were, themselves, not trained paramedics. So, Qantas decided to train their flight service directors (or lead flight attendants) to use defibrillators. Qantas' defibrillators, however, were not really automatic. They had a monitoring device, but it was rarely used. And when it was used, few of the passenger-patients survived.

Dr. Donaldson quipped that those few passenger-patients who had survived their cardiac arrest events were, of course, very appreciative. And in many cases, the relatives of those passenger-patients who did not survive were generally satisfied that everything that could have been done for their loved one was done. Qantas, he added, also had a much more extensive medical kit and drugs onboard than did U.S. carriers at the time to use during emergencies.

American Airlines' Testimony

My Turn

Finally, my time to speak to the subcommittee members arrived. As I was preparing to speak the room was oddly silent. Then, as I began speaking, I noticed in peripheral vision that people all around the room were beginning to scribble notes madly. Also, just as I was beginning to speak I – and everyone else in the room – could hear the start of the Mario Brothers video game music begin on Erin's Game Boy. Chuckles rippled through the room. A little bit taken aback, I turned around as Linda Campbell graciously helped Erin turn off the sound to her Game Boy.

So, I began again.

"Recently American Airlines purchased automatic external defibrillators for installation on its over-water aircraft," I said. "Over-water aircraft are those which fly international routes such as Europe, Latin America and Japan and on certain domestic flights that cross over water. The defibrillator will be onboard all flights of these by July 1 and by the end of the year we plan to enhance our onboard medical kits so that a responding physician may handle at least the first hour of any medical emergency. We want to monitor this facet before expanding to the entire fleet. American will train 2,300 lead flight attendants, known as Pursers, on how to use the device and all (attendants) will be trained by the summer of 1997." I paused and looked around. Everyone was still scribbling. There was dead silence – and no Game Boy sounds. So, I continue, repeating the gospel of sudden cardiac arrest:

"We first must understand the epidemiology of sudden cardiac arrest. More than 1,000 people per day in the United States suffer from it. It is all but impossible to predict who will have a sudden cardiac arrest or where or when it will happen," I testified. "The chances of surviving are 1 and 10 with most persons dying before reaching the hospital. Those who do survive that have a good chance of living many more years. Eighty percent (of those who survive the initial event) are alive at one year and as many as 57% are alive at 5 years.

"The life-saving defibrillation shock must be given within minutes. The chance of survival decreases 7% to 10% for each minute that the defibrillator (shock) is delayed. Even if a passenger experienced a sudden cardiac arrest immediately after a plane left the gate, the time it (takes) for the plane to return to the gate to receive defibrillation from a responding paramedic team would be too late.

"Many physicians, nurses and paramedics are used to the large hospital defibrillators. They are called monophasic defibrillators. It is the form of defibrillator that Dr. Donaldson has for Qantas Airlines. Other folks have seen them in movies and on television or other hospital emergency room settings. Those units, except for Qantas, are cumbersome. They require a physician or trained medical personnel to interpret heart rhythms to use the device.

"This past fall, the US FDA appeared to approve the use of an automatic form of these devices, which does its own interpretation, for commercial aircraft. I carefully studied American's internal medical event and medical diversion data to reach the conclusion that automatic external defibrillators and enhanced medical kits were worthy of implementation. There was a great mismatch between the existing kits and what passengers were experiencing on board.

"Qantas can screen passengers for boarding however domestic U.S. carriers are not able to do so and we can only speculate what might be one reason for the increase in diversion rates.

"The defibrillator costs $3,000 to $4,000. Initially 262 aircraft will have the system and we are purchasing 300 devices for stocking purposes.

"One singular promise was the foundation of our decision to place this life-saving capability onboard. It was based on the aphorism in medicine: 'first do no harm.' Aviation medicine deals not only with the health concerns of people but the unusual environments in which those people go. Ultimately, we felt it was the right thing to do. It was the right thing for our customers, which is of paramount importance at American Airlines."

The room was still silent. I wondered whether I had blown it?

Later I was told that what I shared was so unusual, and so far beyond the safety requirements previously placed on any U.S. air carrier that people in that hearing room did not know what to think. Even the politicians were speechless. Many people also said that those in the room simply could not believe there was no cost benefit or profit motive behind this move coming from American Airlines, always known for its aim to make a buck on everything it does. My "It's the right thing to do" mantra just didn't jive with those folks' deep-seated beliefs about how American Airlines does things.

The silence continued until I asked Chairman Lapinski "May I demonstrate how it works? I promise the device is in a training mode, so unless we have volunteers, I won't shock anybody, really".

The room, mercifully, erupted with laughter.

Rep. Roy Blunt a then rookie Republican from Missouri who now serves as his states' senior Senator, joked: "Well, Mister Pease was here first this morning if he wants to be a volunteer."

Again, there was more tension-relieving laughter. After my demonstration and closing remarks, the subcommittee members began their questioning period. Poor Dr. Jordan from the FAA immediately began being pummeled with criticism for "analysis paralysis." The beating he took lasted for many minutes. I felt badly for Dr. Jordan, yet I was secretly glad the Congressmen and women were pummeling him and not me. Rep. Blunt wound up his time by asking Dr. Jordan, almost rhetorically, "Why study these issues to death? Why do we need a 12-month study? People are dying while we wait. The cardiac problem is well documented by the largest U.S. air carrier, American Airlines. Why not proceed with what American Airlines is doing? American Airlines is ahead of where the FAA is on this and I think we need to be more proactive."

And no one can say that Rep. Blunt was just carrying water for a constituent. American did eventually buy TWA, which operated a hub in St. Louis and a big maintenance facility in Kansas City.

But that did not happen until 2001. In fact, American was something of the enemy for the perennial money-losing TWA because our Chicago and DFW hubs bracketed its St. Louis hub. We attracted lots of passengers traveling from, to or within the central United States who otherwise would have flown on TWA via St. Louis, to connect over our hubs instead. It could be argued fairly that at the time Rep. Blunt's parochial political interests would have been better served had he dismissed American's AED program as a marketing stunt. But he did not. He hailed it as an example of aggressive, positive innovation.

As the session neared its close, Rep. Lapinski said "I want to say to Dr. McKenas, (and) to complement my good friend, Bob Crandall, for once again being an innovator in the aviation industry. You buy in quantities, so I assume he'll get them a little less expensive and Bob's a good negotiator, so he probably even gets that savings."

Now, since I noted that Rep. Blunt had, at the time, no political motivations to support American's move, I must note that Rep. Lapinski's district included Chicago's O'Hare Airport, where we operated our second-largest hub. Would he have supported American's AED program even if we did not have a hub in district? Maybe. Maybe even probably. But, as his reference to Mr. Crandall indicated, he was clearly supportive of American as one of his corporate constituents.

It also was obvious to me throughout the hearing and the questioning that Mr. Crandall was no stranger to Washington D.C. He was well known to these Congress members. So, I couldn't resist throwing them a little surprise by telling them "Actually Mr. Crandall was not even in on our negotiations. He did pick a very shrewd Corporate Medical Director though, and Minette Rich on our committee was a strong acquisitions specialist for American Airlines."

Of course, we all operate under the demanding expectations Mr. Crandall set for how we conducted business. But I wanted to make sure the subcommittee members knew that while Bob Crandall was incredibly important to our success, he did not operate as a one-man show. We put our team together under his direction, and he set the standards of excellence, and expected us to do our jobs well – and we usually did.

With that the day of testimony was complete. As people started to get up, Dr. Donaldson from Qantas immediately sought me out. "I am so proud to meet this 'young whippersnapper'," he said. "I feel like a proud grandfather!" He then gave me a big hug in front of God and Country, and some sleeping senators. He was beyond pleased that American Airlines had taken this important step because, I think, he understood what far-reaching impact it would have on the global airline industry and, eventually, on saving the lives of very ill passengers who otherwise would die.

As Erin and I left the hearing room a pigeon feather fluttered to the ground. It had fallen out of Erin's Game Boy case. I picked it up, hugged her, and gave it to her, bird-germs and all. She eagerly grabbed it and re-tucked it into her Gameboy case. It was as if she was saying that her trip to Washington had been as rewarding as mine.

And with that I knew that it was time to get back to Dallas-Fort Worth where we needed to press ahead with the hard, rapid work of implementing our AED program. People's lives were still being lost at a rate of at least one person per week on our airplanes, even as we worked feverishly to introduce the change that, hopefully, would save many of those who otherwise would die. Meanwhile, we had planted the idea that other airlines, and even other industries should and could move ahead with similar programs, and that Congress could and should make creating public access to defibrillation technology a law.

CHAPTER VII

FINISHING TOUCHES

Our little group left Washington D.C. behind and returned to our work of the final stages of implementing this huge project. So much more needed to be done to start saving lives on board. I reminded the task force repeatedly—"we are losing at least one person every month to the Sudden Cardiac Arrest assassin; we need to save them. *Primum non nocere!*"

Reworking the Chain of Survival

In order to save as many lives as possible from cardiac arrest, the American Heart Association and others had previously come up with the components of an effective cardiac resuscitation program. It is a set of actions, procedures or, to use the clinical word, protocols, generally done in order, that lead to the best survival chance for the patient. It is called "The Chain of Survival."

Prior to the broad introduction of AEDS we only had cardiopulmonary resuscitation, i.e. providing the ABCs: Airway, Breathing and Circulation. Now, we were introducing a D: Defibrillation. And it appeared the D was becoming more important, in terms of time, than either A, B or C. Not only must one respond quickly to someone in cardiac arrest and place the defibrillator on them as fast as possible the need for cardiopulmonary resuscitation continues. That is, when the "smart" AED tells you, the operator, to do chest compressions and mouth-to-mouth breathing [Cardiopulmonary Resuscitation, or CPR for short] someone – a real person living and breathing outside AED box – must be there to do exactly those procedures.

So, we at American had to make significant changes in our accepted resuscitation protocols for whenever one of our passengers goes unresponsive, stops breathing and has no pulse. Under our new AED-aided protocols the flight attendant aiding a passenger will place the defibrillator on the patient first, then will do whatever the box tells them to do (by audio command or digital readout). The AED might tell them to start with CPR, indicating that for any number of reasons the patient's condition is not right for absorbing a shock. Or the AED might tell the attendant to fire away and give the passenger a big jolt (in the case of totally automatic AEDs the defibrillator will fire itself without the attendant or other operator having to act. In any case, the defibrillator is now the boss – the decision maker - in such situations.

The next step in the traditional Chain of Survival was to call for an ambulance help, typically via a 911 call. The thought behind that is that regardless of the outcome of the shock, if someone is in such a condition that they must be shocked by a defibrillator, they are by definition a very clinically unstable patient. As such, they need the attention of paramedic, who will start an IV and medication to support the tenuously stabilized rhythm of the heart of someone who just had to have their heart shocked back into operation. Such a patient also almost certainly needs to be transported to a hospital as soon as possible for more thorough care and observation by heart specialists.

Under American's (and others') old protocols, once paramedics arrived, they would be able to administer drugs to help stabilize the defibrillated heart, boosting the odds for survival. Then they would whisk the patient off to an Emergency Room, and probably hospital admission.

Obviously, those steps in the old protocol were hard, if not impossible to do at 35,000 feet. Ambulances do not have wings and jet engines to reach the plane. Paramedics cannot just materialize out of thin air the way Enterprise crew members on Star Trek simply get "beamed" across long distances. Even Platinum members of our AAdvantage cannot get that kind of service.

So, our team had to think of a way to have a "paramedic in a box." We also had to re-think where, and when we would divert a plane to get a passenger-patient to someplace where they could get follow-up care after being zapped by an AED. Putting a defibrillator on board, even though it would be in well-trained flight attendants' hands, was only part of the solution to the medical problem at hand. Post-defibrillation patients need very specific kinds of medical care that simply could never be delivered effectively onboard a flight.

Another thing we had to re-think was how our attendants would relate to doctors who volunteered to help with a patient in cardiac arrest. Forever we had taught our attendants to defer to the instructions of a qualified doctor or other medical professional, assuming they knew more about medicine and cardiac arrest treatment than our people did. But with the introduction of AEDs and our new cardiac arrest protocols, that was not necessarily true. And in such situations, there was never going to be enough time for the attendant to quiz the doctor about his understanding of our new protocols and AEDs. So, we had to teach our flight attendants to do something very unnatural for them (and for most everybody else, too). We had to teach them to sometimes ignore the advice or directions of a passenger-doctor who volunteered to help.

Traditionally, prior to American's defibrillator initiative doctors and other health care providers were all taught to start CPR immediately. But, based our Medical Department's coordination with Richard Cummings and others at the American Heart Association, it became obvious that if a defibrillator was available, our response steps – and the order in which we performed them – would have to change. We determined the defibrillator must get onto that person as fast as possible. Remember, that for sudden cardiac arrests, every minute of delay to that life-saving shock reduces that person's chance of survival by 10%. It's also important to remember that the AEDs we were putting on the planes also were advanced devices that monitored the patient's heart and other vital signs and, based on its programming, determined whether or not the patient needed a shock, and if so, how much energy should they be hit with.

So, our medical team's instructions to our 25,000 flight attendants were to lay the passenger-patient flat (or as flat as possible given whatever space was available on the plane), check for a pulse and breathing, and then, if no pulse or breathing was detected, to apply the defibrillator's "leads" or wires to the patient's chest at the points they'd been trained to make those connections (and where the AED also instructed them to place the leads). From that point the AED would take control.

But where do you lay a passenger flat on a crowded plane? The aisle might work if the patient is skinny. The flight attendant would then only need to clear some rows of seats of people, and the rescuers could work from either side, in a seat row.

The galley would also be ideal, but American did not want the flight attendants to waste valuable time trying to move an ill customer to the galley. It also might prove to be very difficult or impossible if the patient was large, contorted or convulsing, and if the attendant was small. We had to keep in mind that it can be quite awkward to carry what, effectively, would be a corpse from their seat, past frightened passengers in multiple rows, and all the way up hill to the forward galley, or downhill to the aft galley (remember, planes typically fly in a slightly "nose up" attitude). In our minds we could just see that scene from the rowdy 1980 movie *Airplane!*, a comedic spoof of airplane disaster movies where a flight attendant, holding a guitar, inadvertently (and repeatedly) bopped people on the head as she walked down the aisle. We certainly did not want a repeat of that, only with a "dead" person's feet knocking passengers in the head.

So, we determined doing CPR right at the seat itself might work best and could be done if there was no other option. The armrests do, after all, go up. And passengers can be moved out of the rows immediately in front and behind the 'rescue' row to provide access to attendants and others responding to the situation. It was not a great solution. Seats are soft and do not provide the kind of "counter pressure" you would like to have when performing CPR on someone. But it was the best option available to us, and the quickest, which really matters when every second of delay counts.

So, American became the first large scale entity of any kind to formally change its protocol from the traditional "start CPR immediately" model.

Our flight attendants already were trained in the most well-known forms of cardiopulmonary resuscitation, Mouth to Mouth Resuscitation and Chest Compressions. But, as mentioned, our team instructed our attendants to apply the defibrillator immediately if the passenger-patient met three simple and obvious criteria: they were unresponsive; they had no pulse, and there was no regular breathing.

So, what is "no regular breathing?" Most people breathe in and out repetitively. However, someone who is in the process of dying might still be breathing almost undetectably, or they can still make occasional, irregular agonal "gasps." What that means is that lower centers of the brain that control autonomic functions are still trying to make the person breathe even though other parts of the brain already have started to shut down. Thus, we had to teach this nuance to our attendants: they might hear or see the patient gasp a bit, but if their breathing is not regular, the defibrillator had to be applied quickly.

In the early days of the program American attendants were involved in several cases in which an onboard doctor who had volunteered to help declared a passenger-patient dead and told the attendant not to place the defibrillator on them. Thankfully, in each case the attendants followed their training, followed our protocols, and successfully brought their passenger-patients back to life. Oh, the nasty letters I would get from doctors in those days complaining about insolent flight attendants who did not follow their on-board medical advice. At this phase of the rescue, though, our rule was: do not listen to onboard doctors who tell you to deviate from your training, especially when it came to defibrillator use.

Thus, we at American, in coordination with help from the American Heart Association, had rewritten the first two steps in the traditional Chain of Survival. If there was no pulse, no spontaneous breathing, and the person is unresponsive, the defibrillator was to be applied. Only then were our people to perform CPR, and only if the AED said to do it.

But...what about paramedics or other medical professionals?

Another innovation we made as part of this program was that we at American had made the key decisions to first bring on board our planes all the principle medical tools that would be needed to care for a cardiac arrest patient for at least the first hour of such an event – the AEDs and our new, enhanced medical kits. And we had decided to train and empower our flight attendants to do the initial life-saving work made possible by the presence of those tools. Then we re-thought how we could use most effectively the professional components of this nation's well-developed medical response system. First, as always had been the case, we had to hope and pray that an advanced emergency care or health care provider, like a nurse, paramedic, or a volunteer physician was aboard. But while we advised our flight attendants to steer volunteering doctors away from the defibrillator, we wanted our attendants to make sure the doctors were given our spiffy new Advanced Medical Kits that included lots of really important medicines and medical tools and supplies that could come in quite handy when dealing with patients just zapped back to life by an AED, or patients suffering any number of health crises besides cardiac arrest.

But that also meant American had to figure out a way to get physicians, nurses, and paramedics to come forward and use our brand-new Enhanced Kits. Beyond training in how to treat wounds and basic injuries using the wrappings, bandages and disinfectants in those kits, our attendants were not trained in how use perform more advanced medical procedures such as intubation, or authorized to administer medicines. Only real medical pros could do that. So, the attendants' job in that regard was to get the tools into their hands.

The Enhanced Medical Kit: TED, meet ALICE

Not only did American pioneer on-board defibrillation, it also had to revamp the entire concept of what advanced medical response equipment should be onboard. Our old FAA medical kits, like those of other carriers, were woefully inadequate. My team and I studied the existing FAA medical kit standards and quickly saw they fell significantly short of what we thought we needed to have the most effective medical response program possible. In response we began our new Advanced Life Support Cardiac Equipment kit, a program that ran on parallel tracks to the AED program and which, at its core, was really a part of the AED program.

For the enhanced medical kit, as you may recall, the team dubbed this part of the project "ALICE." That stood for Advanced Life Cardiac Life Support and Cardiac Emergency Equipment. Another "win" for American Airlines was that when the FAA did eventually mandate this enhanced medical kit program for all air carriers too—at the time pretty near the same kit we constructed! "ALICE" was adopted pretty much as the standard name for the kits industry-wide. It is not incorrect to say that we literally set the standard for the industry's new – and still current – enhance medical kits on all U.S. commercial aircraft.

The minimum FAA Medical Kit at that time contained only:

An oral pharyngeal airway. This is a device that holds the mouth open, so the tongue will not obstruct breathing. It is not an optimal device at all. It typically causes a partially-conscious patient to gag, vomit, and aspirate whatever stuff is in the stomach into their lungs. That causes problems that often are worse than the patient's original problem

A blood pressure cuff. Sounds fine to the normal person, but I knew from experience aboard rescue helicopters at Cape Canaveral that it was virtually impossible to hear a blood pressure response in the arm in the noisy environment inside an aircraft, so these cuffs were useless

Antiseptic wipes.

A tourniquet. They both make it easier to stop bleeding, and to get a vein to pop up so it can be seen just under the skin, making it easier to deliver intravenous medicines

A stethoscope. Another useless tool inside a noisy cabin of a plane flying at 400 m.p.h. or whatever

Sterile gloves. This is to protect the provider's hands, and to protect the patient from being in contact with unsterile hands

Dextrose. A sugar solution helpful when someone is having a diabetic shock or insulin reaction episode that causes their blood sugar level to drop too low.

Hypodermic needles and Hypodermic syringes. These let the provider inject and administer medicines into a muscle or vein

Diphenhydramine. This is the same as Benadryl which you can get over the counter. But this is in injectable form, which makes it ideal for use on someone who was having an allergic reaction

Nitroglycerin. This is a medicine that goes under the tongue when a person experiences chest pains resulting from the heart not getting enough oxygen to function properly. The medicine dilates the arteries, so blood with a higher oxygen content can reach the heart muscle

Epinephrine. This is an injectable good for treating both asthma attacks and allergic reactions.

As noted, the critiques of those kits - both my observations in the Air Force, and those of airline docs and nurses - were that a stethoscope is useless in a noisy environment, and that the medications included often were not adequate for the kind of emergencies likely to be encountered in flight. Worse, some of the equipment that was supposed to be packed in those kits often was absent. American's own internal studies that I had spearheaded, as well as independent studies from the vendor, MedAire, showed a clear mismatch between what was happening on board commercial airplanes in the United States and what was being provided (or not provided) in the FAA medical kit.

I repeatedly had advised that a stethoscope was worthless, based on my experience in charge of the space shuttle medical rescue program at NASA. What was needed was a device with a digital readout that did not rely on a doctor, nurse or paramedic must listen for heart or other bodily sounds over the din of wind, passengers talking, and airplane sounds. Also, as Joan Garrett pointed out in her congressional testimony, her company understood there the was a critical mismatch between the content of those kits and the medical situations in which they most likely they would be used.

The three significant points of mismatch were: cardiac events, seizure disorders, and asthmatic disorders. The medical kits provided little or nothing that could be used to assist passengers experiencing those kinds of medical emergencies in flight. We also were becoming aware the problem was getting worse thanks to changes taking place in the demographics of air travelers since FACA study conducted nearly a decade earlier, in 1988. The average age of airline passengers had risen, actually rather significantly, since that study. Thus, the most common kind of medical problems onboard our planes were changing, too. And based on projections, the U.S. population and, therefore, the population of airline travelers was going to continue aging rather rapidly. The vanguard of the huge Baby Boom generation was entering their 50s at that point, and millions more were climbing the age ladder right behind them. So, American, on their own and independent from the FAA, developed its Enhanced Medical Kit.

Beginning in April 1988, American's attendants began getting new training on the use of those medical kits when they made their annual returns to the airline's schoolhouse. For the first time, they were told to deliver the onboard medical kits only to a verified licensed physician or to a medical professional who an American Medical Department physician specifically authorized to use the kit during a radio call from the plane. We did that because of the presence of more powerful, controlled medicines we began placing in those kits.

American also implemented a regime of daily inflight medical kit checks and reporting requirements. That was done not only because it was a simply a good practice to check the emergency supplies every day before a plane made its first flight, but also because those were carrying those controlled medicines like Valium that could become the target of thieves. (Valium is an ideal medicine to stop seizures.) Of course, we did not allow attendants, pilots or even on-board doctors to use the Valium for themselves. But the mere presence of such drugs onboard could have been tempting for any employee who had a substance abuse issue, or for that matter, of any passenger who happened to be aware of the presence of those medications. American was not particularly worried about employees pilfering such drugs because we really did not think it would happen much, if at all. But as with any large organization it was then, and continues to be possible, for a small number of employees to have drug addiction problems. And accessing those drug kits to steal the medications out of them would not be that difficult, especially during the six- to eight-hour stretches when those planes sit quietly empty at airports overnight, or even during shorter down times in the middle of the day. So, our new daily checks made clear to any employee who might try it that they would be caught if they did.

The new kits were originally equipped like what were known as "Banyan" kits, which were commonplace in doctor's offices. Banyan is a company that had been designing medical kits for years. But our more advanced kits were beefed up to include:

- Advanced airway breathing management tools
- Minor surgical instruments
- A digital readout blood pressure monitor
- A manometer, which measures the blood pressure without the need for someone to listen for sounds via a stethoscope
- Intravenous solutions and equipment
- Cardiac medications to treat heart arrhythmias, chest pain and the like.
- Asthma medications
- Anti-nausea medications
- Antiseizure medications, including diazepam, which is a form of Valium.
- Anti-allergy medications
- Anti-pain medication

Those additional tools and medications meant American could provide what was needed to keep a patient going for the first hour after a shock from a defibrillator. It also meant medical people onboard could treat other passengers experiencing serious symptoms of potentially medical maladies other than cardiac arrest.

Of course, the most critical piece of American's in-flight medical response program was, and continues to be, the presence of a doctor, or at least the presence of a nurse or paramedic on board who could get permission or direction from one of our American Medical Department doctors on the ground.

As discussed previously, it was not, and still is not unusual for physicians to be travellers on board our planes. American's internal data told us that at least one doctor was on board around 85% of our flights. Yet, we also knew many doctors were reluctant to come forward when the call went out for a doctor onboard because of their growing fear of lawsuits. Additionally, many doctors on our flights were actually ineffective in providing patient care because they were researchers, administrators or even retired. And many doctors were reluctant to volunteer because of their specialties, thinking they would be of little use in handling a cardiac rescue because they hadn't had any training in that procedure since the first year of med school, or because they practiced a specialty like psychiatry and had all-but forgotten what little they'd once known about cardiac medicine.

Those growing concerns about doctors' liability exposure when responding to calls for help on board airlines made us realize a key element of our in-flight medical emergency plan – dependence on volunteer doctor/passengers, was growing more and more unreliable, and it was something we could fix—the fix had to come from Congress and legislation.

The 1998 Aviation Medical Assistance Act

By this time, I, perhaps mistakenly, had gained more and more recognition in the Aviation Medicine community for our work on the defibrillator and medical kit issues. Somehow, people got it in their head that I knew what I was talking about when it came to in-flight health care. Thus, while I actually tried to hide so I would not be picked, picked I was to chair the Air Transport Association's Medical Committee. Remember, ATA was then the industry's principal trade group and Washington lobby organization. It still is today, but it goes by a different name: Airlines for America, or A4A.

This committee met monthly at the AATA's headquarters in D.C., and it included medical representatives from all the major carriers. Some airlines sent their medical directors like me. They were full-time airline employees who had large medical staffs like I did. United and Delta were two such carriers. Other airlines sent medical directors who actually were contractors, along with, in most cases, a nurse who was an actual employee of that carrier. Continental fell into that category. Still other carriers sent non-medical people from their Safety departments who served as the closest thing they had to being a medical director.

In the olden days, the ATA Medical Committee mostly just determined industry benchmarks for in-flight medical responses so carriers could, as money and management priorities allowed, standardize practices across the industry. In effect, it was a gentlemanly way to let us look over each other's shoulder and copy best practices without the competitive impulses that made doing the same thing in finance or marketing difficult, if not impossible – and sometimes even illegal. For us, such sharing of best practices was a well-intentioned way of spreading improved in-flight medical care across the industry in a way that could only benefit every carrier.

That surprisingly collegial approach was disturbed however when we at American announced our defibrillator and enhanced medical kit (ALICE) programs. Some thought we were grandstanding and trying to gain a competitive advantage over our rivals. Of course, that was never part of our thinking, the way it very well could have been had what was launched been a marketing or financial innovation. But it was all about providing better medical care for sick passengers, and once everyone on the committee figured out, the concerns about American trying to gain a leg up on everyone else quickly evaporated. And once I was appointed to chair the group, our committee quickly discovered, individually and collectively, that we could actually be an honest-to-goodness industry committee with a real operational focus that we could work on together for the benefit of all. We also noticed rather quickly that for the first time, other parts of the airline industry were listening to us medical people! I wish I could claim that was all the result of a well-thought-out plan on my part, and on the part of my team at American Medical, to dramatically change the U.S. airline industry for the better, but it was not. Still, it turns out that the I – or we at American Medical, actually - had successfully linked airlines' internal airline medical resources to their true operational requirements for the first time in history. And we had successfully cross populated that innovation pretty much across the entire industry.

Our committee, now equipped with some real "teeth," started working through the ATA – and with the support Dr. Russ Rayman of the Aerospace Medical Association and Dr. Jon Jordan, the Federal Air Surgeon - to get some new legislation passed that would protect "Good Samaritan" doctors and other medical providers who volunteer to help in a medical crisis on board.

Most doctors are good people. That, for the most part, even includes me, though my wife might at times debate that. Though tales of smart young guys and girls going into medicine only for the money abound, the reality is that most people who enter medical school genuinely want to help people. Sure, they are attracted by the science, and maybe by the social standing that typically accompanies being a doctor, and not every doctor has the people skills that make it obvious that they are really focused on helping people. But doctors, by and large, are in medicine primarily to help people. But in the 1990s, U.S. society was becoming increasingly litigious and doctors were becoming keenly aware they could lose millions of dollars, their reputations, their practices and even their licenses because of liability lawsuits stemming from a well-intentioned Good Samaritan response. Some had begun declining to volunteer precisely for that reason. And that was a potential threat to the effectiveness of our defibrillator and enhanced medical kit programs.

In reality, it was - and still is - pretty easy for our crews (and veteran travelers, for that matter) to pick out the doctors on board a flight when a passenger experiences some sort of a significant medical issues. All you have to do is make an announcement over the PA asking for help from a doctor or any other medical professionals onboard. The doctors are the ones who slump down in their seats, and suddenly find a very interesting article in the American Way magazine tucked into the seat back in front of them. Of course, many doctors do not do that. They immediately stand up and ask how they can be of help. But the liability concerns were, in those days, swinging the numbers toward those who do not want to get involved.

Once, not long after I joined American as a staff doctor, I was flying with my young daughter Erin back to Florida for a visit with old friends. A man a few seats ahead of us suddenly slumped over, and his new bride, who he had married only the day before, started screaming and shaking him. Without thinking I bolted out of my seat to get to him, just as I had always been trained to do whenever I happened to be near when someone suddenly fell ill.

That poor passenger had the look of death. His eyes were glazed, staring up at the ceiling, exactly how Carmen Giggey would describe her husband a few years later. Thankfully, just as I got to him, and before I could even check his pulse, the young man came to. I tended to him the best I could with the limited capability we had on board in those days. Still, I advised the pilot to divert, because we had no clue as to why that happened to him. Though he was awake and seemed okay to the average observer, he was by definition a very unstable patient. He did say he did not get much sleep the night prior—it was after all his honeymoon. I asked a flight attendant to watch Erin and assure her that all was OK, and that Daddy was just helping another passenger. Erin's wee little eyes were peering over the seat, to make sure her daddy was still there. It was that day that Erin understood that M.D. not only stood for "My Daddy" but also "Medical Doctor" (when they became teenagers, my kids again began telling people it stood for "Mentally Deranged"). She also learned that day doctors had response commitments to others that overrode everything else in emergency circumstances.

In that vein – that's a doctor's pun – when I first became American's medical director, I wanted to do something to formally recognize the role of doctors who volunteered to help with in-flight health emergencies. To encourage more of that behavior, we started a "Thank You" program. If American learned a doctor voluntarily had come forward to help in a medical situation, I would write them a personal letter and include 50,000 AAdvantage miles as a way of rewarding them for their service not only that passenger but also to our airline. American, of course, could not pay them cash as that would be like a payment for services and might establish a doctor-patient relationship that could permit the patient to sue the doctor or American. The miles were just a token of American's appreciation. But still, the doctors appreciated the thank you. After all, they had given up part of their trip to help.

Of course, sometimes, doctors would get crass and send me a bill for their time on board. Sometimes, the nasty letters came after they had received their thank you letter with the awards miles. I typically would write back saying that they did not have to respond, and reminded that they had done so voluntarily. Also, I would explain that getting paid for their service meant they no longer would considered "Good Samaritans" and therefore would be subject to potentially tremendous liability. Most times after receiving that kind of letter from me they would back off.

But because not every doctor or health professional would bolt forward to help, for whatever reasons, our industry's Washington trade group, the Air Transport Association, got involved in promoting what became the Aviation Medical Assistance Act of 1998. I ended up being a principal author of the medical components of the draft bill. I wrote my contribution at my office in Fort Worth and took it to a meeting of the ATA's medical committee and to the ATA's leadership, which included the senior staff plus the board members, who were the chairmen or presidents of the various airlines who were members of the ATA. And most of what I wrote survived all the editing and revisions that take place when

Congressional staff members get hold of it and when their bosses, the Representatives and Senators who actually get elected to enact laws, start debating bills in committee and then on the floors of both chambers.

The Act captured a lot of what already was going on in the aviation medical world. It covered a lot of "sins" that came out during the Congressional hearing regarding medical events in flight. The law:

* Directed the FAA to formally re-evaluate the equipment in medical kits carried on commercial planes and to make a decision whether to require automatic external defibrillators be carried on such planes
* Gave the FAA Administrator no more than one year to fully address the medical kit contents issue and the related issue of the training requirements that should be put into place for flight attendants in how to use that equipment,
* Mandated that air carriers make a good faith effort to obtain and submit quarterly reports regarding the number of persons who died on aircraft, or people declared dead after being removed from such an aircraft. This included reporting the victim's age, any information concerning the cause of death, and whether or not the plane diverted as a result of the health-related incident or death
* Stipulated that an air carrier will not be liable for damages in any court action brought in a Federal or State court arising from the performance of the air carrier in obtaining or attempting to obtain the assistance of a passenger in an in-flight medical emergency, or out of the acts or omissions of the passenger rendering the assistance, if the carrier in good faith believes that responding passenger is a medically qualified person.

* Made it clear that any medically qualified responding passenger would not be liable for damages in any action brought in a Federal or State Court arising out of that person's acts or omissions in providing or attempting to aid in the case of an in-flight medical emergency, unless there is gross negligence or willful misconduct.

The Act gave broad leeway in defining a "medically qualified individual" as any person who is licensed, certified or otherwise qualified to provide medical care in a State, including a physician, nurse, physician assistant, paramedic, and emergency medical technician.

Flight Attendants

Perhaps the most important cog in the Chain of Survival was the flight attendant. Not just any flight attendant, mind you, the American Airlines flight attendant, who, based on my interactions with the APFA health and safety leaders Emily Carter, Debbie Luhr, and Kathy Lord Jones, were the best of the best in terms of their training and service to the customer.

I once tried to go to their training program. I figured I needed to be an expert – or at least have a very deep understanding of what they do – if ever I might have to actually disqualify a flight attendant based on their having become a direct or imminent threat to passengers, crew or the plane. I wanted to be as credible as possible should I ever have to respond to the Equal Employment Opportunity Commission in the event of a lawsuit. So, I joined a group of flight attendant trainees going through their initial training classes. And, just like most of them, I struggled with opening doors, pushing galley carts, and learning some of the emergency protocols.

Perhaps most comical was the water slide. They used to have a huge airplane mockup in the middle of a pool at the American Airlines Learning Center down the street from the headquarters building in Fort Worth. I was not, at the time, a small man. Far from it, though thankfully I have lost a lot of weight in the 25 years since then. Well, as one can probably imagine, when I jumped out of the plane door and down onto that slide, it bowed way down, hit the water, and like a trampoline, flung me off the slide into the water. It was not one bit glamorous All my dignity as Corporate Medical Director was lost in that moment. Everyone there – the trainees, the trainers, and a few others watching the training all laughed hysterically at my expense. That, of course, included me, too. Everybody enjoyed the ridiculous site of this big ol' doctor and corporate boss getting tossed like a rag doll into the pool by an emergency slide while trying to pretend he could do a flight attendant's job.

Coffee, Tea or Defibrillator?

As the flight attendant population at American began hearing about defibrillators, and as they started to get placed on board, their response, at least prior to receiving their formal training, was that of curiosity. Over the first year or so, after the defibrillators began showing up onboard our planes, our attendants would get trained a few dozen at a time. But for a while, most of our attendants were flying on planes with equipment they had not be trained to use. That is a very unusual, even uncomfortable situation for them. Thus, the curiosity continued to build for them until it came their time to go back to school in Fort Worth and get trained.

Naturally, whenever I flew in those early days of the defibrillator program, I would check the plane to see if our team of AA Medical nurses had installed one on that plane. Often, I would see the bracket, with the red heart dashed by a golden lightning bolt logo that I had designed. If my girls or wife were flying with me, I would always point it out them. And they would say '" That's nice, Dad/David" and go right back to their Game Boys or Words with Friends. One time, I asked a flight attendant if they had one of the new defibrillators on board, and she looked at me, and at my less-than-impressive physique, with deep concern: 'Why? You don't think you need one do you?" she asked very seriously. That put me in my place, to be sure.

So, the defibrillators were bought, the logistics established, and I got final blessing from our Corporate Insurance and Legal departments to proceed. The Maintenance and Engineering teams were starting to install the brackets on the planes and our team of nurses was beginning to place the defibrillators and enhanced medical kits onboard. The next step was to get all 25,000 or more attendants trained, and do it in a year, or less, if possible.

Most people are used to the term "first responder." These are the EMTs and Paramedics who are trained to respond to emergencies on the ground, in ambulances, on fire trucks and the like. American's venture, however, was the first medical response program ever designed around a large group of non-medical people who would become first responders. And we had to train every one of them from scratch. If any of our attendants happened to have had previous medical training as EMTs, nurses or even as field medics in the military that was a plus, but we could not build a large-scale training program around the few attendants who might fall into that category. So, we trained all our people as if they did not know anything beyond how to apply a Band-Aid. They were to become what the first ever "non-traditional first responders." They were – and are - ordinary people who by nature of their jobs, are the closest to someone having a cardiac arrest or some other life-threatening medical issue in flight. So, it only made sense to make sure they had enough training to place a defibrillator on a sick passenger and follow the machine's instructions thereafter. These days it is not uncommon to find janitors, and building security guards serving as non-traditional first responders. But our flight attendants at American were the first to ever serve in that role in any significant numbers.

A big reason that was possible then, and is possible today is that Automatic External Defibrillators that were beginning to appear on the market in the mid-90s were so darn easy to use. Frankly, they did not require much training to use. Still, being American Airlines, which never has been known for skimping on training and customer safety, the initial training on the program was three hours long – and that is just for how to use the defibrillator. Training the attendants use the enhanced medical kits we also were installing at the same time took more time, even though most of the items and medicines added to those kits could only be used by doctors or other licensed medical pros.

The American Heart Association continued to work very closely with AA Medical. Our lead nurse, Linda Campbell worked with Julie Bourke Suchman, who was the head of American's flight service training department, and then her replacement, Melanie Wahrmund, plus their marvelous team of trainers. Linda also coordinated closely with APFA Union leaders and Dayle Culhane, the chief of American's Pursers (lead flight attendants). Together those folks came up with the prototype flight attendant training program, which soon became the model for all other air carriers followed in training their own attendants to use defibrillators

After their initial shock that American was in fact doing this, and as soon as the FAA started to lean toward making them mandatory, other carriers began trying various tactics to obtain copies of American's training program, our protocols, details about our enhanced medical kit, and anything else they could get their hands on. Our team did not mind, however, because if more lives could be saved by expanding the program, that would just further our success and fully in line with American's only real goal for our AED program. To us at AA medical, it did not matter what airline a passenger's life was saved on. It only matters that their life was saved.

Linda Campbell focused much of her efforts on the logistics of training the first 1,300 pursers – the lead flight attendants on international flights, who would be the first cohort of American attendants to get the new medical training. It was no minor task. Our new medical training took three hours. But the attendants' annual recurrent training in those days was scheduled to last just two hours. So somehow, we had to figure out a way to extend that training time to accommodate the medical training without squeezing out other training they needed to get while back at the schoolhouse.

Pursers are more common on international flights, which by nature last much longer than most domestic flights and require several rounds of food and drink service plus lots of other services steps that just do not happen on your average domestic flight. There is also the natural increased exposure to a potential emergency water landing and all the very demanding training that goes with making sure passengers survive and get out. As a result, our pursers are creme-de-la-crème of flight attendants. In addition to typically serving our first and business class passengers, who pay the most for their travel and expect the best and most personal service, pursers manage whole, enlarged complement of attendants on those long flights carrying 250 to nearly 400 passengers. The purser also is responsible for collecting and being accountable for cash paid inflight for drinks, food and duty-free item. In short, pursers are the attendants whose job includes making sure the customer experience on their respective flights is up to the airline's standards and passengers' expectations.

Flight attendants are trained at an airline's headquarters or training base. Initial training can last anywhere from a few days to six weeks, depending on the level of service detail a carrier wants from its attendants beyond the FAA-required safety training. They must jump into water, deploy rafts, direct mock evacuations of a cabin full of customers, and the like. At American, we had what used to be known as the "Stewardess College" down the street from headquarters, complete with a dorm where flight attendants would live for six weeks until they earned their wings. But as veteran attendants, pursers were based all over the U.S. Bringing them all in to DFW Airport for training not only would be expensive it also would disrupt the relentless training schedule for new attendants, groups of which would begin their initial training only an hour or so after the previous class had their wings pinned on at their graduation ceremony. So, my team and I had to create a "road show" training program so we could move from hub to hub to train small groups of pursers in the field. In that way our "schoolhouse," which is what airline people call their training facilities, became portable.

Thankfully, the pursers were stationed at American's big hubs in major cities where we could fly as a team rather easily, places like Los Angeles International Airport, Chicago O'Hare Airport, New York's John F. Kennedy, and LaGuardia airports, and Miami International. And, of course, we did some purser training at DFW Airport, just across the freeway from our headquarters (little known fact... our training center and operations center actually are on land leased from DFW Airport).

Linda Campbell and I travelled a lot in those days because we two were the primary medical trainers for those pursers who were the first to be trained on the use of AEDs and our enhanced medical kits. Our training team also included several regular attendant trainers. We would spend two or three days at each hub, training pursers in waves.

Most of those training sessions wound up being in some very elegant hotels in beautiful locations. American was making good money those days so, while we were not exactly spendthrifts, there was not any budget pressure on us. And, honestly, no one could put on training session like the American flight attendant training team.

There was music, special backgrounds etc. The receptions and food at break times were wonderful. The parties at night were awesome.

The attendants themselves, in those days, were very cautious in their dealings with me and other members of the AA Medical department. To them, our department always had been the "evil" department that would take them off work for medical reasons or the first to call if they ever had a positive drug test [most often explained by prescription medicines]. So, Linda and I got used to receiving lukewarm receptions at such events, at least initially.

I would begin the training session talking about the defibrillator program and give the program's background. Then I would explain the basic steps in the use of our AEDs. That would take about an hour. The attendants then would practice for two hours. During my portion of the session I also explained sudden cardiac arrest and how this device we were training them to use might one day show definitively to the public what kind of heroes and heroines attendants actually are in terms of passenger safety. In a way it is unfortunate that it would take the introduction of a piece of fantastic technology like an AED and a passenger suffering a cardiac arrest to demonstrate just how important flight attendants are in protecting the lives and wellbeing of airline passengers. They do lots of other things short of hooking an ill patient up to a defibrillator that are critical in establishing and maintaining safe operations. But few of those tasks are as dramatic as using an AED on a passenger, and none are likely to grab headline notice the way saving a passenger's life with an electric shock to the heart typically is. In another sense, its probably good flight attendants do not get a lot of attention for their safety work. That means they are doing their safety jobs so well air travelers do not notice, or even think about, all the things that could go wrong in flight if not for the crew's diligent work. During that time I learned - and re-learned over and over - that flight attendants, and especially pursers are incredible people. I made many friendships in those days of working so closely with our pursers. For the most part they loved their work and loved doing their best for the customers.

During those sessions I had to address the awkward situation of how to take off a customer's shirt or blouse. I would stress that the Flight Attendants were to cast modesty aside in a cardiac arrest situation, because without giving that passenger a life-saving shock as quickly as possible, that passenger most assuredly would die. I also rather sheepishly would share that when the passenger involved was a lady, their brassiere would have to come off as well. I also would caution the attendants about why the bra had to be removed: most of them have metal embedded in them to serve as support wires. If we were to deliver a shock to a woman with her bra still on, that high voltage charge would go through the metal, not the skin.

To hammer the point home, I acquired a bra, and in front, took the wire out from beneath the cup and took it with me into my training sessions. That is where I and Linda Campbell would do a short Laurel and Hardy-style routine.

"Linda," I would ask. "Do you know what this is?"

And she would respond with: "A bra wire from a very well-endowed woman!"

The attendants in the training session got the point. Unless you want an arc of electricity during a shock, the bra had to come off. Be discrete, I would add in my instructions, and give some visual privacy to the victim, but do not be afraid to move quickly. In such situation seconds matter, a lot.

During one of those early training sessions an eager young male flight attendant was sitting in the first row of our training room. And just as I began talking about these special instructions for treating a female and said that the responding attendant would have to remove the lady's blouse and bra, this young man, in a loud stage whisper said: "ALL RIIIIIGHT!" I gave him my best "stern school-marm" look and stressed that we had to remain completely professional. Then I slipped behind the display board during a break so I could let loose with a hysterical laugh I had been repressing.

During those training sessions Linda and I would work together while the regular flight attendant training staff members worked at different stations as we gave them their first opportunities to get their hands on an AED and practice with them – on mannequins, not each other. Linda and I would start that hands-on portion of the training by giving the initial demonstration for all to observe. To keep things light and engaging I'd sometimes let my inner goofball out at this point by pulling the forearm off a dummy and say, "Let's give Linda a big hand for all she does!" while literally giving her a "hand" (and forearm). That is the kind of humor that would cause my wife and kids – and sometimes my colleagues in the AA Medical department to groan. But it always worked well in the training sessions. It always got great laughs from the attendants in training. I guess I had found my audience.

Ready for Launch

With all the legal and insurance matters nailed down, the purchasing and logistics issues sewn up and the training program in place and going smoothly, the defibrillators slowly started showing up on airplanes.

And once those AEDs started going on our planes I began waiting, anxiously for the moment when one of them would be used on a plane for the very first time. After all, American had spent millions of dollars on this program. And I joked that I had begun checking the job listings, just in case no one ever used one of the defibrillators, exposing me as the guy behind a huge waste of the company's money and attention. It was clear, to me anyway, that senior management, no matter what they verbalized, would feel the money was needlessly spent if the lifesaving events I would predict would result from equipping our hundreds of planes with AEDS never happened

So, I became the ghoulish "Dr. Kevorkian" of American Airlines. "Did anyone die yesterday?" I would ask every morning on the operations call that included leaders from every department of the company as a way of making sure everyone was aware of any current disruptions or issues that had to be dealt with immediately. It seemed to me like weeks passed with nothing happening as the devices were slowly being placed on board a few more airplanes each night.

On the night of Feb. 16, 1998, Mija Lee and Barbara Rice, two RNs from the AA Medical department, along with Esther Fieler and Donna Richey, two technicians from American's clinic at our

massive DFW Airport hub, were going about their new nightly duties of installing AEDs in planes parked at the gates during the six or
seven hours each night when flight operations all-but cease. They
were doing the final checks of brand-new AEDs and then installing them in the brackets our maintenance and engineering people
previously had bolted into select planes overhead compartments.
It was kind of an odd sight: ladies in white nurses' uniforms moving
methodically through a largely deserted airport terminal, pushing
a squeaky cart full of defibrillators and supplies down the con-
course, and then down into jet bridges and onto docked aircraft.
These installers had obtained full jet bridge and airplane plane
security access rights after going through careful background
checks just so they could do that job unsupervised by security personnel. We had come full circle as an industry. Nurses were placing medical equipment on board planes; medical equipment that
was to be used by non-medical employees (flight attendants) who
some 60 years earlier had been required to be nurses themselves.
It was on that cold February night at DFW that Lee, Rice, Fieler and
Richey installed an AED onboard a McDonnell Douglas MD-80, or
Super 80 in American's terminology, that was bound the next day
for Mexico City. That same plane would then return to Mexico City
on the day after that, Feb. 18. One of its passengers on the 18th
was going to be large man from North Carolina who was about to
become part of history. His name? Robert Giggey.

CHAPTER VIII

THE SHOCK FELT AROUND THE WORLD
ROBERT GIGGEY 2.0

So much for the huge flashback! Let us pick the story back up, with Shawn Lynn, Don Grohman, Carmen Giggey, and Robert Giggey! So much had happened to get this dream of mine – and of others on my team at AA medical – realized to get this lifesaving equipment on board. Then it happened. This at-first nameless customer, who we obviously did not know, had been shocked by a defibrillator onboard one of our planes.

Bettye Harris burst into the clinic and interrupted my contemplation of the meaning of this historical moment.

"Get your tie and suitcoat. They are coming!" she said excitedly.

"Who is coming?" I asked.

"CBS, NBC CNN and the Dallas Morning News. They are all wanting to interview you!"

"But has he made it? Is he alive?" I said.

We did not yet know.

Back on the airplane, Don Grohman and Shawn Lynn continued feverishly to work on Mr. Giggey. While Shawn relentlessly breathed into Giggey's lungs, and seemingly to have spiritual breath blown into her mind at the same time, Don performed a series of chest compressions.

So, as he worked, with no success, to revive Robert Giggey, Don's training told him to do what he always does when a patient remains unresponsive, unconscious and not breathing: He yelled :

"We need a defibrillator."

He then quickly recalled, out loud, that airplanes do not carry defibrillators.

"This one does!" Shawn responded without missing a beat. She happened to have seen it as she walked onto this very flight, still despondent from her life situation. She ran and got it.

As Shawn got the defibrillator, Don unbuttoned Robert's shirt exposing his chest. It was covered in chest hair and cold, clammy sweat. The defibrillator had a razor in the kit, so he quickly shaved where the two pads would be attached with adhesive. He pressed the machine's on button. It started to talk.

"Apply pads to patient's bare chest," the machine's voice said.

Don even noted there were graphics on the pads saying exactly where they should go on the chest. Because Mr. Giggey's seemingly dead body was covered in moisture, so he used a napkin to get dry off his chest. The defibrillator spoke again.

"Analyzing heart rhythm - do not touch the patient."

Mrs. Giggey, who had been praying for her husband, gave up her grip on his feet momentarily.

Don advised all people to clear the patient, and do not touch him. Then, the device found the lethal rhythm of sudden cardiac arrest—ventricular fibrillation.

"Shock advised, do not touch the patient. Shock advised, press shock button now. Shock advised, press the shock button now. PRESS THE SHOCK BUTTON NOW."

Don made certain all people, including Carmen Giggey who was still touching him and praying at his feet, were clear of Mr. Giggey. He quickly pressed the shock button.

Robert Giggey's corpse jumped up off the seat by about two feet, Don recalls.

Shawn quickly returned to his body and felt for the carotid in his neck.

"He has a pulse! There is a pulse!" she exclaimed.

Indeed, Robert Giggey had come back to life in that moment and began to move a bit.

The passengers in the airplane broke into wild cheers and applause. Tears of relief were streaming down passengers' faces. They would all had been anxiously watching this bit of real-life high drama play out in front of them. They were both metaphorically and, in some cases, physically in shock. Complete strangers began hugging each other in joy as Robert came to and Carmen, weeping, reached over to him with a combination of great relief and shocked disbelief over what she had just witnessed. "Your husband is back with us Carmen!" Don proclaimed. "Please keep praying though, he is not out of the woods." Unashamedly, she said repeatedly: "Thank you God! Thank you for saving my husband!"

Shawn, meanwhile, went numb. What had just happened to her? What was that voice she had heard? She wept, but it was a crying caused not by relief that Mr. Giggey had been shocked back to life, though certainly she was ecstatic over that result. Rather her tears were tears of relief concerning her own emotional, or even spiritual condition. She no longer felt the overwhelming sense of despair that she had lugged onboard with her when she reported for duty a little earlier. New life had just been breathed into her soul and she knew it, not in the way that one knows 2 + 2 = 4, but in the way one knows what it is like to be loved and valued by another. A smile grew from ear to ear as she absorbed what had just happened not only to Robert Giggey but also to her. She had just been brought back to life every bit as much as he had.

By this time, their plane was back at the gate. Mrs. Giggey accompanied the paramedics who had come onboard as they took her husband to a nearby hospital. On the way out of the plane, Shawn told her, "I hope you don't mind that I kissed your husband." Shawn and Carmen, one a woman whose soul seemingly had been dead minutes earlier and the other a woman whose husband actually had been clinically dead just moments before, laughed and hugged each other dearly, both dripping tears of joy onto each other.

Although airport paramedics equipped with a defibrillator also responded, Mike Simpson, a paramedic supervisor at the DFW Airport, later said it took them eight minutes from the time they were dispatched to reach Robert Giggey's side, by which time he had already been revived. Those paramedics did board the plane and they administered cardiac stabilizing drugs before transporting Mr. Giggey to a waiting ambulance that rushed him to doctors - and to awaiting news crews - at the hospital.

John Crewdson, the intrepid Chicago Tribune medical reporter who had been tracking the development of American's pioneering AED program, later reported hospital tests showed Mr. Giggey had a coronary artery blockage that had impeded the blood flow to his heart.

First Reactions

American's headquarters are located just south of DFW airport, across a freeway. Still, because of the length of the airport's runways and the massive amount of land its developers wisely included in the property as safety zone, the headquarters building was about three miles, as the crow flies, from the terminals. So close, yet so far, as they say. While the Giggey life rescue was going on, we at AA Medical had no knowledge of it. Even had someone thought to give us a call during the emergency – and why would they have had such a thought? – nobody had time to make such a call. In fact, it was not until about an hour after Mr. Giggey had been taken to the hospital that Linda Campbell ran into my office and half-shouted "We had a first shock use of the device."

Again, the first words out of my mouth were "Did he make it?"

Linda said, "Yes he did!"

I can be kind of an emotional guy, but I was surprised at how fast tears began welling up in my eyes. and like Mrs. Giggey, who I had never met, I could only say "Thank you ,God!"

Seconds later Bettye Harris reminded me that "Corporate Communications is on the line; several news channels and reporters are out in the lobby for you." Word sure travels fast.

Linda Campbell drove over to the airport to retrieve the AED that was used on Mr. Giggey. She also got the card that went with it and, amazingly, a printout of Mr. Giggey's EKG tracing. Then she took all that to the hospital where Mr. Giggey had been taken to get that medical data to his doctors. At the hospital, Mrs. Giggey was besieged by television camera crews. She and I were both were interviewed for the local news programs that evening.

On their 5 p.m. "early" news show, KXAS Channel 5, the NBC affiliate in Dallas-Fort Worth, reported that "A passenger aboard an American Airlines flight is in serious condition tonight after suffering a heart attack. But fortunately, the airline was not caught off guard. New high-tech equipment, a flight attendant and a paramedic saved the man's life. Here is Texas 5's Debra Damiano" then went live to the field reporter, who said, "You might think it could never happen to you or someone you love in an airplane. A medical emergency that could mean life or death." Mrs. Giggey's first retelling of the story to the news cameras was the simple statement: "They had no heart, no pulse."

"It is definitely something that Carmen Giggey thought would never happen to her husband, Robert," the reporter continued. "Mrs. Giggey said she wasn't running through the airport, but they were briskly walking on a moving sidewalk. She and her husband. She didn't think it was a pace that would bother her or her husband." Carmen, still shaken from the event, said: "When we were on the plane...his eyes! I never... his eyes weren't alive, and his head was back."

Damiano, the reporter, went on to explain Robert Giggey suffered a heart attack but that American was prepared for such event. She noted that American was, at that time, the only airline equipped with automatic external defibrillators... that a flight had attendant grabbed it... and that a paramedic on board helped her revive the 53-year-old passenger.

"According to American Airlines, this is the first time the device was used to shock someone and bring them back to life," she added.

A reporter came to the lobby of our headquarters building to interview me. She asked what, from my perspective, was the most important question behind the whole AED program: "Without the defibrillator what would have happened?"

I was a nervous wreck but I had had enough media training to know I had to be very careful. Plus, I did not yet know the full details of the save. Mr. Giggey, after all, could still perish that night or the next day, despite having received that lifesaving shock. So, I answered the reporter's question rather professorially: "Statistics tell us that Mr. Giggey would not have survived."

I said this in part to justify the program in which I had invested so much of American's money and so much more of my own medical, managerial, professional and emotional interest. I also wanted to protect my hide from the figurative "whuppin" I feared I might get from senior management if things turned out poorly for this program. But I couldn't help myself entirely; I went a little further out on the limb by concluding on camera that "Definitely it was worth it. If we save just one life with this program, it's worth it."

Carmen Giggey, who I'd not yet met, was much more ebullient and said with a huge smile on camera: "They are my heroes, and I don't even know their names. They saved the life of a very wonderful person, very loved, who will have an opportunity to do a few more good things." Although an eloquent and gracious lady Carmen finally got to the point where she had to decline talking about it anymore that day. Good Morning America also sent a reporter and crew to interview her at the hospital. But she asked them to go away for the time being because Robert was in surgery at that moment and, as she told them, she needed to "be in prayer in the hospital chapel with the hospital chaplain - to keep praying for his successful recovery."

Some of her quotes in the interviews she did give were classic:

"*For a few minutes I was a widow. I think if we had been any-where else, I would still be a widow. The flight attendants (and Don Grohman, the on-board paramedic) acted so quickly (it) was just amazing. I'll never fly another airline.*"

She also said:

"*I'll never get on a plane again doesn't have one of these machines. American Airlines did this voluntarily. No one forced them to. I do not know why other airlines have not done this. I mean I don't care whether we get peanuts or not!*"

So, Mr. Robert Giggey came back to life that day thanks to the heroism of Shawn Lynn and Don Grohman, backed by a cast of hundreds at American Airlines who made the program come to pass. He was the first passenger on board a commercial aircraft in the United States to be saved by a defibrillator.

The story immediately caught the media's attention.

Of course, John Crewdson of the Chicago Tribune - that per-sistent investigative reporter who I once suspected of having hidden microphones in my office, and a Pulitzer Prize winner – wrote a story about the historic event. It ran under the headline Defibrillator Saves First Life Aboard a U.S. Plane, and his byline on Feb. 20, 1998. It read:

"If Robert Giggey had chosen any other airline for his Mexican Vacation, he would very likely soon be dead. Instead Giggey, a 53-year-old North Carolina businessman, Wednesday became the first person to be revived after experiencing cardiac arrest aboard a U.S. airliner.

Following a brisk walk to the gate, Giggey and his wife, Carmen had just taken their seats aboard an American Airlines flight from Dallas Fort Worth Airport to Mexico City, when Carmen Giggey turned to speak to her husband.

"He was sitting by the window" she said. "We were buckled and ready to go."

"I turned my head and said, 'Honey' and he didn't respond. His eyes were dead just dead. His skin was clammy. His teeth were clenched. Nothing moved, no response. I never saw anything like that before. I must have screamed for help."

"The next thing I knew the stewards were all around us... a steward and a stewardess." They just zoomed in. They got me out of the way and got to him. He had no pulse, no heartbeat. They had this thing they called a defibrillator. I didn't know what a defibrillator was."

Fortunately for Robert Giggey, who suffered a sudden cardiac death, American carries battery-operated defibrillators, making it the only United States airliner that currently does. The machines can restore normal heartbeat in cases of cardiac arrest by delivering a strong electric shock.

"He was still in his seat, leaning over with his head in the aisle", Carmine Giggey recalled Thursday.

"My husband is a big man-he is 6 feet 4. We call him 'Big Gig'. They pulled his shirt apart, they cut his T-shirt out of the way and they hooked up the machine"

The defibrillator used by American is a portable model called the Heartstream Forerunner, and it analyzed Giggey's heart rhythm and concluded he was experiencing what Dr. David McKenas, American's corporate medical director, described as a classic ventricular fibrillation a condition in which the heartbeat is too rapid and irregular to pump blood to the brain.

"Giggey was by all appearances dead: Unconscious, no pulse, no breathing," McKenas said.

Carmine Giggey stood by and watched. She kept praying, "Please God give me my husband back" she recalled.

Then one of the stewards said he is going to be all right.

"It was a wonderful thing...for a few seconds I was a widow." she said.

According to the Forerunner's internal computer, Giggey's heart rhythm returned to normal less than 20 seconds after the defibrillator's electrodes were attached to the chest.

"Just 1 shock was all it took because they got to him so fast" McKenas said. "The Captain said it was all very, very dramatic."

American declined to make any of the flight attendants involved in the event available to reporters. But the account provided by one of the attendants to Heartstream executive credit the role of an off-duty paramedic from the Garland, Texas fire department was also a passenger.

"She said the paramedic answered the call for assistance" said the executive who asked not to be named.

"The paramedic started CPR and mouth-to-mouth resuscitation while the attendant ran to get the defibrillator. When she got back, they reversed roles, and he attached the electrodes and delivered the shock".

The paramedic, who remained on the flight to Mexico City, could not be located immediately. According to American officials the flight attendant recently had been trained to operate the defibrillator in the absence of medical assistance. The airlines said that 20,000 of its flight attendants will be given such training.

In cases of cardiac arrest, the chance of survival drops by about 10% with each passing minute. Unless defibrillation occurs within the first 10 minutes it is not likely to be successful.

"The key is that the defibrillator got there early" said Dr. Ted Bronson a cardiologist at the Baylor Medical Center in Irving Texas were Giggey's condition was described as serious but stable.

"Even in the hospital it usually takes several shocks with someone his size."

Although Airport paramedics equipped with a defibrillator also responded according to Captain Mike Simpson, a paramedic supervisor at the Dallas Fort Worth Airport, they did not receive the call until some 8 minutes after Giggey had been revived.

The paramedic boarded the plane and administered cardiac stabilizing drugs before transporting Giggey to an awaiting ambulance.

Airlines are not required to carry such drugs in their onboard medical kits, but American has announced plans to begin adding them in April along with medications to treat other acute illnesses and several pieces of hospital-style emergency equipment used in cardiac emergencies.

According to Bronson, hospital tests showed Giggey was suffering from a blockage of his coronary arteries that impeded the flow applied to his heart. The condition had been exacerbated by the Giggey's haste, which then caused the heart to begin fibrillating.

Then there was this report from The Dallas Morning News:

New Defibrillator Saves Airline Passenger

By J. Lynn Lunford and Joy Dickinson, The Dallas Morning News

A passenger who suffered a heart attack Wednesday on board an American Airlines jet liner has apparently

become the first person to be saved by a newly installed automatic defibrillator, an official said. A flight attendant used the device which delivers an electric charge to restart the heart on Robert Giggey, 52, after he collapsed following a rush to catch a 9:30 AM flight to Mexico City from Dallas Fort Worth international Airport. The airplane was still at the gate, but officials said without the defibrillator, Mr. Giggey could easily have died.

"People on the airplane were able to give him the same treatment we would have begun as soon as our ambulance got there" said Kathy Dotson, Director of DFW Department of Public Safety.

"I cannot overstate how important it was that they were able to start that treatment immediately."

Mr. Giggey, who owns a small manufacturing and fabric business near Raleigh, North Carolina, was in serious but stable condition Wednesday night at Baylor Medical Center at Irving, said his wife, Carmen Giggey.

"His spirits are up and is trying to get a game on TV", she said.

A Garland paramedic who was on the flight as part of the mission trip to Mexico played a key role in helping Mr. Giggey, Mr. Dotson said. Paramedic firefighter Donald Grohman, who had received training in Garland using the device, identified himself and immediately began helping.

"We are very pleased with the outcome," said Dr. David McKenas, American's corporate medical director. This does appear to be the first case that the defibrillator has brought someone back on an airplane.

In July, American became the first domestic airline to install the automated defibrillators which are about the size of the laptop computer. The airline installed them onto 142 airplanes that are used for over water flights and plans that to have them on all 640 airplanes in the Fleet by November.

Delta Airlines and United Airlines have since announced that they will outfit their fleets with the devices, which are not required by the Federal Aviation Administration.

Before the devices were installed, it was not unusual for passengers who suffered heart attacks on long flights to die before the plane could land at an airport, particularly if the flight was over water. Neither the FAA nor the airlines have developed an accurate way to track medical emergencies, but planes are diverted every day because of heart attacks and other ailments.

"Every minute you delay applying a defibrillator decreases the odds of survival by 7-10%"'s, Dr. McKenas said.

The automated defibrillators used by the airlines have sophisticated sensors that can determine when or if to shock the patient. Electrodes are attached to the patient's chest enabling the machine to track a patient's heart rate. When a patient's heart has stopped or it is beating irregularly, the machine sends out electrical impulses that can correct the problem.

All of American's flight attendant pursers who fly on planes equipped with defibrillators are trained to use them. An American official said that by November. all 20,000 of the company's flight attendants will receive the training.

Mrs. Giggey said Wednesday night that her husband had no memory of boarding the plane or having a heart attack.

"For a few minutes I was a widow. I think if we had been anywhere else, I'd still be a widow" she said.

"They acted so quickly it was just amazing. I'll now never fly another airline."

Mr. Grohman, the 33-year-old Garland paramedic continued to Mexico City and could not be reached for comment Wednesday.

And this article was in DFW People, a small paper for DFW-based workers:

AA Flight Attendant's Training plays Major Role in Saving Man's Life on 727,

by Bill Leader

Shawn Lynn, 39, an American Airlines DFW-based flight attendant played a role in saving a man's life. On Wednesday, February 8, while on American Airlines Boeing 727-200 was packed preparing to depart for a flight from DFW international Airport for Mexico City, a man collapsed with a heart attack. Garland firefighter paramedic Don Grohman was on board and like a team which included Miss Lynn, to provide and ultimately save the life of Robert Giggey, age 52, from North Carolina. Angie Bolivar, spokeswoman for Baylor medical Hospital of Irving said Monday, February 23 that Giggey's condition had changed from critical to serious. Grohman believes Miss Lynn should receive some recognition for her efforts. "Shawn was excellent. The whole crew was excellent. I was highly impressed" said Grohman, who had been a paramedic for 12 years.

After hearing the call for a doctor or paramedic, Grohman, who was seated near the back of the airplane, came forward. He asked one of the flight attendants for a mask. A mask is a device which healthcare people use when administering mouth-to-mouth resuscitation. The mask equipped with the valve was placed over the patient's mouth and allows the person administrating mouth-to-mouth to breathe oxygen into the person's mouth. However, the mask valve prevents any fluids from the stricken person's mouth entering back into the oxygen-givers mouth.

"I asked for a mask. Some others went looking for one 1 and then I said he needs mouth-to-mouth resuscitation. Shawn didn't hesitate. She just said, 'I'll do it'. And she

started immediately. I was highly impressed. I have been in this job for years and it something that bothers many people. She just did it. This was impressive."

In the meantime, another flight attendant had brought the AED machine to the area. While Miss Lynn was breathing life-saving oxygen back into his lungs, Grohman had time to set up the AED machine.

"If it were not for Miss Lynn giving mouth-to-mouth, the outcome of this might have been considerably different." Grohman said.

He explained that when a person suffers a heart attack, normal breathing is restricted. Without oxygen to the brain, a person becomes brain-dead.

Grohman is a member of the Ridgeland Bible Fellowship church's missionary group. He was on his way to Cordova, Veracruz in Mexico to help repair the mission's flat root church which had developed leaks. He said to the man seated next to him: it looks like we are leaving on time. They were firing up the engines. The flight was scheduled to leave at 9:26 AM and finally pushed back to a 10:12 AM. And then Grohman heard over the PA system that either a doctor or paramedic was needed.

"I was seated in the middle seat, and I just got up and jumped over him. I don't remember any of that. It's kind of a blur now.", Grollman said.

He ran forward to find that a doctor from Mexico was on the scene taking the man's pulse.

"I immediately recognized what was wrong. I've been many on many of these calls. His color was really bad."

Giggey was seated at a window seat. Grohman went behind Giggey and tilted his head back and cleaned his airways. With the assistance of the flight attendant, Grohman then laid Giggey down flat along the seats. He asked for a mask and while one of the flight attendants was searching for it, Grohman said the stricken man needs mouth-to-mouth resuscitation now. Ms. Lynn stepped and without hesitation.

One of the flight attendants produce the AED machine which Grohman used. He explained the machine had 2 pads. He first removed Giggey's shirt. He then took out the pads which are attached to the machine with wires. He removed the protective paper from the pads sticky surface and then affixed the pads to the man's chest.

The AED machine is also a heart monitor and automatically informs the operator when the patient needs an electric shock to assist her heart to function correctly.

Grohman said he had to give Giggey two shocks and then the machine's monitor system indicated the man's heart was beating normally. When he saw that his heart was beating, he told Ms Lynn that he would take over *mouth-to-mouth. He explained that Giggey had bitten his tongue. There was some blood said Grohman and I am used to it. In the meantime, DFW Department of Public Safety brought an ambulance onto the ramp and were ready with a stretcher inside the aircraft. Giggey was loaded onto the stretcher and Grohman recalls the heart-stricken man had already opened his eyes and said a few words to him. He was still groggy*

Grohman believes Giggey was close to dying because he had started agonal breathing. Grohman said it is like a snoring sound and is an automatic reflex of a dying person who is still trying to breathe in oxygen but at the same time not having the strength to pull the oxygen into their lungs. Sometimes it is referred to as a death rattle.

The Saves Continue

That was one fantastic day. Then the floodgates opened as American learned of more and more lives being saved in the next few months. Here are some more reports.

Portable Device Restarts Hearts

CBSnews.com, *November 30, 1998.*

A 62-year-old man from New Hampshire was aboard and American Airlines flight on November 22, 1998 when he went into cardiac arrest. An automated external defibrillator brought on board only days before saved Michael Tighe's life, reports CBS this morning: Anchor Russ Mitchell.

American Airlines is the first carrier to begin installing the portable defibrillators onboard domestic flights.

Dolores Tighe was with her husband on the plane when she found she could not wake him. Alarmed that he was not responding, she called the head flight attendant. Both the attendant and other passengers helped get Michael onto the floor.

His pulse was weak, and it was clear he was having difficulty breathing. Dolores and the flight attendant began performing CPR on Michael. When he didn't respond, the attendant called for the defibrillator.

After placing pads on his chest that attached to the device, the attendant was able to monitor Michael's heart rate. The machines reading suggested that they defibrillate Michael using an electric shock to activate the heart.

This time, it took five shocks. But after 5 attempts, Michael revived. The plane, going from Boston to Los Angeles made an emergency landing in Denver where Tighe was taken to a nearby hospital for cardiac care.

Ironically Michael worked for the Boston public-health commission, which has been pushing the city to install automatic portable defibrillators in office buildings, hotels and on fire engines.

"I certainly not only agree that the defibrillators are important, and that they saved lives, but it has saved my life and I am now a missionary for them!" Michael told CBS This Morning.

Now, Michael says his prognosis is excellent. Although he will probably have a defibrillator put into his chest and he should be able to resume sporting activities, he has enjoyed such as running and cross-country skiing. The doctor's say the portable device used to restart Michael's life is one of the biggest medical advances in recent years.

"This device will take an electrical current and put it through the patient when his heart has stopped and has become erratically beating as it helps that heart get back to its normal rhythm" explains Dr. John Brennan, chairman of the Emergency Services of the American College of Emergency Physicians.

Dr. Brennan explains the device had 2 pads which are placed on the patient, one on the heart and the other on the right side of the person's chest. If the pads are in the wrong place, the machine will not administer a shock. The machine is turned on and the 'analyze' button is pushed. A computer chip inside will analyze the patient's heart rate. If the machine indicates the heart is in ventricular fibrillation, meaning the heart has a lethal rhythm, then the patient needs to be shocked. The machine has a computerized voice which will ask the operator to stand clear if it is preparing to generate electricity discharge the patient. The person administrating the aid then pushes the shock button. As a safeguard, the machine has an automatic control so that the shock button will not operate if the machine does not find a lethal rhythm. After shocking the patient, the defibrillator will begin analyzing the patient's heart rate then advise administrating either another shock or CPR as necessary.

Dr. Brennan says the defibrillators cost between $3,000 to $5,000 and weigh about 6-1/2 pounds.

The Federal Aviation Administration is considering whether to recommend that all airlines have the devices on their planes. Dr. Brennan says that it is very likely that the FAA will pass legislation in the future that requires the defibrillators to be installed on commercial planes. In the meantime, other public institutions have begun to use the machines. This has been shown to work in stadiums, and this works in community homes with retired people and this has worked in airlines, per Dr. Brennan. A person must go through 4 hours of training to operate the defibrillator. After that, the person operating the machine must file regular reports with a doctor to confirm it is being used correctly.

John Crewdson, of the Chicago Tribune, captured Mr. Tighe's save, and others. In the following article he noted that at almost the same time that Tighe was being revived aboard his flight, another a doctor aboard another American flight over central Nevada was using cardiac drugs obtained from the airline's newly enhanced medical kit to revive the dwindling heartbeat of a 73-year-old California man who had collapsed while reading a newspaper. "The two incidents, which were only a few minutes and perhaps 1000 miles apart, provided a dramatic illustration of American's pioneering efforts to treat critically ill passengers in-flight contrary to the airline industry's traditional maxim that it is always better to land the plane and then to minister to sick passengers," he wrote. The story continued:

"It was luck" said Dolores Tighe. "A lot of luck."

Tighe and his wife Dolores, a registered nurse, were aware of what defibrillators can do. One of Tighe's responsibilities, as Communications Director for the Boston Public-Health commission is to publicize the city's efforts to place automatic portable defibrillators like this one that saved his life in office buildings and hotels and on fire engines.

When they made the reservations for a trip to Los Angeles, where Dolores Tighe planned to attend a nursing conference and the couple hoped to visit one of their 4 daughters. The Tighes did not know American currently is the only United States carrier to carry the life-saving defibrillators.

Since American began carrying the devices 18 months ago, they have been used to shock 6 passengers of whom three, including Tighe, have survived. Tighe however was the first passenger whose life has been saved in flight.

"I was not wanting to be the world's first" said Tighe, "But I am grateful".

His wife was more than grateful. "It was a miracle" she said. "The fact that he is alive is a miracle."

It was a greater miracle than she realized. Although American now has defibrillators on more than 400 widebody transcontinental planes, they still are being installed on the remaining 200 narrow body domestic jets. According to American spokesman, John Hotard, the Tighe's plane was equipped with its defibrillator, a $3000 Heartstream Forerunner, only days before.

"God was with that man" said Dr. David McKenas, American's medical director who spearheaded all airlines in the U.S. to upgrade their onboard medical services.

Except for that singular coincidence, Michael Tighe said he would have died in a Boeing 757 somewhere over the Plains East of the Rockies.

"I had my feet on his lap", recalled Dolores Tighe. He was watching the TV and suddenly, his arms swung out into the aisle, followed by his head. I knew something was wrong. I yelled at him and he didn't respond. I started hitting his face and calling his name and he was not answering me."

269

"I started screaming for help. I was hysterical. The flight attendants came and asked for help to get him down onto the floor. Everybody was helping, passengers as well as flight attendants. It was obvious that he had stopped breathing and I started CPR."

When the flight attendants arrived with the plane's defibrillator, one of the new generation portable machines the size of the laptop computer, Dolores Tighe didn't recognize it at first.

"All of a sudden this box appears" she said. "I had no idea what it was. They put the leads on him and shocked him. Every time he came back but reverted back. The last time he stayed. He then began to respond and wake up. He kept trying to sit up. He had no idea who he was or where he was."

According to the Forerunner's internal computer, which reads a patient's heart rhythm and decides whether to transmit a strong burst of electrical current designed to normalize a fibrillating heart, only 4 minutes elapsed from the first shock Mr. Tighe received to the last.

The next 30 minutes, until the plane landed in Denver, were described by Dolores Tighe as the longest of her life.

"They had called for an emergency landing by that time", she said. "We just had to wait to get to an airport so we could land. It seemed like it was taking forever."

At the same time, but on another flight, Dr. John Roach, a surgical resident from the University of California at Davis who was en route from Sacramento to Dallas aboard American flight 1158, was answering a call for a physician from flight attendants who had discovered in unconscious passenger.

"He had no pulse and no blood pressure" said Roach who connected the passenger to the plane's defibrillator, which also contains a small cardiac monitor.

The monitor showed not a ventricular fibrillation as it did with Michael Tighe, but a dangerously slow heart rhythm of 40 beats a minute.

No shock was advised by the machine.

Roach, however, viewing a picture of the man's heart rhythm on the screen was able to diagnosis condition as hypotensive bradycardia, a condition that also results in death if not quickly treated.

The prescribed treatment for bradycardia is a heart stimulant, atropine which is commonly available in hospital emergency rooms but not on airplanes. Roach's plane, however, was one that had installed the new Enhanced Medical Kit that McKenas had designed. It contains a much wider variety of medicines and equipment, including intravenous needles and tubes and airlines than are required to carry by federal law.

"I put in an IV" Roach said, and I gave him 1 mg of atropine. At that point he got his heart rate up to about 60 and he developed a blood pressure and regained consciousness".

"By the time of flight did an emergency landing in Las Vegas, the passenger was doing fine", Roach said.

"But without the IV equipment and the atropine he could've died."

American is so far the only US carrier to carry enhanced medical kits which have been available for many years on many European and Asian airlines. The kits contain drugs to treat cardiac arrest and a wide variety of other acute conditions including diabetes, congestive heart failure, seizures, asthma, postpartum bleeding and allergic reactions.

Hotard said the enhanced kits so far have been opened 14 times but until Thursday only for non-life-threatening conditions such as abdominal cramps, nausea and acute asthma. These are conditions that nevertheless cause distress and discomfort for passengers untreated that often results in emergency landings that inconvenience passengers and cost airlines money. Dr. McKenas recalled a case the month prior in which a young woman onboard a flight bound for Chicago experienced a severe asthma attack.

"I was the physician on the radio" McKenas said, "and we were very close to advising the plane to divert since her *vital signs were so abnormal. Luckily, that plane had an advanced kit, and I ordered that the kit be opened. She used the Ventolin inhaler with such great improvement that a diversion was avoided."*

McKenas said that the airline fleet will be fully equipped with defibrillators and enhanced medical kits by March.

"This has been a huge undertaking but with very great rewards" he said. "All it takes is one phone call from a passenger's family who survived a cardiac arrest through these efforts to know the program is worth it".

The enhanced medical kits cannot be opened by flight attendants without a physician present or an order from an American Airlines ground physician by radio. But nearly all of Americans 24,000 flight attendants have been trained to use the defibrillators even without a physician's order.

Last month a 70-year-old passenger aboard another Chicago bound plane was successfully defibrillated by an American airlines flight attendant while the plane was waiting to take off from North Carolina Raleigh Durham airport.

"It said to push the button and that's what I did" recalled the flight's purser, Ray Bayless, who was among the first flight attendants trained to use the machines when they went into service last year.

"It's nothing to be afraid of" Bayless said.

"It's the best friend we've got on that airplane. I am so thankful American put it on board. It saved this man's life."

News of American's second and third successful defibrillations spread quickly. The first was Robert Giggey, who last February was headed for a Mexican vacation with his wife Carmen when he suffered a cardiac arrest on the runway of DFW airport. They called me and told me Mr. Giggey, who owns a small Manufacturing Company in Mebane, North Carolina, recently returned to work after a quadruple heart bypass.

Giggey was contacted for his comment on these saves.

"I was very happy to hear that" he said. "If they had not done this with these machines of course I would not be here either. I was the first, but the big thing is I'm alive."

Current federal regulations require airlines to carry only minimal emergency medical equipment: A stethoscope and a blood pressure cuff, two medicines for treating acute allergic reactions, nitroglycerin tablets for angina sufferers and dextrose for diabetic passengers who accidentally take too much insulin.

American's chief competitors, Delta and United, initially said they too would begin carrying defibrillators and enhanced medical kits this past summer. Both airlines now say they have delayed their plans and will begin installing the machines early next year.

A spokeswoman for Northwest Airlines the nation's fourth largest commercial carrier says that it more likely than not will also begin carrying defibrillators but is still evaluating the equipment.

Other airlines that have begun carrying defibrillators or have plans to do so include Varig, the Brazilian airline, Hong Kong based Cathay Pacific, Air Zimbabwe, Finnair, and Alaska Airlines

Last month, Karen Henser, a British flight attendant with Emirates airlines used the defibrillator to save the life of a passenger on a flight from Dubai, United Arab Emirates to Karachi, Pakistan.

"I was nervous at first" she said, "but the training then took over and everything went smoothly."

In December of 1997, a flight attendant for London based Virgin Atlantic airways which has carried defibrillators for years successfully revived a 73-year-old Alex Tweedy aboard a flight from London to Miami. After recuperating for two weeks in Charleston, South Carolina, Tweedy returned home to Scotland to see his newborn granddaughter for the first time. Reached Friday at his home on Scotland's north coast, Tweedy said that now at 74 he was doing fine and "everything is perfect, just lovely."

In the last 18 months American has deployed its defibrillators nearly 100 times though in most instances only as a heart monitor.

According to Hotard, on 14 of those occasions by showing a non-life-threatening heart rhythm the monitor helped to prevent an unnecessary emergency landing. In 8 other cases, he said it helped airline medical personnel decide to divert the plane.

While defibrillators are useless in treating heart attacks, other drugs and treatments are available. But these depend on a correct diagnosis of a heart attack and progress which can only be provided by cardiac monitor more sophisticated than those built into the portable defibrillators.

The Australian airline Qantas, pioneered the use of in-flight defibrillators in 1992 and has saved the lives of at least two of its passengers.

Because US airlines have not been required to record or report in-flight medical emergencies, the paucity of data had made it impossible to know with any precision how often airline passengers get sick or die in the sky.

In April, President Clinton signed the Aviation Medical Assistance Act which requires some 30 domestic airlines to begin reporting passenger medical emergencies to the Federal Aviation Administration. It also requires the FAA to decide by next year whether to make it mandatory for

US *airlines to carry defibrillators.*

In the 1996 *report,* Code Blue Survival in the Sky, *the* Chicago Tribune *estimated the annual number of in-flight deaths at between 114 and 360...more deaths, on average, than result from aircraft accidents.*

Although older passengers get sick more often than younger ones, cardiac arrest which kills an estimated 350,000 400,000 Americans each year often strikes those with no prior symptoms of heart disease, as in the case of Michael Tighe.

While her husband was being defibrillated by the flight attendants, Dolores Tighe talked to physicians who happened to be passengers aboard the plane, and they started asking her questions about his medical history.

"He really doesn't have a medical history she said". "He exercises every day. He runs a lot. He takes care of himself. We thought he was in relatively good shape."

The Golden Heart Club

Soon after American started saving lives, I had an idea. I know, that can be dangerous sometimes, but this was, I think, a good one. I asked myself, and others, "Why not bring the flight attendant hero or heroine into DFW along with the person whose life they saved?" We wound up creating something we called the Golden Heart ceremony. At the time I was still working to get all flight attendants to embrace this program, so I wanted to publicize the good coming out of our program.

We made it a fancy event, usually at the American Learning Center, where we train all our flight attendants and do training for other employees, including some non-flight training for our pilots. A trophy was designed, and is given to each flight attendant who played an important role in saving the life of a passenger. Being a musician, I picked out heroic Olympian-type music to play in the background as I introduce the flight attendant to the rescued person. It never fails. There's not a dry eye in the entire room when those two people meet.

At one of the first ceremonies, American brought Roger Shorack, Robert Giggey and others into DFW. Mr. Shorack had suffered cardiac arrest while putting his bag above his seat before a scheduled flight from New York to Paris.

Mr. Shorack said, "I am not much of a praying person. I had prayed that when I died, it would be sudden, quick and complete. And it was. But thanks to American Airlines I've had to revise that prayer to 'Whenever I die again.' "

I said at that time: "This is really a club to celebrate bringing people back!"

Carmen Giggey was there at the first celebration, too. She told us that "At the time my husband died on the plane, ambulances and fire trucks in North Carolina (where the Giggeys live) did not have portable defibrillators. Now they do. We have changed our state and local laws so people may use portable defibrillators."

At the first Golden Heart ceremony, Laura Griffin quoted my first observation:

"American's statistics showed we were losing too many passengers to sudden cardiac arrest. We decided we really should do something. We thought if we save one person, it will be worth it".

At the ceremony, Mr. Tighe noted that it took 5 shocks to save him. He was a runner, a swimmer and nonsmoker, and the furthest thought in his mind was I wonder if this airplane has a defibrillator."

Flight attendant Elaine Mueller used a defibrillator on a passenger who collapsed at DFW Airport. She said she could only think of her own father. "I would want someone to help my father if something happened to him," she said. "I was not going to let this man die on a dirty airport floor. You just think that whoever this is, they could be someone's mother or father or special person in someone's life".

I also designed a pin to award to flight attendant rescuers, which they receive at the Golden Heart ceremony after they meet the person they saved. The person they saved would pin it onto the flight attendant's lapel.

The whole intent of this kind of recognition was not only to recognize these wonderful flight attendants for their heroic efforts, but to encourage other flight attendants through word of mouth not to be afraid of the device. Word got out that the person who would get a pin would be the person who pressed the shock button. Soon enough, flight attendants were jockeying for position, and competing as to who would push that button when the machine told them to do it.

Robert Giggey, being the first person saved by a U.S. airline's on-board defibrillator, was very emotional when he appeared at his Golden Heart Ceremony. He gave a signed picture to flight attendant Shawn Lynn, with this beautiful inscription:

Robert Loomis Giggey
Born 2-21-44
Died 2-18-98
Revived: 2-18-98
Because of you!

AFTERSHOCKS

On July 29, 2003, seven years since American first placed defibrillators on board its jets, the industry recorded its 50th save. Furthermore, we knew at that time about 56% of those who experienced cardiac arrest aboard a U.S. airline flight were surviving vs. a survival rate of only about 5% before defibrillation was added to the equation. By 2007 the number of in-flight saves had jumped to 76 with a 63% survival rate.

Those aren't big numbers in the grand scheme of global or even just U.S. air travel. But tell that to those who survived, and to their loved ones. Each one of those lives is precious, and each represents the type of heart events that always have been survivable if only there had been the right technology available to treat them in the first critical minutes of a cardiac arrest.

And when you evaluate American's survival statistics in light of overall cardiac arrest survival rates you will see that they truly were – and continue to be - remarkable. Whereas ground paramedics were only getting perhaps 10-15% survival rates in such cases, American was registering a 63% survival rate. Clearly the difference-maker was not the plane, or the fact that attendants are trained now. It was the ready availability of an AED within seconds of a person going into cardiac arrest. Remember, time is the single most critical factor in treating such a patient. A patient's survival chances diminish by about 10% every minute that passes before a shock is delivered. And the environment in planes is ideal for spotting someone entering cardiac arrest very quickly. If flight attendants, who typically are up and, in the aisles, do not see someone pass out and respond immediately, chances are very high that their seatmates will. And that starts the response to a cardiac arrest event faster than a response in other locations likely would get started. Then, because an AED is onboard it can be hooked up to the stricken person in as little as one minute's time. Its built-in intelligence can determine within just a few seconds if, and how much of a shock is needed. Nobody wants to have a cardiac arrest, anywhere. But the technology, the situation and the number of trained first responders is now developed to the point that you could argue that if it's absolutely inevitable that you're going to have a cardiac arrest the second best place to be when you have one would be aboard a U.S. commercial aircraft (the best place, of course, would be in a hospital, already hooked up to a heart monitor).

But that was, by no means the case, as recently as 1997. On July 6 of that year, New York Times writer Betsy Wade, the author of The Practical Traveler, wrote in a column headlined Airlines Adding Defibrillators that: "The FAA, according to Dr. Jon Jordan the Federal Air Surgeon, is not ready to order more elaborate medical equipment aboard planes because, just as it had claimed to the Congressional Subcommittee, it did not know what was needed.

"The chief medical officer for the FAA said in testimony to Congress and still made the arguments that had been advanced that planes should not be flying hospitals, and too much equipment might discourage pursuit of the proper course of action, namely getting the plane down and the passenger to a hospital."

Wade opined however that "the FAA may be overtaken by events in the marketplace." She noted that on July 1, in 1997, American Airlines began putting defibrillators aboard 242 jets, or 40% of its fleet. These were the planes that fly over water, with the rationale being that an emergency landing is not feasible over the ocean. She reported that American had trained 2,300 pursers to use the devices and that the airline was pressing Congress for a federal Good Samaritan law to indemnify medical professionals from malpractice suits.

She also went into the history of their use. Virgin Atlantic put defibrillators on virtually all its planes in 1990, but the devices had only been used 10 times, with just two passengers being revived and surviving. In 1991 Qantas put them aboard 53 of its fleet of 93 planes. Air Zimbabwe put defibrillators on its 3 wide body planes. She added because of the information that defibrillators provide, new prescription medicines for cardiac care and perhaps breathing devices were to be added to plane's in-flight medical kits later that year. She also explained the FAA did not require flight attendants to know CPR. Though the total number of cardiac cases among the reported 14,334 in-flight emergencies the previous year was unclear, anecdotal evidence and common sense indicated the number was large and that the condition was the most serious medical event that could happen to a passenger in flight. People – flight attendants and passengers - trying to help a sick passenger typically cannot diagnose accurately the sick passenger's underlying ailment. Thus she, like many others before her, speculated that the reason for the jump and emergencies overall may be due to the American's with Disabilities Act in 1990 which said no persons could be denied full access to public transportation due to a disability, meaning airlines had begun carrying passengers who in earlier years they would not have agreed to carry because they were so ill or invalid.

While there may have been some validity in such thinking, I was not at all certain that simply carrying more passengers who in the old days we might have turned away was a major factor in the number of passengers having major health events occur while flying. Indeed, it is not as though airlines were in the business of turning away passengers before the Americans with Disabilities Act was passed then began carrying anyone who showed up at the airport afterward. Very few people were ever denied travel for health reasons, ever. It happened, but those were rare and extreme cases, and usually only because the level of care or the amount of space needed to carry them onboard was just insufficient.

I recognized via such concerns and other factors that we needed more scientific legitimacy to our program. Although I had sizable academic credentials, I knew I could not provide that kind of legitimacy and credibility on my own. But Rick Page, the PhD/MD electrophysiologist at UT Southwestern Medical School, could. Rick reviewed every onboard shock event and use, and spearheaded the writing of a medical research paper. The idea was promptly accepted by the *New England Journal of Medicine*. So, numerous saves later, a thoroughly researched and professionally vetted evaluation of the performance of American's AED program Airlines was captured in an article that appeared in that esteemed publication.

What had started out as a curious and perhaps meaningful data anomaly that I shared with my CEO while I had him down to skivvies in my exam room for his annual physical, eventually was being given very serious attention by the world's most highly-regarded medical journal. As a budding pianist in Oneida NY, I had certainly never dreamed of co-authoring an article for this journal. The article detailed the stunning success of the program, which was far greater than had ever been seen in the world of emergency medical response.

The paper found that there had been 250 uses of AEDs by airlines from July 1997 to around December 1999, or about 7.6 uses per month. It was mostly used as a cardiac monitor. A total of 15 unnecessary flight diversions were avoided and 13 diversions were recommended because the AEDs' monitoring tools and programing detected medical issues serious enough to order the plane out of the sky immediately. Out of 19 shock opportunities that grew out of those 250 uses, resuscitation was successful 11 times, or in 58% of the cases, at least in terms of immediate survival. The long-term survival rate of 47% actually was a little higher than most of us had anticipated. These results, obviously, were far better than the 10% survival often seen from use in the field with paramedics on the ground. The much higher success rate, of course, correlates directly with the much quicker response time on planes, where a defibrillator was exactly where it needed to be the moment the need for one presented itself. Now, of the 19 shock events, 16 were not in flight (but either still aboard planes at the gate or taxing to or from the runway, or in a jet way or terminal near a gate. Three shock events actually happened in the air. In 11 cases, the passenger/patient initially was resuscitated. Of the 19 who were shocked by one of our AEDs, nine are still alive and ten are deceased. Most of the events occurred in the passenger's seat. One event occurred in a jet bridge during the boarding process, one in the terminal, one in the aisle of a plane, and one in a plane's lavatory. The cases were predominantly male.

Finally, other airlines formally followed American's lead. Crewdson of the Chicago Tribune reported on Dec. 10, 1998 that US Airways would become the second U.S. domestic to begin carrying portable cardiac defibrillators on some of its planes and the first to install hand-held heart monitors that can tell when a passenger is suffering a heart attack or other cardiac abnormalities. Delta and

United then quickly announced plans to begin installing defibrillators and enhanced medical kits on their fleets the following year.
United's announcement came less than two weeks after the carrier
was sued by the widow of a 37-year-old United passenger named
Steven Saunders. Saunders had died of a cardiac arrest in 1995
aboard a United flight from Boston to San Francisco. Northwest,
Continental and TWA all said they were studying the issue.

Then on January 8, 1999, Crewdson reported that British Airways
would become the first large European airline to begin carrying
portable cardiac defibrillators.

Then the FAA came through, albeit belatedly. On April 15, 2001,
the Associated Press reported the FAA finally was ordering defibrillators be placed on board all U.S. airlines' planes. The agency gave
airlines three years to put defibrillators on all domestic and international flights and to get flight attendants trained in their use. It
also was significant – just as significant as the defibrillator mandate – that the FAA at the same time order airlines to upgrade their
medical kits modeled like American's new enhanced medical kit.

Later that same year, on Nov.8, a trade journal reported that
more than 20 people were still alive at that time thanks to defibrillators on American's aircraft alone. The most recent save, at
that time, had come on Halloween, Oct. 31, at a boarding gate at
Chicago's O'Hare Airport.

"These devices are proven invaluable in saving lives" that trade
journal quoted me as saying.

"Passengers can travel with an added level of comfort knowing
that every American and American Eagle aircraft has a defibrillator
and flight attendants are trained to use them."

Okay, maybe that was laying on the corporate promotional bab-
ble a little thick. The truth is, very few travelers ever think about

the availability of a defibrillator onboard the planes on which they will be flying, even in those days when the idea was still relatively novel. But in a way, that is a good thing. It means our customers trust airlines to be as well-equipped, as well-trained, and as ready as possible to handle even the most serious medical emergency that can happen to an individual aboard a plane. Anything worse almost certainly would have to be the result of some sort of violent attack by a terrorist or madman.

Finally, the Federal Aviation Administration issued a final rule on April 12, 2001 requiring US Airlines to carry defibrillators on all domestic and international flights within 3 years. American was already 100% in compliance, and led the cause to make it mandatory. We finally won! And the good thing about our introduction of AEDs and advanced medical kits to the U.S. airline industry is that the saves just keep on piling up, even today. By April 2004 American chalked up its 50th passenger saved. It was fitting, then, that American issued that news release on Feb. 14, Valentine's Day, the holiday whose very symbol is a heart.

I left American in 2002. Times again were changing. The 9-11 terror attacks had occurred on, of course, Sept. 11, 2001, sparking a total shutdown of the U.S. airspace for several days and an unprecedented and huge drop in demand for air travel as passengers shied away from flying for fear they, too, could be killed in a suicide attack. That event nearly brought the entire industry to its knees financially, and several carriers were forced into bankruptcy or saved from that fate by a government-backed loan guarantee program that Congress passed in recognition that our industry had been a direct economic victim of acts of war.

Meanwhile, the industry was entering a time of severe turbulence because of their own precarious finances and big fights with their unions looming on the horizon. The medical department for which I'd fought so hard continued to operate after I left, but in those days of tight money and some big losses, the medical departments budget and its operations were whittled away some each year until what was left of it finally was outsourced. But before I left, I was invited to speak at the American Heart Association's Annual Conference. There were thousands of doctors and health professionals in the audience.

When they heard the name "American Airlines" prior to my introduction and presentation there was an immediate standing ovation from the mammoth crowd filling the ballroom where we met. The applause was thunderous. I fought hard to hold back my tears, though a tear drop or two did escape. Experiencing that massive affirmation from my colleagues for the initiative taken by our medical team at American was, quite frankly, overwhelming. And the applause would not stop. It probably only lasted for a minute, or less, but to me it seemed like 10 minutes. There were foot stomps, and cheers. All coming from stodgy doctors, no less! In the event's program the American Heart Association noted in the section "Comments from Emergency Cardiovascular Care Programs," written by Dr. Richard O. Cummins, MD: ECC Senior Science Co-Editor:

> "For United States airlines, the true pioneer company was American Airlines, under the innovative medical leadership of David McKenas, MD, and Linda Campbell, RN and the corporate leadership of Robert Crandall, company president. They stand at the highest tier of heroes because they first recognized 'it is the right thing to do,' and they 'just did it.'"

AUTHOR'S EPILOGUE

The dramatic story of Robert Giggey's heart attack aboard American Airlines Flight 2017 on February 18, 1998 was the first of tens, even hundreds-of -thousands of similar medical events now commonplace on airplanes, in shopping malls and office buildings, at sporting events and schools, and in all sorts of public places over the last couple of decades. It is more than a little gratifying to have been a key person behind the simple-yet-complex, small-but-enormous change in one airline's operating procedures that ultimately brought about such a remarkable and wonderful development in the lives of thousands of individuals plus their families and friends, and, ultimately in the lives of people all over the world.

It would be dishonest of me to pretend that it was part of some grandiose plan that I had all along. The truth of the matter is I just stumbled across some numbers in my work that most any other physician in the world would have overlooked or dismissed. And it is only thanks to my unique and very roundabout path into the medical profession, and into my position as chief medical officer for the world's largest airline, that even I paid attention to those obscure numbers.

This story continues to shock me. How could an ordinary life like my own make a change in the world and make the world a better place through a seemingly small step? Just by looking at some numbers, and questioning what was going on, it is now reported thousands of lives had been preserved and changed. Just by talking to an astute company CEO who was always willing to test new ideas, during his physical exam, no less, a dramatic change resulted. How people were cared for in flight when an unthinkable medical emergency happened in flight was forever changed. I am deeply humbled.

It amazed me that despite the FAA's initial opposition, and based mostly on American Airlines' pioneering experience, the FAA finally mandated on board defibrillators, and enhanced medical kits for all commercial air carriers in April 15, 2001. They became common place in other ground-based industries following American's example. The lives saved are estimated to be in the thousands, though no one really knows the total. It amazed me, too, that the FAA also mandated the enhanced on-board medical kit that I and our American Airlines team had designed, with the same contents that are the core of what is found now on all US air carriers. It amazed me too that President Clinton, too, signed the Aviation Medical Assistance Act we developed which required some 30 domestic airlines to begin reporting passenger medical emergencies to the Federal Aviation Administration and indemnified Good Samaritan doctors to help an ailing passenger aboard an airplane.

Now age 66, as I look back, I too am "shocked" about what I perceived to be an "unseen hand" working in and through the entire program and throughout my life. It is remarkable to me the role of "coincidences" in this program, and that thousands of lives saved, all based on a simple cog in a corporate world that looked at statistics of on-board deaths. The Merriam Webster Dictionary defines coincidence as: the occurrence of events that happen at the same time by accident but seem to have some connection. There were so many coincidences that point to some "other" power beyond what we can know and understand as humans. For example:

How does one explain an uncanny repetitive dream predicting to the exact day of the death of one's father?

How does the path of anyone's career shape them to become what seems to be the perfect fit, at the perfect time, under the perfect management, to affect a program on a scale never seen before, to lead the way to saving lives worldwide from sudden cardiac arrest? I could not have plotted a more bizarre but more perfect course for my life to achieve this one bit of important success had I tried. And I certainly did not try.

Perhaps you feel the same way at times. Perhaps you do not. You might not see it now, but when you can look back on your life, you will see how your miracle unfolded across your own life history. Even the bleakest moment, I have learned, can prepare you for important moments or opportunities you will encounter in the years ahead. I know that despite some initial ridicule, and some bleak times, I saw it.

Shawn Lynn, the flight attendant who was extremely despondent, also saw it. How is it that a suicidal flight attendant came to her senses, and functioned at 100% of her capabilities to save the life of a kindly man like Robert Giggey? How did she pull it together to find the strength and fortitude to do so? What was the voice that she heard? Was it God?

What was the remarkable transformation that would bring her back to enjoy a wonderful life, from an imminent suicide to following a call to the mission field where she would minister to Christian Missionaries in Africa?

How was it that Carmen Giggey's prayers, clinging to the man that she loved while he was dead on a plane, were heard such that he came back to life?

Though I am a scientist by profession, I know enough about that subject to know that we do not, as scientists, have enough information to dismiss the existence of a power in this world that is beyond our understanding. If anything, what we do not know points us – me, certainly – to God. And as a Christian doctor I can say I am quite happy that there are explanations for things that happen regarding the health and lives of my patients, and my family, that simply cannot be fully explained by science. That is a source of great comfort and hope. It seems to me that there is a veil surrounding our day-to-day lives that sometimes, we are allowed to see through, or at least briefly to push it aside before the wind blows it shut again. The Apostle Paul said it best in 1 Corinthians Chapter 13, verses 12 and 13:

> "Now we see but a dim reflection as in a mirror; then we shall see face to face. Now I know in part; then I shall know fully, even as I am fully known. And now these three remain: faith, hope, and love; but the greatest of these is love...."

WHERE ARE THEY NOW?

In closing, I want to let you know where our key 'actors' in the opening chapter are now.

I am pleased to report that as of this writing, Robert Giggey is still alive, enjoying life with Carmen, and living in Roxboro, NC. He commented when I spoke to him last (in 2019) that American Airlines gave him 23 more years of life, and he is still going strong. This year, when I went out to North Carolina to move my daughter, Catherine McKenas, now a PhD in Chemistry at Duke University Shared Materials and Instrumentation Facility. Carmen and Robert drove from Roxboro, to meet us for dinner. He is still alive, 23 years later. I was so proud my daughter Catherine could meet them. We had a blessed time together.

Carmen Giggey went on to be a public health activist in the state of North Carolina in support of public access defibrillators. She did a film for the Red Cross re-enacting what had happened that day and has had numerous speaking engagements for the Red Cross and other groups advocating for public access defibrillators. In part, because of her public health activism in North Carolina, all public laws in that state regarding public access defibrillators were put in place and/or strengthened.

Don Grohman reported that on his return to the DFW area after his mission trip to Mexico, Mrs. Giggey got in touch with him to thank him. She and Robert wanted to take him to dinner. He subsequently discovered his cousin was the doctor who received Mr. Giggey once he arrived at the hospital emergency room that day. Don was at the Garland Fire Department for 17 years, 16 of them as a paramedic. He trained at the UT Southwestern Medical School. After the event, Don went back to work as a firefighter-paramedic but was injured in an ambulance run in 1999 and suffered some paralysis. He had surgery on his spine in 2002 but because he had fractured his neck, he was unable to return to duty as a fireman-paramedic. So, Don went to college part-time and completed an accounting degree at the University of North Texas in 2003. He joined a large accounting firm before moving to Denver in 2005, and then to the Washington, D.C. area in 2006, all with the same accounting firm. He works today as an auditor for a US Government agency.

Shawn Lynn (now Verkerk) no longer affords the thought of suicide any merit. She went back to church, recommitted her life to her faith, and in fact, eventually went on to do Christian missionary work. She was planning to help start a Women's Center in South Africa but got re-directed to Zambia. She assisted missionaries in various life changing outreaches and organized and directed teams that came from America to build church structures there.

Shawn made history that day, on her darkest of days, by being the first flight attendant in the United States to be involved in an on-board defibrillator resuscitation. She recalls Don Grohman's last words to her, as they deplaned in Mexico City: "What you did today separated the men from the boys!" Shawn was psychologically healed that day. Her life took on a new sense of purpose, direction and a new joy. And after Mr. Giggey's save, Shawn stopped being haunted by those CPR dreams.

Ten years after Mr. Giggey's historic shock and save there was a reunion of the major players in that event. It was held at the Raleigh Durham Airport. Don Grohman was not able to attend. Shawn Lynn Verkerk was surprised to get the call to come to the reunion. She was all set to retire from her job as American flight attendant in just two weeks so she could start her mission work.

One of 'Big Gig's' grandchildren, born after Mr. Giggey's "resurrection" saw Shawn, ran up to her, and gave her a big hug.

"Thank you for saving my Pap-Pap!" she said.

Shawn hugged her back, but then looked straight at Mr. Giggey. Tears were in both of their eyes. She said,

"No. Thank *you* for saving me."

Photos and news videos regarding the program, the people saved and other details my be found on the Author's page at Amazon.com.

CPSIA information can be obtained
at www.ICGtesting.com
Printed in the USA
BVHW011648190621
609851BV00014B/268/J